A RADICAL ARISTOCRAT

A RADICAL ARISTOCRAT

The Rt Hon.
Sir William Molesworth
Bart., PC, MP

of

PENCARROW

and his wife

ANDALUSIA

– by –

Alison Adburgham

TABB HOUSE

First published 1990

Tabb House Ltd, 7 Church Street, Padstow, Cornwall, PL28 8BG

British Library Cataloguing in Publication Data
Adburgham, Alison
    A radical aristocrat: the Rt. Hon. Sir William Molesworth, Bart, PC, MP
of Pencarrow and his wife Andalusia.
    1. England. Social life, 1820-1910. Biographies
    I. Title
    942.074092

ISBN 0 907018 84 X

Typeset by St. George Typesetting, Redruth, Cornwall
Printed and bound by Bookcraft (Bath) Ltd. Midsomer Norton, Avon.

CONTENTS

SIC FIDEM TENEO

INTRODUCTION

IT has been my endeavour to trace the threads of Sir William Molesworth's political career as they interwove with his personal life in Cornwall and in London. His was a short life. He died at the age of forty-five in the year he was appointed Colonial Secretary in Lord Palmerston's Cabinet at the height of the Crimean War. The appointment was hailed, both in England and in the colonies, as the right man in the right place at the right time. That he should die within a matter of months was ironic.

The man himself, all his life, was a paradox. He had the disinterested intellectual curiosity usually attributed to men of the eighteenth century, yet a driving urge for the practical social reforms associated with the first half of the nineteenth century. A brilliant scholar, happy when losing himself in philosophical, mathematical and scientific problems, he yet threw himself energetically into the earthy practicalities of creating the exceptional beauty of his garden and grounds. His health was delicate from childhood, but he was possessed by an inner energy that drove him to ignore fatigue, both physical and mental. Spontaneously generous in initiating and funding any enterprise he believed in – the *London and Westminster Review*, the Reform Club, the Bodmin and Wadebridge railway – he was meticulous in accounting the small expenditures of daily life, a characteristic inherited from his Scottish mother. He was an aristocrat to his finger tips, an exquisite in dress, yet many considered him an almost revolutionary radical, a traitor to his class.

In 1901 Mrs Millicent Fawcett published a biography of Sir William Molesworth. It was the time of the Boer War, and she thought that 'an account of his work for colonial reform might reinforce those who believed in a generous settlement for South Africa when the war should be over'. Her late husband, Henry Fawcett, MP, described himself as a political follower of Sir William when he stood as an Independent Radical in Southwark, Molesworth's constituency at the time of his death. Mrs Fawcett herself never met Sir William, but she was fortunate in having the cooperation of his sister Mary, Mrs Richard Ford, who was still very much alive in her eighties. Her most necessary cooperation, however, had one great disadvantage. This was Mary's intense bitterness towards Andalusia, her brother's wife, whom she considered, as did many others, responsible for his early death. This hostility inevitably meant censorship; and Mrs Fawcett's life of Sir William contains but one paragraph mentioning the wife to whom he was married during the most important years of his political career and who caused him to change his whole personal life style.

Thirty-four years before Mrs Fawcett's biography, twelve years after Sir William's death, a book was printed for private circulation: *The Philosophical Radicals of 1832 comprising the Life of Sir William Molesworth* by Mrs Grote. Harriet Grote, ardently committed with her husband George Grote, MP, to the aims of the Philosophical Radical group, was a forceful lady, unique in her generation. She was a presence in Molesworth's life from the time when he, at the age of twenty-two, took his seat in the Reformed Parliament of 1832. She regarded him as her disciple. She scolded him, teased him, was more than a little in love with him. She became William's confidante at the time when he was tormentingly frustrated in serious love affairs. This intimate friendship ended abruptly after twelve years when he married Andalusia, Mrs Temple West, a widow whom society, including Mrs Grote, considered unsuitable. Mrs Grote's life of Sir William, also the many letters exchanged between them, throw much light upon his personality; but the book cannot be regarded as factually impeccable, nor unbiased. Neither is it any help in getting to know Andalusia.

Andalusia's family background and brief concert and stage career have not been difficult to trace; but the seven years of her marriage to a Worcestershire gentleman three times her age, followed by her eight years as his widow before meeting Sir William, remain obscure. If there were any of her letters or personal papers at Pencarrow, they must have been destroyed by Mary Ford. Recollections of Andalusia in contemporary memoirs are many, all relating to her years as a hostess to distinguished personalities in politics, fashionable society, literature and the musical world, both at the great London house in Eaton Place and at Pencarrow house-parties. From these it can be deduced that she was an expert in the delicate art of putting herself across, and had the even more valuable talent, in a hostess, of drawing out others to sparkle. But beneath the surface? How deep was the bond between her and Sir William? I have said that he was a man of paradox – she was one of his contradictions.

The eleven years of their marriage were followed by thirty-three years when Andalusia reigned alone – but never lonely – as mistress of 87 Eaton Place and of Pencarrow in Cornwall. My last chapter covers those years. An account of them is necessary to complete Sir William's story.

ACKNOWLEDGEMENTS

THIS book could not have been written had not Lieut-Colonel Sir Arscott Molesworth-St Aubyn, Bart. given me freedom of access to everything contained in the Pencarrow archives, and I would like to thank him and also Lady Molesworth-St Aubyn for their warm welcome at all times. Nor could I have written the book without the help of Mrs Joan Colquitt-Craven, Pencarrow's honorary archivist. She has been an invaluable collaborator, giving me the benefit of her extensive knowledge of Molesworth history and also of local history. Her companionship and enthusiasm on the trail of relevant details in many localities has been a very great pleasure to me during the years of research. She also spent considerable time reading drafts of my manuscript at various stages, making helpful comments and suggestions. I cannot thank her enough.

To Mr Brian Roberts I must express deep gratitude for his generosity in giving me the results of his own research, in both London and Bath, into the early life of Andalusia Lady Molesworth, her musical career and first marriage. This has indeed been of inestimable value to me. Dr Kathleen Barker, Hon. Secretary of the Society for Theatre Research was most helpful in tracing Andalusia's years at the Royal Academy of Music and on the stage – as also was Miss Betty Matthews, Hon. Archivist of the Royal Society of Musicians of Great Britain. Miss Alyson Cooper, MA, consultant to the Devon and Cornwall Division of the Historic Buildings Re-survey of England, gave me interesting information about Costislost as well as Pencarrow. Mrs D.M. Sandoe has been infinitely generous in the time she has spent burrowing in old local newspapers, even transcribing by hand whole stretches of almost indecipherable newsprint – a dedicated voluntary sleuth. I would like also to thank Sir Brinsley Ford, CBE, FSA, grandson of Mary Ford's husband Richard Ford, for sending me recollections of his grandfather and the Ford family home.

Miss Janet Arnold, FSA, has made an invaluable contribution to the book with her skilled photography of portraits at Pencarrow and of drawings from the Visitors' Book, for which I am most grateful. In addition, she read the book closely and critically in manuscript, as did Dr Ann Saunders, FSA, who was very helpful indeed on various specialist details. Mr C.B.M. Heywood gave much encouragement from the beginning by his interest in – and discussion of – my original conception of a new approach to Sir William's life. Finally, I would like to thank the librarians of the London Library, St James's Square, for their assistance, and express my admiration for the British Library Lending Division. This wonderful service has brought me, through the Padstow Public Library, volumes of 19th century letters, diaries, memoirs etc. from university and county reference libraries in many parts of the country. Where I have quoted from published books they are acknowledged in the text, with details of publication given in the bibliography at the end of the book. All previously unpublished quotations and extracts come directly from letters and documents in the Pencarrow archives.

Alison Adburgham
1990

LIST OF ILLUSTRATIONS

PLATES

IN THE TEXT

1 Sir William Molesworth, Bart, aged 22, at the time of his entering Parliament. Portrait by George Hayter.

II Pencarrow at the time when Sir William was planning his Italian garden. From a water-colour, c. 1833.

PART ONE

1810 – 1844

EARLY YEARS

A young very rich man, named Sir William Molesworth, pleased me considerably. I liked the frank manners of the young man . . . I pitied his darkness of mind, and heartily wished him well.

Thomas Carlyle, Letter to his mother, May 30 1834

An undercurrent of energy and action flowed deep and strong beneath a delicate and aristocratic person, which in no way displeased the masses, ever glad to be led by a gentleman.

Richard Ford, Unpublished sketch of Sir William Molesworth

I would do anything, not dishonourable, to gain the lady. I have softened down my opinions to the verge of falsehood; but that barrier I will not pass.

Sir William on his suit for the hand of Juliana Carew

CHAPTER I — 1810-1831

ON the day in 1837 when Disraeli made his ill-received maiden speech in the House of Commons, T.P. O'Connor, MP, noted in his diary:

'Of all the groups in the House, the one that strikes you as containing the youngest and best-dressed men is the Radical Group. At their head sits Sir William Molesworth, who does not look more than twenty-eight, a dandy in dress, and somewhat Dundrearyish in delivery; fair in complexion, and with hair approaching in colour red; eye-glassed, and altogether like a Radical leader who has a rent-roll of £12,000 or £14,000 a year'.

O'Connor was not far out in assessing Sir William's age. He was twenty-seven and had been a Member of Parliament for five years, having been adopted as candidate for East Cornwall upon his coming of age. O'Connor was also right about his being wealthy; at the age of thirteen he had succeeded, on the death of his father, to the extensive Molesworth estates in Cornwall and Devon, also wealth originally derived from property in Huntingdonshire, sugar plantations in the West Indies, and mining interests in Cornwall leading to the founding of a banking-house which eventually became Lloyds Bank.

Young, very rich and a bit of a dandy – always an attractive combination – Sir William's scholarly attainments were far greater than those of most aristocratic young men, his intellectual interests wider and deeper. This can to some extent be accounted for by the fact that a brilliant brain was accompanied by a delicate constitution which prevented his education from following the usual upper-class course. Strong constitutions were not a characteristic of Molesworth males. Although William died at forty-five, his life was longer than that of any of the seven Molesworth baronets who preceded him. Both his younger brothers died before him. His father, Arscott Molesworth, died aged thirty-three, having married at nineteen and begotten five children. William, the eldest, was born in 1810.

1

Sir Arscott had entered him at birth for Eton, where he himself had been; but since William suffered severely from scrofula it became evident that his health would not stand the rigours of a public school. Harshly unsympathetic to his disappointing heir, Sir Arscott dispatched him to a private boarding school at Putney, where he was miserable and became seriously ill with inflammatory diathesis.

When his father died, his mother rescued him. Dr Lecke, the family doctor, advised he should 'avoid all Causes of high Excitement both corporal and mental . . . Sir William's great Vivacity, very good Humour combined with no ordinary Talent render some Direction of his pursuits to a right Course highly desirable at his Time of Life. His future Health and Happiness all greatly depend on this. It appears therefore to Dr Lecke to suggest to her Ladyship the advantage that must be derived from the immediate assistance of an able Tutor. Boys of 15 or 16 are generally above the Restraint and Coercion from Females however much they love and respect them. Often when they are placed at Eton they fall sacrifice to ardent dispositions unless corrected by some Mentor who takes more than an ordinary interest in their Fate'.

This letter of June 18th 1824 enclosed what Dr Lecke called a 'Scheme' of lessons and play hours to be followed under the tutor. Lady Molesworth would have none of it. She was Scottish, descended from the Hume family and, besides being of sturdy stock (she lived till her ninety-eighth year), possessed undoubted mental distinction. She had also inherited considerable comeliness from her grandmother, Betsy Hume, a celebrated Edinburgh beauty. And it was in Edinburgh that she decided the young baronet should be educated. With characteristic thoroughness she transplanted from Pencarrow the whole family – William, then aged fourteen, his two younger brothers and two sisters – to live at 97 George Street, Edinburgh.

In the first years after their migration from Cornwall William was often in bed with inflammatory attacks; but he was able to join some university classes, and also studied modern languages – Italian, French, German – before entering the University as a full-time student. His Italian tutor was Gaetano da Marchi, erstwhile statesman in Piedmont, who had expatriated himself to avoid prosecution when a revolution had been attempted in 1821. He had settled in Edinburgh and was influential in forming William's philosophic turn of mind. At this time Edinburgh was regarded as the 'Athens of the North'. It was the birthplace of 'philosophical radicalism'; and the intellectual atmosphere was reflected in the Whig-supporting *Edinburgh Review*, founded in 1802 by Francis Jeffrey, Henry Brougham and Sydney Smith. In William Molesworth's time it was still edited by Francis Jeffrey and was publishing the radical ideas of some of the most admired men of letters of the day. It was inevitable that William should turn away from the conservative thinking of his land-owning ancestors, many of whom had represented Tory constituencies in Parliament. The Molesworths had been in Cornwall since the reign of Queen Elizabeth I, when a John Molesworth had purchased Pencarrow from an Exeter family called Walker. He was recorded in the Heralds' Visitation of 1620 (the MS is now at Pencarrow) as the younger son of John Molesworth of Helpston, Northamptonshire. He married Catherine, daughter and heiress of John Hender of Botreaux Castle near Tintagel, and became the Auditor or Commissioner for the Duchy of Cornwall to Queen Elizabeth.

ANOTHER young Cornishman who, like William Molesworth, was to become a leading Radical in politics, was Charles Buller; and he also spent the formative years of his education at Edinburgh, where Thomas Carlyle was his tutor from 1822-'23. Charles was four years older than William, but they were life-time friends, since the Buller family at Polvellan and the Molesworths at Pencarrow were comparatively near neighbours. Carlyle described Charles Buller as 'a most manageable, cheery, and altogether welcome and intelligent phenomenon; quite a bit of sunshine in my dreary Edinburgh desert'. After his years at Edinburgh, Charles Buller went on to Cambridge; and this may well have influenced Molesworth's decision to leave Edinburgh for Cambridge in 1827. He was entered at St John's College, but very soon moved to Trinity, which he considered had more style. Writing to his mother he said, 'I like Cambridge very much but detest St John's . . . not gentlemen . . . things greatly altered since my uncle was here. All those with whom

I am intimate are at Trinity, including Charles Buller.' In another
letter from St John's he says he has had a quarrel with his tutor
Gwatkin 'arising from him saying he would not allow me to have
a beef steak for breakfast'. After he had moved to Trinity, another
letter says Gwatkins had presented him with a long bill relevant to
his time at St John's – £46.8.0. He was borrowing to pay it off. No
doubt Lady Molesworth forthwith despatched the money to settle
the bill. The very idea of William borrowing would be obnoxious
to her – as he well knew.

William Makepeace Thackeray, one year younger than Molesworth,
entered Trinity two years later; and in *Pendennis* he has given
an exaggerated account of undergraduate fast-living at Oxbridge
– Thackeray surprisingly used that term, now generally thought
to derive from the time of the twentieth century building of
'red-brick' universities. Perhaps he thought it prudent not to
specify Cambridge as young Pen's university, so high were the
jinks he describes. He himself studied little while he was there,
lived extravagantly, and went down in 1830 without a degree.
It seems that Molesworth, when at Trinity, was caught up into
the same kind of fast-living as was Thackeray after him. Away
from the intellectually élitist atmosphere of Edinburgh – also
away from his mother's restraining presence – his natural high
spirits at last burst free. There were frequent letters to Lady
Molesworth asking for more money; and in this lies a similarity
in the circumstances of Thackeray's young Pendennis and that
of young Molesworth – they both had widowed mothers who
controlled their allowances. One gets the impression that Mrs
Pendennis, by no means rich, was far more indulgent to
her darling son than was Scottish Lady Molesworth in the
allowance she granted to William out of his own considerable
wealth.

In particular William needed money for fox-hunting. In spite
of his delicate health, he had from boyhood ridden to hounds.
Pencarrow is not in fashionable hunting country, but the
Molesworth's Devonshire seat at Tetcott is in the country of
the famous fox-hunting parson, Jack Russell. A favourite meet
was at Tetcott House. Now at Cambridge, William wrote to his
mother: 'If you do not wish me to have my neck broken you

must consent to let me have good hunters, for not to hunt is out of the question.' He did, in fact, break his collar-bone – remounted and rode on fifty miles after his fall. Later, an almost fatal fall was the beginning of a life-long friendship with Edward Duppa, son of the artist and author Richard Duppa, who himself became a portrait painter. When William fell, the rest of the hunt rode on regardless; but Duppa dismounted and came to his aid. William felt he owed his life to Duppa; and this led to an unfortunate sequel when Duppa became involved in a quarrel over a gambling incident. William, although he himself was not involved in the incident, took up Duppa's cause and thereby got into trouble with the college authorities. Whatever were the facts of the case, the bizarre outcome was that William challenged his tutor, Mr Henry Barnard, to a duel. On April 30th 1828, he and Barnard were bound over by the Mayor of Cambridge to keep the peace for twelve months, and Molesworth was sent down from the University.

Lady Molesworth was determined William must continue his education, and arranged for him to go to Germany accompanied by an old family friend, General Sir Joseph Straton, who would act as counsellor and guide – he had commanded the Enniskillens at Waterloo, but no doubt had other qualifications for conducting a high-spirited young man through the temptations of foreign lands. William's personal servant Duncan Maclean went with them – it was the start of a life-long servant-to-master devotion. Everyone who knew Molesworth knew Maclean. Before setting out William, who did not consider that leaving England released him from the challenge to his tutor, arranged an assignment at Calais to be kept at the end of their year of 'keeping the peace.' That would be on May 2nd 1829, just three weeks before William's nineteenth birthday.

The expulsion from Cambridge, disastrous-seeming at the time, was possibly all for the best. At Cambridge the fast life of wealthy undergraduates on pleasure bent could well have swept William happily along, leaving little time for study. But William was essentially a scholar – a born scholar. As a small boy his family had nicknamed him 'the philosopher' because of his interest in physics, botany and metaphysics, his love of poisonous chemicals, and his habit of spending all his pocket-money on books. Later, when in Edinburgh, he had nearly died from inhaling chlorine gas in a laboratory he had himself constructed in the suburb of Portpello. Even at Cambridge, with all its tempting distractions, he determinedly devoted most mornings to work – pure mathematics at that time were his favourite study. Now in Germany, while continuing his study of mathematics, he worked hard to get complete command of the language and a wide knowledge of German literature and philosophy.

He and General Straton spent some time in Frankfurt, then went on to Offenbach, and from there to Spa. William dutifully wrote frequently to his mother – and rather more frivolous letters to his sister Elizabeth. From Spa he reported: 'Only one pretty girl in the whole town – with a disagreeable old father.' He escorted the pretty girl for long walks, permitted by the disagreeable old father when he learned that the young English baronet was very rich . . . In one letter home William wrote: 'General Straton says reports of my fortune have begun to be ingeniously misquoted.' From Spa they went on to Munich, where the General recommended William should make a long stay. An introduction to the British Minister, Lord Erskine, gave him the entrée to Munich society. The Erskine family invited William to make the British Embassy his home, but General Straton, fearing too many social distractions there, arranged private lodgings for William and Maclean before himself returning to England. Before leaving, he wrote to reassure Lady Molesworth: 'William is steady, proper, and gentlemanly – never plays [gambles] though everyone else does. No turn for any form of dissipation.'

The fashionable craze in Munich at the time was dancing – hardly a form of dissipation. William wrote home: 'A good dancer is looked upon as a Deity and a bad one is esteemed amongst the d – d.' He was asking for more money, for with his characteristic determination to do well in whatever he attempted he wished to engage a dancing master. On November 28th 1828, he wrote: 'My dancing master is as good as a language master – I shall have a whole month to practice before the gay season which begins next month.' When the season was in full swing he told his sister Elizabeth: 'The ballroom presents an appearance more like the

betting ring at Newmarket than anything I am acquainted with.'
He didn't think much of the fillies: 'German women all damned
ugly – but married women much more pleasant than misses.' His
daily routine was: German philosophy in the mornings, dancing
lessons, fencing and sledging in the afternoons; in the evenings
the theatre, then dancing until three in the morning. He also
reported that he was 'becoming a very good rifle shot.' Having
mastered the grammar of the German language, he hoped his
conversation would be perfected just by mixing in society. How
provoking then to find that all fashionable Germans talked in
French. 'It is a nuisance', he wrote to his mother on February
18th 1829, 'that in society there is hardly a word of German
spoken . . . The natives always speak to each other in French,
and many openly declare that they prefer it to their own language.
And if you address them in German they always reply in French.'
The last festivity he took part in at Munich was a fancy-dress ball
given by the Electress, after which William boasted to his sister,
'The public chose to affirm I had the most splendid costume in
the room!' A few days later he left Munich with Maclean to make
the thirteen-day journey to Calais to keep the duelling assignment
with Barnard on May 1st 1829, at which Lord Queensbury acted
as his second.

Mr Barnard's aunt, Miss Charlotte Barnard, had towards the end
of the previous year discovered what was afoot; and on December
5th 1928, wrote to Lady Molesworth:

                              Withersfield, near Haverhill, Suffolk
Madam,
    It is, I assure you, with reluctance I enter upon a Subject which must,
as the Mother of Sir William Molesworth, be a painful one to you, yet as
it also deeply concerns my own Family, I cannot allow myself to shrink
from it, feeling as I do most strongly that as a Female, I may be excused
the Anxiety it causes me; and that as a Christian, I am bound to take any
Steps in my power to prevent a Duel. You are probably informed that last
year, several young Men were expell'd from Cambridge, in consequence of
a quarrel at a Gambling party, which produced a Challenge, and would
then have terminated in a Duel, had not the Mayor of Cambridge put
a stop to it, binding Sir William Molesworth and Mr Henry Barnard (my
nephew) to keep the Peace for twelve Months – at the end of the Period

it is, I find, determined by what the World calls the Rules of Honour, a Duel *must* take place between them. By mere Accident I find that the time fixed for their Meeting is the 1st of next May, the place, Calais – I do assure you I have not learnt these particulars from my Nephew, or censure that of Sir William Molesworth . . . but I cannot answer it to myself hereafter, should fatal Consequences ensue, to either, not to have made some attempt to prevent it, by stating the Circumstances to some of Sir William Molesworth's family, who may have the influence with him, or Authority sufficient to enable them to do so – With my Nephew I am well convinced I have no chance of Success.

I am told that it is no difficult matter to prevent the Duel. If information were laid before the Police at Calais, who would on arrival of the Parties, and the production of their Passports, arrest them and bind them to keep the Peace. I have only now to add that I very sincerely regret being obliged to lay these painful Circumstances before you and that I am, Madam,
Your obt. Servant, Charlotte A. Barnard.

In her reply to this letter, Lady Molesworth made it quite clear that she blamed the whole episode upon Mr Barnard, and that it was up to him to withdraw – moreover, she would never attempt to influence her son to take a course that could be considered injurious to his honour:

. . . It would be senseless for me to occupy your time by expressing the great painful anxiety I experienced during my son's short residence at Cambridge. Your feelings are most deeply awakened at the sense of your nephew's danger, how much more acute then must be a Mother's for a son who till he went to the University hardly gave her a moment's uneasiness, apart from the state of his health. Your nephew much his Senior and [bred] to the Church must have been fully aware of the inevitable consequence that must follow the conduct he pursued towards my son who had not then attained his eighteenth year. Melancholy and deplorable as the termination may prove of this lamentable quarrel, I have no hopes of averting the evil except by your Nephew [making a reparation?] commensurate to the injury done.

You declare you have no chance of success with Mr Henry Barnard & I feel that whatever influence I might possess over my son, I never could exercise it until such took place, for altho' his Mother and a woman I never could advise what hereafter might be deem'd injurious to his honour. It now rests entirely with your Nephew's friends who appear perfectly conversant with all that has taken place and what can be done under such circumstances to take the measures they think most [provident?] to avoid the impending duel.

As far as is known, no measures were attempted. The next letter in the archives addressed to Lady Molesworth, 97 George Street, Edinburgh has a postmark May 2nd 1829.

It is from William, at Stephens Hotel, Clifford Street, London, and begins:

I am happy to inform you that I am alive and well. I could not hit my adversary all I could [would?]. I am excessively obliged to you for sending Leach [the family attorney] to Calais and am under the greatest obligation to him. I came up to town with him and arrived here this morning. I have left my servant and baggage at Calais. I am most infernally tired of travelling all alone and nothing whatsoever should induce me to return to travel alone. The distance from Munich to Calais is above 700 miles and took me 13 days all alone with my servant, nothing but an affair would ever induce me to take such a journey alone. . . I shall stay in England till either you or the General or someone else will go with me.

. . . Leach has informed me of a demand made upon me by a Cam. banker. I am excessively astonished, but it must be pay'd; such conduct is too bad. I shall write to his brother whom I had informed of the existence of the bill and who had assured me it should be pay'd. I shall cease acquaintance with the whole family. Love to all.

I am my dear Mother,
          Your affectionate son, William Molesworth.

The brief period as a Cambridge undergraduate had caused many debts as well as a duel. It is frustrating that no fuller account of the duel than in this letter can be found. Maclean, no doubt, enjoyed giving many vivid verbal accounts with much embroidery. It is known that he told Lady Molesworth that when he accompanied Sir William to the 'affair' he had a loaded pistol in his pocket, and if Barnard had killed his master he, Maclean, had determined to murder Barnard. We cannot doubt the pistol in the pocket. Maclean, after all, was a Highlander.

William remained in England until late Autumn before setting out for Rome – travelling alone, except for Maclean. It seems from his letters home that social life in Rome was even more demanding than in Munich; it included a costume ball at which he was dressed as Ivanhoe. Nevertheless, he assured his mother, he was keeping to a strict routine – 'to bed at three and rise again at nine'. To his studies he had now added Arabic and Oriental languages, in which he was instructed by 'a master with a long beard, from Chaldea.' His ambition was to extend his travels to the Near East. Lady Molesworth with her two daughters later joined him in Rome, and remained in Italy for the rest of 1830, visiting Naples, Castellmare, Bologna, and all the essential cities of the Grand Tour. William, who had taken lessons in drawing and painting in Germany, had by this time considerable artistic ability, as is shown in a volume of his Italian sketches at Pencarrow. It was the gardens of the noblemen's villas that were his chief fascination. They stimulated and fertilised the interest he had always had in plants, trees and garden architecture, an interest which continued for the rest of his life. Immediately on returning from Italy to Pencarrow, he designed an Italian garden in the form of an amphitheatre with terraces of grass, its centre-piece a fountain, its basin copied from that of the Piazza Navonna in Rome.

This return was early in 1831, in good time to prepare for the celebrations of William's majority on May 23rd. They found that in England all the talk was of the controversies and agitations aroused by the Reform Bill then before Parliament.

CHAPTER II — 1832-4

THE Reform Bill presented to Parliament in 1831 was passed on its second reading on March 23rd by a majority of just one vote. It was quickly defeated in Committee and the Prime Minister, Lord Grey, instantly resolved on a dissolution of Parliament. Writs for the General Election were issued in April – too soon for Molesworth to offer himself as a candidate, as he did not attain his majority until May 23rd. But inevitably he was caught up in the political excitement of the time. The radical ideas first acquired during his Edinburgh education, followed by his mingling with free-thinking young intellectuals in Germany, combined to make him feel he should lend active support to those who were dedicated to bringing about a more just, more representative administration of Great Britain. He was against established aristocratic institutions despite himself representing a centuries-old family. It was nothing to him that the Reform Bill proposed the extinction of many pocket boroughs* in Cornwall under one-family control – some of which had been represented by his own relatives. His like-minded friend Charles Buller, who was in the un-reformed Parliament of 1830-'32 as a Member for West Looe, his family pocket-borough, had voted in 1831 for its extinction. Thus it was that William abandoned his dream of travelling in the East, at least for the time being, and agreed to stand as Liberal candidate for East Cornwall at the next General Election.

In his address to the electors in June 1832, after the Reform Bill had been passed, he promised to support 'every species of just and salutary reform in Church and State'. Among the reforms he advocated was that education should not be under the exclusive control of the clergy, and that far more money should be spent

---

*Pocket boroughs – Parliamentary constituencies with few voters, usually rural, in which one family had the inherited right to propose the candidate for election.

on national education. He declared his support for the Ballot, for
triennial parliaments, free trade and tithe commutation; and he
boldly stated his belief that the Reform Bill did not go nearly far
enough. In spite of such very radical declarations, he was returned
unopposed for East Cornwall, his colleague being William Salisbury
Trelawny. Charles Buller, whose address to his electors had been
equally radical, was returned for Liskeard. William Makepeace
Thackeray had stayed with the Buller family at Polvellan for a
fortnight to help Charles in his campaign, and it was there that
he met William Molesworth for the first time.

Thackeray's diary gives details of his journey from London to
Cornwall, which are of interest since it was the same journey that
Molesworth would be making so often after his election:

Tuesday May 19th 1832: At 8 o'clock we set off by the mail outside, and
after a dull, cold, hot, damp, dusty uncomfortable ride of four and twenty
hours arrived at Plymouth – Fare £2.14.0. expenses £1.6.0.
Wednesday 20th: We dined uncomfortably and then were glad enough to
go to bed. My sleep was pleasantly diversified by bugs and lasted till seven.
Bill etc. 15s.
Thursday 21st: Crossed the water to Torpoint and set off to Liskeard by
the mail.

Molesworth, not being hard up like Thackeray, would not travel
outside on the mail. Nor would he put up in Plymouth in an
hostelry with bugs in the bed. But he would have an additional
fourteen miles by mail from Liskeard to Bodmin, where he would be
put down at the Royal Hotel, headquarters of the mail coach from
North Cornwall to Truro. There his own carriage from Pencarrow
would meet him.

Thackeray's diary continued:

July 11th: At Polvellan all day eating, sleeping and dawdling; there
arrived Mrs and Miss Hillier of the Caledonia, and Sir William Molesworth
who is standing for the county – the first two strike me as being fools, the
last a sensible fellow enough.
July 12th: Set off with Mrs Hillier, her daughter and Miss A. Buller
to Liskeard where we found young women in waggons singing hymns,
charity children, banners etc. – all awaiting the arrival of Sir William
Molesworth and Charles Buller who with Mr and Mrs Buller were dragged

into the town by the enthusiastic populace. 400 sat down to dinner at
1 o'clock . . . We adjourned to the town-hall where the members
and attorneys and a farmer called Greig made speeches, this latter as
fine an orator as ever I heard; came home at about eight and spent
a pleasant evening – Sir William Molesworth went away. He made a
wretched speech as did everyone excepting C.B. [Charles Buller] and
Greig.

WHEN the House of Commons assembled for the first session
of the reformed parliament, Molesworth and Buller took their seats
amongst the Whigs. But Molesworth was a rebel to party discipline
from the start, twice voting against the Government of which he
was a nominal supporter on amendments to the Address. . . the
Government was proposing to bring in a new Coercion Bill for
Ireland. Sir William had written of it to his mother: 'I will oppose
this infernal Bill, engendered in Hell (i.e. the House of Lords) to
the last.' Lord Grey, the Prime Minister, must have thought the
unruly young member to be a bit of a nuisance; but George Grote,
Member for the City of London, regarded him with a speculative
eye. This wealthy baronet could be a valuable member of the
group of MPs calling themselves the Philosophical Radicals. He
would bring them the support of a name influentially connected
with the landed interest and with the associations of hereditary
descent, yet eager to crusade against aristocratic privilege. Grote
himself, a City banker, although nominally a Benthamite was by
no means belligerent. He believed in working for gradual reform
that would lead to quiet, unrevolutionary progress to a more just
and balanced society: the Ballot, Triennial Parliaments, extension
of the suffrage, reform of the House of Lords – *not* abolition of
the House of Lords as some of the Radicals, including Molesworth,
believed necessary. Grote was temperamentally a scholar, absorbed
in writing a history of Greece. It was his wife Harriet who was heart
and soul a political animal. Sharing her husband's beliefs and aims,
she promoted them energetically. Indeed, one might call her, in
modern terms, a public relations officer for the Philosophical Radical
Group, which was made up of intellectuals impatient for changes
far beyond those brought about by the passing of the Reform
Bill.

When George Grote told his wife of the intriguing arrival in
Parliament of a very young baronet, said to be extremely wealthy,

rather too exquisite in dress, delicate looking but seeming to be driven by an inner fire, she scented a promising recruit and demanded that he be introduced to her. The friendship which swiftly developed became so much a part of Molesworth's life for the next twelve years that it is necessary at this point to describe further this female politician, unique in her generation.

Harriet Grote, outspoken and quick witted, was unselfconsciously abrasive in thrusting repartee, even to the occasional stab with a slang expression. She was said to have never felt shy. Conspicuously eccentric in dress, she was the subject of innumerable quips. Sydney Smith declared that Harriet Grote was the origin of the word grotesque; and summed up Mr and Mrs Grote after a visit they had paid him in his Somerset vicarage: 'I like her, she is such a gentleman, and I like him, he is such a perfect lady'. Augustus Hare in *The Story of My Life* wrote: 'I was enchanted with Mrs Grote, whom De Toqueville pronounced "the cleverest woman of his acquaintance", though her exterior – with a short waist, brown mantle of stamped velvet, and huge bonnet, full of full-blown roses – was certainly not captivating.' Lady Eastlake, in an affectionate sketch of Mrs Grote published after her death, wrote that 'her blue eyes were so large and luminous that someone likened them to carriage lamps. She had a passion for discordant colours, and had her petticoats always arranged to display her feet and ankles, of which she was excessively proud.' She drew further attention to them by wearing white socks and red shoes.

Had Mrs Grote lived in the twentieth century she would without doubt have become a Member of Parliament – although her unpredictable eccentricity and fearless tongue might have prevented her from becoming a Cabinet Minister. John Stuart Mill deplored that her husband did not have the same energy and drive. Son of James Stuart Mill, the utilitarian philosopher and promulgator of Benthamism, himself an ardent, impatient philosophical radical, he wrote in the *London & Westminster Review*, October 1835, that the one thing needed for the Philosophical Radical party in Parliament was a leader, a man of action – 'Why does not Mr Grote exert himself? There is not a man in Parliament who *could* do so much or who is more thoroughly the people's friend'; and Francis Place who, like John Stuart Mill, was not a Member of Parliament, declared that there was not a man in the Radical party with the exception of Madame Grote.

When Madame Grote's carriage-lamp eyes first lighted upon Sir William Molesworth, they perceived a young man of pent-up intensity, on tip-toe for action. She and her husband introduced him to those of the group that he had not already met, and she came to regard him as virtually her disciple – a willing disciple, for there seems to have been immediate rapport. As a married woman, eight years Sir William's senior and known to be excessively devoted to her husband, she could be teasingly affectionate in her letters to Sir William, and he could be flippantly flirtatious in his. She reproved him for being unsociable. When he first entered Parliament he restricted his social life to the small circle of his political colleagues, feeling that it would be illogical for one of his radical beliefs to mingle in the extravagant gatherings of high society. When he could not avoid them, he tended to be awkwardly aloof, standing on the outskirts. Mrs Grote, who did not allow her radicalism to conflict with her delight in aristocratic society, sent him 'a good scold for his rude and uncourteous habits'. In another letter she alleged to have heard complaints of his being insolent, rude, and vain, 'to which defects I own on your behalf, but add that these defects form the safeguard to your political virtue'.

William's friendship with both Mr and Mrs Grote had become one of easy familiarity by the time he accompanied them on 'a little rural tour' in Surrey and Hampshire during the Whitsun recess of 1833. He and Mr Grote rode on horseback; and Mrs Grote, driving her phaeton, was accompanied by Mrs Austin, wife of John Austin the eminent jurist. William's twenty-third birthday was celebrated during this excursion, and we have a description of him as Mrs Grote saw him then: 'He had a pleasant countenance, expressive blue eyes, florid complexion, and light brown hair; a slim and neatly made figure, about five feet ten in height, with small well-shaped hands and feet. He rode well; and his manners were, when he took the trouble, those of a man accustomed to good company and assiduous to please.' After this rural idyll, William became a frequent Saturday to Monday guest at the Grote's house in Dulwich Wood.

IN addition to his radical stance in politics, Sir William had a radical attitude to religion. His studies in theology had ironically led him to repudiate the Christian mysteries and refuse to attend any church; while his studies of philosophical works and his contacts with free-thinking scholars in Germany, had influenced him into becoming an agnostic – he never allowed himself to be called an atheist. This attitude to religion was viewed unfavourably by the land-owning gentry in his constituency, and was deeply distressing to most of his family. Many of his Molesworth relatives were in Anglican livings. His father's brother William was Rector of the parish of St Breocke comprising all Wadebridge west of the bridge, and was also the incumbent for St Ervan, a village just a little further away. The Revd Paul William Molesworth was Rector of Tetcott, the Molesworth seat in Devonshire, prior to becoming in 1854 a convert to the Roman Catholic faith. The Revd John Molesworth was rector of Redruth and Crowan, his brother Hender of St Erney and Redruth. Hugh Henry Molesworth, Sir William's first cousin, became Rector of St Petroc Minor, Little Petherick near Padstow, in 1848.

Uncle William at St Breocke was not only distressed at his nephew's denial of Christianity, but also by his political stance. He himself was a dyed-in-the-blood Conservative. When his nephew had first been adopted as a Liberal candidate he had written to him asking what caused him to take such a distressing step, and what aims he would have in the Liberal Party. Sir William had replied on April 9th 1831, giving a full account of the reforms he would aim to bring about should he be elected. His letter ended:

'If, however, I am disappointed in my ambition I shall resume my plan of journeying in the East and quit the shores of Europe for three or four years. Thus explicitly, my dear Uncle, I have answered your letter and although we may disagree on the subject of politics believe me to be most sincerely, most truly, your affectionate nephew – William.'

The rift caused by religion and politics was not bridged in the ensuing years. Uncle William was not one to compromise for the sake of peaceful relations with his sister-in-law and her family. After all, he was a Molesworth and had the same unswerving commitment to his beliefs as did his Molesworth nephew. Four years later he was writing to Lady Molesworth:

January 6th 1835

My dear Mary,

Perhaps you may wonder why you have not seen me lately at Pencarrow, but I trust you do not and will not set it down to the least diminution of my affection and attachment to yourself or my Brother's family. But the truth is, that our views on those questions which now agitate the Kingdom from one end of it to the other, are so totally dissimilar that on the principle of the least said is the soonest mended I account for my absence. Believe me that I am truly grateful for the uniform kindness and respect you have always shown me, I value so highly your esteem and regard that I will not run any risk of forfeiting them by discussing political questions.

It seems from this letter that Lady Molesworth held the same views as her son on political matters – although, with her Scottish upbringing, probably not the same on religion.

UNFORTUNATELY William's beliefs in politics, and lack of belief in religion, were not only of family concern. At this time they were affecting, and were fatally to frustrate, his suit for the hand of Juliana Carew. She and William had known each other since childhood, the Carew family seat being at Antony, near Plymouth. In the interval between the Molesworths returning to Pencarrow from Edinburgh and William starting on his European travels, he had been in the habit of riding over to Antony accompanied by a servant with saddlebags containing his clothes for a visit of two or three days. After his return from Europe, his first election to Parliament, and then his unopposed return at the General Election of 1834 – all ideas of travel in the East by then abandoned – he set his heart upon marriage to Juliana – Julia, as she was called by family and close friends.

Indeed it was high time for him to marry and start the next generation of Molesworths. The aristocracy believed in early marriage, as soon as their sons had sown their wild oats and when a young bride had plenty of child-bearing years before her to ensure a sound sequence. Although parents did not, as in France, arrange marriages without considering the feelings of their sons and daughters, there was a tendency to consider fortune and breeding to be as important as mutual love. For example, Maria Josepha Lady Stanley wrote to her daughter-in-law with reference to the engagement of a relative: 'I am not one who thinks worldly advantages and plenty of money is the *chief* thing needful, although it does make up for deficiency in blood.' And Bulwer-Lytton wrote cynically in his *England and the English,* published in 1833: 'We boast that in our country, young people not being affianced to each other by their parents, there are more marriages in which the heart is engaged than there are abroad. Very possibly; but, in good society, the heart is remarkably prudent, and seldom falls violently in love without a sufficient settlement: where the heart is, *there will the treasure* be also!'

Treasure was not lacking in the case of William and Julia, and their hearts were truly engaged. Religion and politics were the barriers that Julia's family considered insurmountable. William was not at all reticent about his *affaire de coeur* and wrote frankly about his suit's progress and set-backs to his mother and his sister Elizabeth; but the depth of his feelings, the times of hope and then of despair, were most fully confided to his dear friend and confidante Mrs Grote. She wrote of them in her *Life of Sir William* published for private circulation ten years after his death.* Maybe she embroidered a little; but she was writing when the principal characters, except William himself, were all still alive – which will have curbed any wild flights of fancy. She tells how, since the Carews at Antony were close friends of the Bullers at Polvellan, William asked Mrs Buller's help to bring about opportunities for him to meet Julia when they were all in London for the season. This Mrs Buller did; and at the first of the Bullers' London parties Mrs Grote's keen curious eyes observed William talking to Julia, and noted that 'his manner and the animation of his countenance lent a singular charm to his whole appearance.' On that evening 'he obtained permission to visit at the house of the Countess St Germans (half-sister of Miss Julia Carew) in Park-crescent, Portland-

---

The Philosophical Radicals of 1832, comprising the Life of Sir William Molesworth and some Incidents connected with the Reform Movement from 1832 to 1845, published Anon. for Private Circulation in 1866. In subsequent references to, and quotations from, this book, it is referred to simply as Mrs Grote's *Life of Sir William Molesworth.*

place.' There, it seems, Julia consented to marry him if he could obtain the permission of her kinsman, Lord Lyttleton, and:

Accordingly, without a moment's loss of time, to Hagley flew the impatient lover, as fast as four post-horses could convey him. Lord Lyttleton received him with polite hauteur; Molesworth addressed him in very earnest language beseeching him to terminate his anxieties by a favourable reply. His lordship said that he understood him to be both a Radical in politics and an infidel in religion. Molesworth rejoined that he did not see what that could have to do with his conduct or character, upon which he challenged scrutiny. His lordship remained inflexible, saying he could never advise his niece to unite herself with a man of such obnoxious opinions.*

Mrs Grote's narrative continues by relating how Molesworth travelled back from Hagley to London overnight and then 'jumped into his tilbury and drove down to our house at Dulwich Wood.' Mrs Grote was not there, having gone up to London for a concert in the Concert Room at the Opera House in the Haymarket. So, 'Back to London he drove, and straight to the Opera House . . . there he whispered to me, "Pray come out into the ante-room, I have much to tell you." He was in a perfect fever, his eyes flashing fire and fury, his voice full of emotion; and when at length we parted, he exclaimed, using a vehement gesture with his arm, "I vow to pull down this haughty aristocracy of ours, or perish in the attempt!" '

After that drama, Molesworth addressed himself assiduously to parliamentary matters. In the summer recess he met Julia at the Plymouth races and balls. Her brothers spent a week-long visit at Pencarrow and gave William an invitation from their parents to visit Antony. He went, but when there made no progress, embarrassed by the constant presence of the observant family circle. He met Julia again at the Bullers' in Polvellan, and Mrs Buller intimated that he might yet succeed in his suit were he at least to modify his sceptical opinions. This he felt would be dishonourable. He wrote from Pencarrow to Mrs Grote in October 1834: 'What between the various alterations of hope, fear, and anxiety, I have been so

*Juliana's father, the Rt Hon. Reginald Pole Carew, had died in 1836. Her mother, Caroline Ann, was daughter of the 1st Lord Lyttelton; so the 2nd Lord Lyttelton was Juliana's uncle and guardian.

annoyed and vexed that I am completely disgusted with myself and irritated at my folly. I would do anything, not dishonourable, to gain the lady. I have softened down my opinions to the verge of falsehood; but that barrier I will not pass! I have been living a great deal in the wide world and on horseback. Years have elapsed since I have led so reckless a life. In spite of it – in spite of the deepest potations – in spite of the severest fatigue – I never was so well in my life!'

Clearly, he was forcing himself onto the road to recovery. How long the road to recovery was for Juliana can only be surmised. At any rate, it was not until nearly five years later, in 1839, that she married Thomas James Agar Robartes of Lanhydrock, near Bodmin, the great seventeenth-century house that is now the National Trust headquarters in Cornwall. It was a marriage to which Lord Lyttleton will most certainly have given his blessing.

CHAPTER III — 1835-6

THE idea of starting a monthly Review began to be discussed by the Philosophical Radicals in 1833. It had become clear to them quite early in the first session of the Reformed Parliament that Lord Grey's government was not going to engender any enthusiasm for further reforms. Indeed, the Whigs seemed quite ready to defeat radical proposals with the help of Tory votes. Thus the true Radicals found themselves fighting the Whigs as much as the Tories. In their frustration they felt a Review would serve as a mouthpiece to expound their beliefs and proposals beyond the Palace of Westminster. John Stuart Mill, Charles Buller and J.A. Roebuck, the Member for Bath, had held informal meetings about the project over a long period. Mr Grote was far from enthusiastic and refused to join them.

Lack of finance was, as ever in such ventures, a damper to enthusiasm; but when Molesworth heard about the idea he immediately supplied both fresh enthusiasm and substantial finance. Thomas Carlyle in his *Reminiscences* wrote an engaging account of Molesworth's high-handed way of setting the new Review afloat: '"How much will your Review take to launch it, then?" asked he (all other Radical believers being so close of fist). "Say £4,000," answered Mill. "Here then," writing a cheque for that amount, rejoined the other.'

John Stuart Mill wrote in his autobiography that one of the main purposes of the Review 'was to stir up the educated Radicals, in and out of Parliament, to exertion, and induce them to make themselves what I thought by using the proper means they might become – a powerful party capable of taking the government of the country, or at least of dictating terms on which they should share it with the Whigs.' One of the 'educated Radicals' that Mill felt needed stirring up was George Grote; and once the *London Review* was launched Grote wrote approvingly of it in his diary, January 1836: 'The chic organ of the Radical party at this period is the *London Review*,

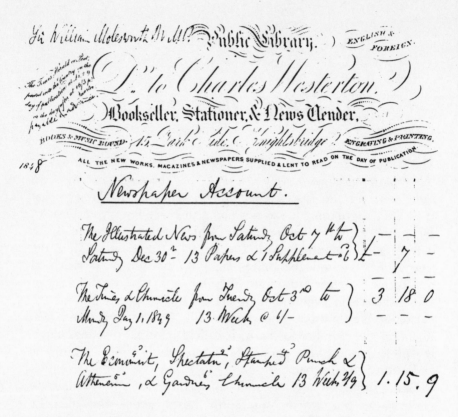

Part of Sir William's quarterly newspaper account. Note that his regular reading included the Gardener's Chronicle.

being the old *Westminster Review* under a new direction; the funds supplied by Sir William Molesworth, MP, with John Stuart Mill for the editor. The list of contributors comprises some of the most able pens of the day, and the Review is undeniably superior in quality to any of its rivals. J.A. Roebuck also issues political tracts, at the price of three halfpence – extremely clever and instructive – selling as many as ten thousand a week.'

Roebuck's tracts were weekly *Pamphlets for the People*. The first was published on June 11th 1835, and they continued for 36 numbers, some written by Roebuck himself. Molesworth contributed £50 to the working capital. In February 1836 he wrote yet another cheque. This was for £1,000 to buy the *Westminster Review*; the first joint issue of the *London and Westminster Review* appeared in April 1836. Mr Grote's diary entry quoted above seems to have anticipated this take-over.

Thomas Carlyle had met Molesworth for the first time in the year before the launching of the *London Review*. Their meeting was at a dinner at the Bullers' London house, which Carlyle wrote about to his mother on May 30th 1834:

Radical members and such like . . . among whom a young, very rich man, named Sir William Molesworth, pleased me considerably. We have met since, and shall probably see much more of one another. He seems very honest; needs, or will need, guidance much, and with it may do not a little good. I like the frank manners of the young man; so beautiful in contrast with Scottish gigmanity. I pitied his darkness of mind, and heartily wished him well. He is, among other things, a vehement smoker of tobacco.

It is interesting that Carlyle detected that 'darkness of mind' which lay under the surface of Sir William's spontaneous enthusiasms. Carlyle's usual stance was to be bitingly critical of aristocrats, abruptly dismissive if they were lightweights. But he discerned that Molesworth was no lightweight. After meeting him again at another Buller dinner party in February 1835, Carlyle noted in his diary: 'Sir William Molesworth with the air of a good roystering schoolboy pleased me considerably more [than Roebuck]. A man of rank can still do this, forget his rank wholly, and be the sooner esteemed for having the mind equal to doing that.'

Although Sir William, as Carlyle's account shows, thoroughly enjoyed the Bullers' parties, he was still being constantly chided by Mrs Grote for being unsociable. At the Bullers he was amongst close friends, so could be relaxed. Mrs Grote considered he should move in wider circles. Often in his letters, Molesworth teased Mrs Grote about her efforts to coax him out of his surliness in society. From Pencarrow in the summer recess of 1836 he wrote 'I am well pleased at your determining not to attempt any more the hopeless task of reforming me, for your reproaches grieved me, though for reasons oft stated they could not have the effect you desired. I can however sometimes be agreeable in the most general society. In proof of which I may state that I have been paying a visit to some of my neighbours for three days, and offended nobody.'

His sister Mary also used to reproach or tease him about his dour manners, and there are many letters to her in which he exaggerates for her amusement his attempts to be gallant and daringly flirtatious at London parties. For instance, in June 1836: 'When does my flame Mrs Chowson come to town? I have fallen in love with one of Mrs Ward's daughters – a young lady between 13 and 14, from whom, under the influence of her father's sherry I stole a lock of hair.' Lady Molesworth does not seem to have brought her daughters to London for the season at this time, although they were both of marriageable age. Most parents considered it a necessary duty to transplant daughters from their country houses to enjoy the fashionable round and meet eligible young men. Perhaps Lady Molesworth could not persuade William, who of course was in *loco parentis* to his sisters, to play his part in introducing them into the circles he himself preferred to avoid.

IN JANUARY 1836 Molesworth travelled to Birmingham with Joseph Parkes to speak against the Orange Lodges* at a public dinner and meeting of the National Political Union. This Union was an association which was taking a considerable part in the continuing battle for further reform. To get to Birmingham meant a long exhausting journey by mail coach – with no rest at the end of it before attending and speaking at the public meetings. The exact timing of the three stressful days can be learned from a letter William wrote to Lady Molesworth. He and Parkes left London at 8 o'clock on the Wednesday evening and reached Birmingham at 12 noon next day – 16 hours on the road. They attended that same day, Thursday, a public dinner at which a thousand people sat down – at the end of which Molesworth made a speech and then went straight on to the National Political Union meeting, at which he spoke again. He and Parkes left Birmingham at one hour past midnight of that same day, and arrived in London at five o'clock on Friday evening – another sixteen hours on the road. Thus they had spent thirty-two hours in a rattling coach, the eleven hours between the journeys being spent at public meetings. Sir William's health might be frail, but there were times when through sheer will-power

*Orange Lodges: secret political branches of supporters of the ultra-Protestant party in Ireland.

he ignored fatigue. He had not been impressed by the big-wigs of Birmingham. 'Shrewd but uneducated men,' he described them in a letter to his mother; 'few of them could pronounce their 'h's – though the younger men were a much better set . . . surprisingly mild in their speeches.' He himself 'was the only one who "spoke out" '.

Following the Birmingham meetings, there was a debate on the Orange Lodges in the House of Commons on February 23rd, the motion being proposed by Hume, seconded by Molesworth. The resolution proposed an address to the King praying him to discharge all Orangemen and members of other secret political associations from all offices, civil and military. The tremendous success of Molesworth's speech which, as was his wont, he had prepared most carefully, is documented in three letters at Pencarrow. The first, dated February 24th, is from William to Lady Molesworth. It begins triumphantly:

We have destroyed the Orangemen. Last night I seconded Hume with a success which exceeded my most sanguine anticipations. The House was full, 400 at least present. Hume made a long and confused speech. He contrived woefully to tangle and to confuse the clearest subject. The House was weary when I rose. I contrived quickly to excite their attention and to stimulate their feelings. I could hardly finish a sentence, so loud and enthusiastic were the cheers: never even amongst my most ardent followers was I so much applauded. When I finished I was congratulated by every one. It would be too egotistical to repeat all that was said to me in praise by the leading men . . . The Tories said it was a most infamous speech, and cursed me cordially for it.

The letter ends 'Thus we have slain the Orangemen.'

His brother Arscott was in the gallery of the House, and wrote to Lady Molesworth on the same day 'I went to hear William on the Orange Lodges, and splendidly he spoke, with a great deal of animation and without that false voice which whenever I have heard him before he used to have.' Arscott's letter continued with criticisms of other speakers, and ended 'Austin and everybody who was near me agreed that it was one of the best, tho' most audacious speech ever delivered. The Tories say it was the most rascally. It quite slagged them, to use a slang expression. Austin said to a friend of his while Wm. was speaking on the *law points.* "He is a d – d clear-headed fellow this." This I overheard.'

Charles Austin was a very distinguished lawyer, so his approval of the law points was particularly gratifying. The third letter was from Edward Duppa to Lady Molesworth, written on February 26th, a very long letter from which but a few passages can be quoted here:

You have, I doubt not, read over William's speech *more than once,* and are in consequence acquainted with the matter, though not perhaps with the manner of his delivery. He rose, not with the diffidence which generally characterises and so well becomes one of his age, but with a degree of self-confidence worthy the Great Dan himself, and spoke with wonderful energy – failed neither in quotation nor reference until interrupted by Mr Randal Plunkett. He begged some explanation, which you will find in the report. Well, explanation given, Wm. stuck his glass firmly in his eye, transfixed the Hon. Member with his look, and said, with a *sang-froid* of which the most experienced debator might well have been proud: "I hope the Hon. Member's memory is refreshed.". . . He then expounded the laws relative to Orange and other societies using secret signs and oaths, told them those who frequented such societies subjected themselves to transportation – that the Duke of Cumberland and his clique ought not to be spared because they were rich and well educated, whilst the poor ignorant Dorchester labourers [the 'Tolpuddle Martyrs'] were suffering for the infringement of those laws which they were unable to understand. William gave out the names of the titled criminals, as he termed them, with exquisite bitterness, and clenched his red pocket-handkerchief in his fist towards the conclusion of his address as though he were tearing up Orange societies by the root. Tremendous cheering followed his speech. In fact, he *distinguished himself,* and I have little hesitation in saying that if he goes on as he has begun he will one day make about the best, though not perhaps the most prudent, speaker in the House.

Duppa's letter ends:

Arscott and myself were in the House from 4 o'clock in the afternoon until 2 in the morning. Arscott turned very pale when his brother rose . . . After *the* speech, for it was assuredly *the* speech of the night, William, Arscott, and your humble servant adjourned to Bellamy's kitchen, where we demanded sundry mutton chops, Welsh rabbits, bottle of porter and sherry – no bad finale to the night's fatigue, for, by Jove, it is a monstrous bore to sit in the same place for ten consecutive hours. Thank God, I am not an MP.

An intriguing outcome from the Orangemen speech was an invitation from the Duchess of Kent, Princess Victoria's mother, to a party at Kensington Palace – 'I suppose,' wrote Sir William, 'in consequence of my proposing to transport her brother-in-law [the Duke of Cumberland].' He goes on to say that he was sure he was pointed out to the Duke of Cumberland, 'as he looked like the devil at me, and I laughed . . . I went with Grote and there was a strange mixture of Rads, Whigs, and Tories. Grote, Pattison, Crawford, Bannerman and myself placed ourselves for some time near the entrance to see the people coming in and going out, and it was excessively funny to see the stares of astonishment of the Tories in finding us there in force. We were presented to the Duchess of Kent, Princess Victoria and Prince Ferdinand.'

TWO months later, on May 3rd 1836, another Molesworth speech was not received with the acclaim that was given to his Orangemen speech. Although it was delivered with equally passionate sincerity, it disastrously lost the motion Molesworth was putting forward. The circumstances are described at length in Cecil Woodham-Smith's *The Reason Why*, the gist of them being that Lord Brudenell who, following court-martial for misconduct had been removed from the command of the 15th Hussars, had subsequently been gazetted to the lieutenant-colonelcy of the 11th Light Dragoons – for which appointment the purchase price was said to have exceeded £40,000. The Press, led by *The Times*, indignantly demanded to be told who was responsible for reversing the decision of the court martial . . . how could a man pronounced to be unfit to command one regiment be fit to command another? Sir William Molesworth gave notice of a motion in the House: 'That a select committee be appointed to enquire into the conduct of the Commander-in-Chief of the Forces in appointing Lieutenant-Colonel Lord Brudenell to the Lieutenant-Colonelcy of the 11th Light Dragoons'. The motion was brought forward on May 3rd. Molesworth made a long speech which was a withering attack on the appointment. He read out the verdict of the court martial, listed the distinguished services of the 11th Light Dragoons in Egypt, in the Peninsula, at Waterloo and, for the last seventeen years, in India. The two Dragoon Majors had served with the regiment for thirty and twenty-five years respectively. The speech ended:

> With what feelings will they view the advancement over their heads of this young officer, who has never heard the sound of a musket, except in the mimic combats of a review . . . who was removed from command for alleged misconduct, and is now deemed the fittest and most proper person to command their regiment? They will say that which is said in every part of this town when the question is discussed . . . courtly influence, courtly favour and courtly intrigue have biased the otherwise sound judgement of the Commander-in-Chief . . . It is an appointment that cannot fail to produce the painful belief – that, provided an officer possesses wealth and influence, it matters not what his past conduct may have been.

Cecil Woodham-Smith relates that when Molesworth sat down there was no applause; 'Indeed, he had been frequently interrupted by cries of "Oh! Oh!", "Question, question", and "Divide, divide". The incredible had happened, and the House of Commons was taking Lord Brudenell's side.' This historian goes on to explain that the reason for this disaster, which was to prove so fatal during the Crimean War, was the choice of Sir William Molesworth to bring forward the motion: 'He was a fatal champion. Personally he was unpopular, politically he was regarded as a most dangerous man. It was only four years since the Reform riots, the Chartist movement was now reaching its height, and an active fear of revolution was common to Whig and Tory. True, the measures he advocated, the abolition of transportation for convicts, have been adopted and today seem commonplaces of good sense, but to his contemporaries he was a revolutionary and a traitor to his class. The friend of Bentham, John Stuart Mill and Grote, he had violently shocked public opinion by denying the divinity of Christ . . . The effect of Sir William Molesworth on the Army authorities was electric. Always jealous of their powers, a public attack made in the House of Commons by a Radical on their administration was unendurable to them. It was one of the Duke of Wellington's cardinal principles that the Army must be kept free from the faintest suspicion of political control. When Joseph Hume, the celebrated Radical, rose to support Sir William Molesworth, the outcome of the debate was a foregone conclusion, and Hume, who had earned the particular detestation of the Army authorities by his efforts to abolish flogging, made himself heard with difficulty. When a division was taken, the result was Ayes 42, Noes 322.'

The chagrin, the rage, the outrage, that Sir William felt at this inglorious defeat was immediately blotted out by a message he was handed as he left the Chamber. Elizabeth, always his most dearly loved sister, was dangerously ill at Pencarrow.

CHAPTER IV — 1836 Cont.

ELIZABETH, twenty-four years old, had been ill for some time; but knowing how involved William was in that first Parliamentary session of 1836, she would not allow their mother to tell him how serious her illness was. She knew that, were he told, he would abandon everything and come to Pencarrow. So it was not until death seemed inevitable that Lady Molesworth sent for him – in fact it was only the night before she died that the message reached William. He caught the first mail coach to Exeter, but at the long journey's end found he was too late to see his most cherished sister alive. Two days later, before the funeral, he wrote to Mrs Grote:

Pencarrow, May 6th

My dear Mrs Grote,

I write to you as you are one who can and will sympathise with me without uttering that conventional jargon of sorrow which to me is disgusting and makes me savage to listen to. I arrived here last night, my sister had ceased to breathe the middle of the day before. She died quietly from the effusion of the water on the brain; calm and collected, though frequently in torture; without a murmur; well aware for some time that death was approaching, she never expressed a fear nor an apprehension, and longed for dissolution as the tranquil sleep from agony. One single thought filled her mind, and that was of me and what I was doing. Even her delirium consisted in a fancy that she was going to hear me speak; and her anxiety was to hear what I said. Not once did she express a wish for me to be near her. She knew I could not leave town with honour, and her entreaties to her mother were to conceal the extent of her danger lest I might be tempted to bring myself into trouble on her account; all proved that she loved me with an intense affection which I felt in return for her; others may love me as well, but no one can ever feel with me like her, for she alone could appreciate my sentiments and opinions. She shared in all the good and bad qualities of my temper and character. I had educated her and well, for in mental resources she found a resource in long years of suffering . . . I feel this blow more than I can express, more than I should like any one to know except yourself. The only tie of really strong affection is broken asunder. I had hoped that we should never have been separated. I looked forward to her rejoicing in my renown and glorying in my honour.

III Lady Molesworth, née
    Mary Brown of
    Edinburgh,
    William's mother.
    Portrait by
    Bryan E. Duppa, 1835.

The Dowager Lady Molesworth
aged 96 — still retaining much
of her celebrated comeliness.
Photograph taken in 1875.

IV Elizabeth Molesworth, William's
    elder sister. Portrait by Bryan E.
    Duppa, 1835, the year before
    she died, aged 24.

Mary Ford, née Molesworth,
by Da Monte, 1859.

Her last consolations were the praises which I have in some slight degree earned this year, though to her they seemed not adequate. I feel paralysed for the present . . . do write. I have one more trial to undergo, the horror of which to me is inconceivable to you – that of hearing the burial service read over her, and bearing a part in that hideous mummery. I would give anything to bury her in a favourite spot in my grounds, under the clear sky, and erect a tomb for myself alongside of her. The baneful and noxious aspect of my ancestral tomb creates in me a loathing which I cannot understand. For myself I will force my heirs under enormous penalties to bury me in this manner. Would that I could devise any means to place her there too. I am afraid there are none. I can write no more.

Believe me, dear Mrs Grote, your ever sincerely grateful
William Molesworth.

Mrs Grote's reply to that letter revealed her deep understanding: 'It is one thing to bear calamity with courage, and another to pretend that bad is good, and that bitter anguish is a source of happiness.'

He could not, of course, at this time of family grief, express his revulsion about burial in the family vault to his mother, nor indeed to any near relative. His resolve that his own burial should be in the grounds at Pencarrow was not relinquished for a very long time, indeed never really relinquished, as is shown by a letter his sister Mary wrote to Lady Zetland at the time of his death. To some insensitive friends it became a subject for jokes, as in a letter from Charles Austin quoted in Chapter VI.

AS SOON as William felt he could leave his mother after Elizabeth's funeral, he returned to London and immersed himself in all the preparations for the opening of the Reform Club in Pall Mall. The Radicals had felt the need of a club such as the Tories' Carlton Club for a long time, and by the end of 1834 plans for one were being seriously discussed. Molesworth had outlined its purpose in a letter to Lady Molesworth on February 19th 1835: 'As another means of attacking the Tories a Liberal Club is to be formed, of which the more liberal Whigs, Radicals etc. will be members. Lords Durham, Mulgrave etc. are anxious about it. It will be like the Athenaeum – a good dining club. The great object is to get the Reformers of the country to join it, so that it may be a place of meeting for them when they come to town. It is much wanted.

Brooks's is not Liberal enough, too expensive and not a dining club.'

Disagreements and covert manoeuvres prevented the plan from maturing smoothly. It was a whole year later, in February 1836, that Molesworth in another letter to his mother told her: 'I have been much occupied in establishing a political club to be called the Reform Club, the history of the transactions with regard to which will amuse you.' He went on to narrate the many negotiations with the more liberal members of the Whig party, and the devious ways by which they were persuaded to support the project: 'I doubt whether we could form a club without the assistance of the Whigs. Most of the Cabinet are now original members: the Dukes of Sussex and of Norfolk etc. We have admitted already above six hundred persons. Our success is certain. It will be the best club in town, and the effect will be to break up the Whig party by joining the best of them to the Radicals, and the club will be the political centre of the Empire, and augment our power immensely. All we want is organisation. This we shall now obtain. We had no place of meeting. The Radical MPs were never to be found together except in the House, consequently no one knew what his neighbour was about. This disorganisation the Whigs desired, and on this account they have always in secret been opposed to a club. Now their only remaining hope is to join us in such numbers as to have the predominance; they will fail in this respect.'

Roebuck was also confident of Radical membership outnumbering the Whigs. He wrote triumphantly to Napier: 'Brookes's [sic] will be done for, and we shall be great and regular opponents of the Carlton.'

Louis Fagan, the first historian of the Reform Club, writing in 1887 gives the credit for both the conception and subsequent foundation of the Club to the Whig MP for Coventry, the Rt Hon. Edward Ellice, 'In whose residence, 14 Carlton House Terrace, the preliminary meetings were held in the year 1836.' But George Woodbridge, writing another history of the Club in 1978, disputes the claim of Ellice, citing various evidences, including an undated letter from Joseph Parkes to Lord Durham:

The most important move lately is the club. Three months before

Parliament a dozen of us of the movement revised it. *You* know when and by whom it was last bruited. Ellice, from Paris, wrote to me and others violently against it . . . The first circular Molesworth, Grote, Ward, self and others cooked up a day before Ellice returned home . . . We are now all cordiality – the Whigs *forced* in, except that Rice, Lord Lansdowne and Lord Bowick have not joined yet. [Those three were in Melbourne's Cabinet and joined later.] We have nearly two hundred and fifty Members of Parliament and a thousand members . . . Ellice having taken it up, pets the child (adopted) as if he begat it himself.

Despite all the leading Whigs becoming members, Molesworth, Roebuck and most of the really hard-core Radicals were confident that their standards would prevail over those of the more luxury-loving Whigs. Their confidence was over-optimistic. In Thomas Duncombe's biography of his father, *Thomas Slingsby Duncombe, MP for Finsbury*, he wrote: 'Notwithstanding the democratic tendency of some, they appear to have soon got reconciled to the palatial luxury with which they found themselves surrounded.'

This 'palatial luxury' was the creation of the distinguished architect Sir Charles Barry. When the Reform Club first opened in 1836, it was in a large house, 104 Pall Mall, previously occupied by the Countess of Dysart, but for the last five years used for storage and exhibition of the King's pictures. Then in 1837 there was the chance of leasing the site of Nos. 101, 102 and 103 Pall Mall, small shops and houses which were due to be demolished. A Club Building Committee was set up, and six architects invited to submit plans. Those of Sir Charles Barry were chosen – the previous year he had gained first premium in the competition for the design of the new Houses of Parliament. The initial cost of the building and its equipment was met by the sale of 5% debentures (all taken up by members) and also loans made by various members of whom Molesworth, of course, was one.

Alexis Soyer was appointed head chef. He was the great rival of the other celebrated chef of the day, Louis Eustache Ude, who reigned at the Carlton Club. Soyer is believed to have been consulted by Barry from the very first stages in the planning of the kitchen quarters and their equipment. Other skilled staff were appointed to ensure the smooth working demanded of a gentlemen's club. Handsome furniture and furnishings were bought; also the essential books for two libraries – reference and general, political and philosophical.

A circular invited members to donate books, pamphlets, maps, documents, parliamentary papers and so on. Everything from cellars to bathrooms was planned to the very highest standards. Molesworth and his radical friends were riding on the crest of a wave that they believed would submerge the Whigs. But the Whigs, appreciating the luxurious amenities of the Club, soon outnumbered the Radicals; and it was not long before the Reform Club became a recognised club of the Liberal party – as it still is today.

In the history of gentlemen's clubs, as in the history of society hostesses, a reputation for *haute cuisine* has always been an important factor. Soyer had come from Paris after the 1830 revolution, and had been employed in various ducal houses. He was brilliant at creating menus for the splendid banquets held at the Club for distinguished guests. Nevertheless, as with some of the Club's members with radical consciences, he was not blind to the world beyond Pall Mall. In the harsh winter of 1846-47, he created a soup costing three-farthings a quart, which was distributed daily to the London poor. The medical profession doubted its nutritive value, but Soyer asserted that his recipe had 'been tasted by numerous noblemen, Members of Parliament and several ladies . . . who have considered it very good and nourishing' – and claimed that a meal of his soup with a biscuit once a day could sustain a man's health. The 'noblemen, MPs and several ladies' who tasted it are unlikely to have made it their one meal that day; but from Ireland, stricken by the potato famine, the Lord Lieutenant asked Soyer to go over and superintend distribution of his soup to the starving. Ten years later, he went out to the Crimea with the official backing of Lord Panmure, but at his own expense, to supervise the insanitary Barrack Hospital kitchens and produce nourishing soups and stews from army rations. As he walked through the wards with his tureens, the stricken soldiers cheered him from their palliasses. A far cry from the Reform Club banquets.

BY THE END of the summer session of 1836, William was on the verge of a breakdown. It had been a year of emotional stress: the final extinction of his hope of marrying Julia Carew; the death of Elizabeth. Then there had been the physical fatigues of his journey to Birmingham and the public meetings there, the mental strain of his two major speeches in the House, on the Orangemen and on Lord Brudenell. Constant meetings in connection with the founding of the Reform Club increased his work load. And to add to all this, he was being made increasingly aware that he was alienating his constituents in Cornwall. His views were not their views. The landed Whigs as well as the Tories, had always disliked his vehement expression of extreme radical views, especially that of reform of the House of Lords, which he considered should be deprived of the absolute veto. The small farmers and their work people, who were mostly his own tenants, had always supported him; but now he sensed that even they were nervous about his political views – in particular those on Free Trade and abolition of the Corn Laws. They were telling him that he had not enough regard for the agricultural interest.

Another factor was Sir William's close association with the *London & Westminster Review*. Everything that appeared in it was attributed by most people to him, whether he had written it or not. John Stuart Mill's unsigned diatribes against this 'devil-worship that went by the name of religion' were particularly offensive. The leader of the Whigs in the East Cornwall constituency, Sir Colman Rashleigh, challenged Molesworth to deny certain opinions in one of Mill's political articles. He refused. Rashleigh then wrote immediately that he could not support him any longer.

The accumulating stress of all these factors on his always frail physique led to his complete collapse after Parliament dissolved for the Summer recess. The dangerous illness which followed seems to have been a form of erysipelas in the region of the brain. In August, when the crisis was past, he decided to resign from the representation of East Cornwall and go abroad to seek physical and spiritual renewal; it was not so much repose he craved as change of scene. Before setting out, he wrote a rough draft of a retiring address to his constituents, leaving it with Charles Buller to correct and then to consult with other radical friends whether it should be issued. Buller considered the address carefully, made some modifying alterations, and wrote to Molesworth: 'As you have no right to attack on the present occasion any but the Cornish Whigs, all attacks on Whigs in general must be struck out.' Buller was always a moderating influence on his friend, advising him to temper his most extravagant expressions, urging him not to ride too hard at his fences. The final draft of the retiring address, issued on September 7th 1836, was a dignified document but sufficiently outspoken to be characteristic of Molesworth. It stated the main points of his political creed: the ballot, free trade, national education, reform of the House of Lords, no religious discrimination, household suffrage, improved government for Ireland, self-government for the colonies, the end of transportation. It was, the address said, by supporting measures with these ends in view that he had alienated many of his original supporters, and he must therefore, in any future election, expect their hostility rather than their aid. For this reason it was his intention to retire from his representation of the constituency. The address concluded by advising the voters, not as their Member but as a brother elector, to consider the ballot a test question: 'That question is now the test of Liberal principles. He mocks you who talks of Freedom of Election, and at the same time refuses to protect you by secret suffrage. He neither deserves the name of a Liberal, nor the support of Liberals, who will consent to leave you at the mercy of your landlord when so easy a remedy can be obtained.'

Thus spake the landlord of great properties.

WITH his retiring address in Buller's hands, William left for Germany accompanied by his mother and remaining sister, Mary, now aged twenty. At Frankfurt they were joined by his brother Francis, eighteen years old, for whom he was guardian as well as brother. From Germany he wrote to Mrs Grote: 'My brother and I are going to read Greek together on the outside of the carriage, and we have got a brace of Thucydides in order to study history.' Then in another letter, 'He is an excessively fine boy, and speaks German like a German. He will fill my shoes well, for I feel that my career will be a short one . . . I like the system I have pursued in educating Francis abroad; it gives him an independent feeling and self-reliance which is most valuable.'

For some time William had been saying that it would not be long before Francis replaced him in Parliament – after all, he himself had become an MP when only twenty-two. But why *replace* him? Why not join him? It was this that William's friends felt to be strangely foreboding. Mrs Grote in her *Life of Sir*

William quotes a letter to her from Henry Warburton, MP who, she says, had been aware of Sir William's growing disinclination to continue in public life, and of her endeavours to counteract it:

What you say about Molesworth, or rather what he says about himself, is so far satisfactory that he has not deserted politics, though there is an absurd morbid feeling about him, as being for this world but for a short period, and speaking of his brother as a 'promising successor.' What is this language in the mouth of a young fellow in the flower of youth? He must have been courting and disappointed in love, or he would never talk after this fashion.

Well, of course he *had* been courting and *was* disappointed in love; but undoubtedly political disillusionment was another element in his depression. Nevertheless he was, as Warburton wrote, 'in the flower of youth.' Travel amidst fresh scenes soon restored his health and spirits. Soon he began to feel thirsty for the stimulus of taking part in the shaping of his country's future. It is said that no man who has once tasted the elixir of political life in the magic circle of the House of Commons can voluntarily abstain from it. Also, Elizabeth would have wished him to return. Thus in September he wrote to Mrs Grote from Prague:

I think you are wrong in accusing me of an absolute wish to shrink from the combat; on the contrary, I stated my anxious hope of being of service to the cause through *The London*, and as long as that Review is carried on with energy you cannot accuse me of deserting the party. I did certainly indulge in a feeling of pleasure at the idea of being once again free from the trammels of Parliament, and sought out reasons for justifying this feeling in your eyes; but, in truth, I will do exactly as you like, for you are the only person who is invariably kind to me whenever I commit follies or errors, and whose reproofs even sound to me more pleasing than the praises of others. I will come into Parliament again if you wish it, and if I can get a constituency that will take me with a clear declaration of my opinions. I am glad that I am free from Cornwall, for I was in a most painful position there, with hardly a gentleman to support me.

He was later disturbed by letters from political friends giving the impression that the Philosophical Radical group was disintegrating for lack of firm direction, some members losing their identity and tending to merge with the Liberals. They lacked a strong leader. Francis Place, who was not an MP but an urgently active speaker at outside meetings, wrote on September 22nd 1836, a long letter to Thomas Falconer, of which this is the last paragraph:

It is a somewhat curious circumstance that Madame Grote should scold at Molesworth and talk of a band of heroes. Where she found one of them I cannot tell. *She* yes *she* was the only member of parliament with whom I had any intercourse in the later third of the session, we communicated freely, but we could find no heroes, nor no decent legislators. We found that the supineness and truckling of the so-called radicals in the House of Commons were the cause of what is called the apathy of the people, and sure I am that we both wished in our hearts that the reformers should be well 'cart-whipped' and that Whigs and Tories were dead and damned. Often indeed have I ejaculated Swift's benediction on them; 'While the devil upon the roof etc. etc.'

Yours truly, Francis Place.

I think you may as well forward this letter to Molesworth.

On October 24th, Sir William decided to take the bull by the horns – or more specifically to write to Mrs Grote. In a letter from Berlin he begged her to use her influence to stop the rot: 'The Radicals in the House are losing their hold over the nation . . . Pray stir them up . . . *Now* is the time . . . Oh for some respectable man of action!' Molesworth knew what everyone else knew, and what Mrs Grote deep down in her must have known, that George Grote would never be a man of action. Someone else must lead the attack. Why not Molesworth? His letter to Mrs Grote ends with a clear sign that he intended to return to the battlefield: 'Pray write me a line at the Reform Club . . . I hope to be in town on the 29th, as I shall leave Hamburg on the 26th at two o'clock in the morning. I will dine with you on Monday the 30th. Ask some Rads. to meet me, honest men and true. Six is your hour?' And after reaching London he lost no time in giving out that he was looking for a constituency.

His friends started enquiring for possible openings in all parts of the country. A letter from another seeker for a constituency, a radical named Ward, shows how far distant Molesworth was prepared to go from Cornwall:

November 23rd 1836

My dear Molesworth,

You are by far the greatest borough monger, or borough monopoliser now in existence. Go where you will, North, South, East or West, one is sure to fall in with you. I had a very snug settlement in Westminster, but Sir Wm. Molesworth has ousted me! I was talked of once with some favour at Newcastle, but Sir Wm. Molesworth has got a requisition in his pocket from all my quondam well-wishers! I might seek refuge in Leeds, but Sir Wm. Molesworth's name again stares me in the face! Now I want to know where you fix yourself, and more particularly what you intend to do about Newcastle, where I think I might have a very fair prospect of establishing myself comfortably. Of course I do not dream of this until I have clearly ascertained your decisions etc. etc.

Newcastle had indeed been mooted for Sir William, but his heart was set on Westminster, the most prestigious – and the most expensive – constituency in the country. Hopes of Westminster, however, were disappointed and Mrs Grote declared he had better settle for Leeds – a quixotic choice, surely, for someone whose home was as far South-West from London as Leeds is North. Even when by the 1840s it became possible to travel from Euston to Leeds by railway, the journey took approximately eleven hours. Mrs Grote's letter to Molesworth reveals both her political influence on him and her affectionate solicitude for the health of the young man she had come to love very dearly and whom she thought of as her devoted disciple:

Well, this opening [Westminster] being proved hopeless, will you try Leeds? Warburton dined here yesterday, and is all for your going into the facts connected with the registrar and ascertaining the ground for expecting a sure return. He wished you to go down in person, but *I* object to that, because I am anxious about your chest. I do not like the idea of a mid-winter travel for you just now. Better send Mr Woollcombe [Sir William's solicitor], and let him overhaul the books and communicate with the Big Whigs on the subject. Mr Marshall is a very discreet safe guide, as to the facts, and being no wise extreme in his opinions, is the more trustworthy as to forming an opinion of 'Rad' strength. Don't go, *I beg of you,* but persevere in the temperate system – you will lay up store of fine health and be as much more *lovable* as healthful – when the tobacco no longer exhales from your person.

Not even Mrs Grote could stop Molesworth smoking cigars. Her

letter continued with a great deal of political gossip. Spurred on by
it, Molesworth sent an address to the Chairman of the Liberal Party
in Leeds, making it quite clear that he would support only measures
that he himself approved in Parliament, while toeing the Whig line
when it met with his approval. 'If by supporting Ministers you mean
that I will support them in opposition to the Tories – undoubtedly
I will. If you mean that I must abstain from expressing my opinions
in speeches, motions, or by amendments, through fear of *indirectly*
destroying the present Administration – then I must tell you I will
not give that species of support . . . I will consent to no compromise
of any kind. Till I receive such an explanation, I cannot accept the
invitation.'

He thought that such an uncompromising expression of his views
would probably destroy his chance of being accepted as a candidate;
but after another meeting had been called in Leeds on January 20th,
it was agreed to accept his candidature on his own terms, disclaiming
any intention or wish to restrain him from the full expression of
his political opinions either by speech or vote in the House. This
satisfied Sir William, and he was adopted. He then sent to the
constituency copies of his political speeches and press articles so that
the voters could have some knowledge of the man whom they had
adopted as their candidate.

In March, Molesworth made his first visit to Leeds, accompanied
by his youngest brother Arscott and Thomas Woollcombe of
Devonport who was a close friend as well as being his solicitor.
Mr Woollcombe wrote to Lady Molesworth from there giving
an account of the visit. Sir William had found Leeds to be
another country, inhabited by another race of men . . . 'We
arrived last night at Pomfret, and this morning were waited on
by a deputation of would-be constituents – the dirtiest-looking
dogs you ever beheld, but they say all mighty rich. Leeds itself
is anything but a handsome place. It is, if possible, twenty times
blacker than the blackest parts of London.'

In contrast to the foreign country he found himself in at Leeds,
Molesworth was in his own familiar element on Nomination Day at
Bodmin, when he was there to support Trelawny who was standing
to be his successor in the East Cornwall constituency. Sir William
wrote to his sister:

My dear Mary – Well, this is fun. Yesterday was the nomination. I gave a large breakfast to anyone who would come so did Vivian. In consequence of which we marched into Bodmin at the head of 600 horses and as many foot . . . [our adversaries] certainly cut a good figure with *squires* and *parsons* and serfs. We were the yeomanry and democracy . . . I made an oration . . . Told them the value of their land depended upon the wealth and numbers of the population, and these upon commerce and manufacture, asked the lords of the soil if they were so short-sighted and so bigotedly attached to their absurd prejudices as not to perceive the truth of this.

Molesworth always enjoyed castigating his fellow landlords.

CHAPTER V — 1837

IN the autumn of 1836 the Grotes had moved from their house in Dulwich Wood to Eccleston Street; and for Sir William their door was always open. Mrs Grote liked to think that her house had become his second home. She was now launching herself with quite a splash in the role of political hostess, and claimed that Sir William was a conspicuously brilliant catch in her social whirlpool. It was thanks to her, she implied, that his stiff, reserved attitude at parties had undergone a sea-change. On February 7th 1837, she wrote to her sister in Stockholm, Mrs Frances Eliza von Koch:

Since we finished furnishing I have had two *soirées politiques* numerously attended, and highly interesting, affording commune; lawyers, citizens, MPs, merchants and a sprinkling of women. Molesworth is the *Mirabeau* of the day, and is completely intoxicated by his success. Never do I remember so rapid a rise into Fame, and deservedly so, as Sir William Molesworth. His able paper in the last *London* has given him a high reputation among our Philosophical Radicals. He is in tearing spirits, and comes here often plaguing me to give another party. I fear I help to puff up his vanity; for I admire his principles, his courage and his talents sincerely.

It was at about this time that the sixteen-year-old Lucie Austin, niece of William's friend Charles Austin, requested in a letter to Mrs Grote that she would give her love to 'that exquisite puppy William Molesworth'. Three months later Mrs Grote, in another letter to her sister on May 11th, reported 'Sir W. Molesworth still principal attaché here. He is now plaguing my heart out to go to the Derby, and I dare say I shall be fool enough to give way. He is to provide a barouche and four – the party is to be three girls (pretty of course), Charles Buller, W. Prescott and Joe Parkin; eight of us in all.'

Mr Grote was evidently not to be included – for which exclusion he was no doubt profoundly grateful. Nor was he always present at the Eccleston Street gatherings. Besides being Member of Parliament for the City, his directorship of a City banking house occupied much of his time – and then there was that great literary work that he had set himself to achieve, his *History of Greece*. Mrs Grote, intensely proud of her husband, always referred to him in conversation as 'The Historian'. Nevertheless, he was a conscientious parliamentarian, and was unhappy about his lack of effect when speaking in public. In her *Personal Life of George Grote*, Mrs Grote relates that 'he took some pains to cultivate the art of speaking in public, by putting himself under the teaching of an elocution master, Mr Jones . . . Mr Grote, indeed, was not the only man of the Radical party who attended to this valuable element in a public career. Sir W. Molesworth, J.A. Roebuck, C. Buller, T. Gisborne and others did so, and to good purpose.' A distinguished class of pupils for Mr Jones.

Richard Cobden, who was to become one of the most brilliant orators of the Left, was not yet in Parliament; but in 1837 he met Molesworth at the Grotes' house and wrote a first impression of him in his journal: 'I met at their house (which by the way, is the great resort of all that is clever in the Opposition ranks) Sir W. Molesworth, a youthful, florid-looking man of foppish and conceited air, with a pile of hair at the back [finished] like a sugar-loaf. I should say that a cast of his head would furnish one of the most singular illustrations of phrenology. For the rest he is not a man of superior talents, and let him *say* what he pleases, there is nothing about him that is democratic in principle.'

Cobden also noted the contrast of Mrs Grote and her husband; 'Had she been a man, she would have been the leader of a party; he is not calculated for it'. But his unfavourable first impression of Molesworth's talents and democratic drive soon altered. Three months later, he wrote a long letter to him concerning the idea of employing a lecturer to go through the North of England towns giving addresses on the ballot, education, free trade and other political and economic topics. This project never got off the ground; and Cobden and Molesworth, although they fought mostly for the same causes, had little empathy. They never became close friends; and on colonial matters they disagreed fundamentally. Cobden believed that the colonies should eventually be completely separated from the mother country, declaring it to be a lesson England should have learned from the American War of Independence. Molesworth and the 'Colonial Reformers' group of which he was a member, believed that the colonies could be content and would prosper peacefully as constituent members of the British Empire were they offered self-government on democratic lines, without severing all connections with the mother country. Colonial self-government became Molesworth's major concern. Outside Parliament the most forcefully outspoken support for his views came from Edward Gibbon Wakefield, John Stuart Mill and Robert Stephen Rintoul, founder (in 1828) of the *Spectator*, also its Editor. The *Spectator* of this time played a prominent part in the discussion of all questions of social and political reform. Within the House of Commons, Molesworth's chief ally on colonial matters, indeed virtually his only ally, was Charles Buller.

ON JUNE 20th 1837, William IV died and Victoria came to the throne. Parliament was dissolved, the constitution requiring a general election on the accession of a new monarch. Molesworth's chance of being elected for Leeds would now be put to the test. Woollcombe accompanied him to Leeds for the period of the election in the last week of July; and it was Woollcombe who wrote to Lady Molesworth describing the scenes on polling day, Sir William's triumph and the rapturous cheering. It may seem strange that a wealthy baronet with all the bearing of a landed aristocrat, fastidiously dressed to the point of dandyism, should be so enthusiastically welcomed to represent a wholly industrial constituency. It was said that the number of his acres gave power to his democratic utterances; and perhaps the explanation lies in something Richard Ford wrote in an unpublished sketch after Sir William's death: 'An undercurrent of energy and action flowed deep and strong beneath a delicate and aristocratic person, which in no wise displeased the masses, ever ready to be led by a gentleman'.

Woollcombe's letter to Lady Molesworth also described the return journey to London – by post-chaise to Manchester, whence they travelled on the new Grand Junction Railway. Their post-chaise halted at Huddersfield, where they had been warned there would be hostility if Sir William were recognised by Tory supporters: 'you will probably get killed by Oastler's men'. He *was* recognised . . .

and such a scene ensued as only Cruickshank could do justice to. We were very popular, however, and glasses of brandy and water were proffered in abundance. They insisted on a speech, which, when horses were to, the Baronet gave them, and such an effusion of Radicalism you never heard. Nothing Sir Francis Burdett ever said came the least near it . . . It took beautifully, however, and we were permitted to depart with sound heads amidst the enthusiastic cheers of the populace. At Manchester the town was in a dreadful state: the military galloping in all directions . . . The scenes of violence in the North seem to have been quite unparalleled, and the loss of life has been serious. We came from Manchester to Birmingham on the Grand Junction Railway at the rate of 25 miles an hour. The only pleasant part of the performance is the saving of time. The motion is disagreeable, as is the noise; and on the whole I confidently predicted that *our* steamers will bear the bell from the railways.

Sir William, unlike Woollcombe, no doubt enjoyed travelling on the Grand Junction Railway, for he was already a railway enthusiast. He had inspired and largely financed the Bodmin to Wadebridge railway, personally engaging Robert Hopkins, civil engineer, to survey the district. Thomas Woollcombe had been the solicitor at the forming of a Company in 1831, and drew up the prospectus - but the railway's original purpose was not to carry passengers. It was visualized as a means of transporting, at low cost, sea sand from the Camel Estuary to the inland farms bordering the course of the river Camel, sand then being the principal manure used in growing corn. The northern terminus of the line was at Wenford Bridge, on the edge of Bodmin Moor.

The official opening was on September 30th 1834; but as Sir William could not be present, Parliament being in session, another 'formal opening' was arranged at the beginning of December, after Parliament had risen. He, with his mother and sister Mary, travelled in one of the seventeen waggons, all decorated with flags and green branches, one flag bearing the motto SCIENCE, PRUDENCE, and PERSEVERANCE. Another waggon contained the band of the Royal Cornish Militia playing patriotic airs. Roger Hopkins the engineer, with Thomas Woollcombe, rode in the tender behind the locomotive, in front of which a waggon carried the block-layers who had been employed on the project. Cheering people lined the whole twelve miles from Wadebridge to Wenford Bridge. The speed was mainly six miles an hour, occasionally increased to about ten miles; and stops were made to take in fresh water at Dunmeer and Tresarratt. The account in the *Morning Post* of December 5 1834, ended, 'We are most happy to add that not the slightest accident occurred to damp the universal satisfaction'. That evening 'upwards of seventy gentlemen sat down to an excellent dinner at Oliver's Hotel, Bodmin, Sir William Molesworth in the Chair, his brother Arscott Molesworth Esq. Vice-Chairman, and the band of the Royal Cornish Militia enlivened the scene.' After-dinner speeches and rousing toasts went on into the small hours of the morning. No ladies present, of course.

The success of the Bodmin and Wadebridge Railway enthused Thomas Woollcombe into taking an active part in promoting the South Devon Railway, and for many years he was Chairman of its Board of Directors. Sir William's romantic imagination did not stop at railways – he conceived a project for a working canal from St Breoke (near Wadebridge) to Lostwithiel. This, however, had to be abandoned when it was found that it would entail a long tunnel at one point. That would make it too expensive, even with all the financial backing that Sir William was prepared to give to his dream of a beautiful working canal. His belief in railways extended to foreseeing them playing a crucial part in colonial development. One of the last letters he wrote as Colonial Secretary, in August 1855, shortly before his final illness and death, was in reply to a note from T. Slingsby Duncome, MP for Finsbury, who with a few other enthusiasts was promoting a project for a railway in Ceylon: 'My dear Duncombe, I am inclined to look very favourably upon the establishment of railways in Ceylon, and will give the subject an early and careful consideration.'

ALTHOUGH Molesworth had been elected for Leeds, the General Election of 1837 brought about the rout of the Radicals. Amongst their many defeats, Joseph Hume lost his seat, also Roebuck at Bath. Grote retained his seat, but only just. From being head of the poll for the City of London at his first election in 1832, he now crept in at the bottom with a fragile majority of six votes. Indeed Mr Grote and about five others, according to Mrs Grote, alone survived to sustain the Radical group. Some of those few others lamented, but

V *The Reform Club in Pall Mall, 1843. Lithograph by T. Shotter Boys.*

Sir William's duelling pistols. Bought from Forsyth & Co. of Leicester Square, London, for the assignation with his Cambridge tutor.

VI *Bodmin and Wadebridge Railway crossing the River Camel at the celebratory opening, 1834. 22 trucks conveying over 400 passengers.*

Hot-houses at Pencarrow built by Sir William in 1835. Photographed by Mary Ford in 1902.

*VII Band of the Royal Cornwall Militia in the centre truck.
Contemporary drawing in the National Railway Museum at York.*

*The Molesworth Arms, coaching inn, Molesworth Street,
Wadebridge. From Hilda Hambly's 19th century collection.*

VIII 'A Leading Article of the Westminster Review'. Cartoon by John Doyle, 1838.

Sir William playing chess with Caroline Trelawney. Pencil sketch at Pencarrow.

not in Mrs Grote's hearing, that Grote himself was too passive to count as a support.

It was not only the Radicals who were ousted. The Whig majority was reduced to just twelve seats and would have to rely on the Irish members to maintain them in office. Moreover the Whigs themselves, in Molesworth's opinion, were becoming increasingly conservative. In the arrogance of his heart he despised them for being neither one thing nor the other. He himself, although temporarily dismayed as news of all the radical defeats came through, rather than disheartened was rekindled for the fight. The Grotes had gone to Switzerland after the election, and from there Mrs Grote wrote several letters to Molesworth, all containing passages of fond solicitude – 'Take care of your health, and don't sit smurring indoors, but take air and exercise I entreat you.' Regarding politics she was pessimistic. On August 13th she wrote: 'I don't see how we Radicals are to make head this coming Parliament at all. Our ranks are properly thinned out . . . The brunt of the battle will have to be sustained by Grote and you, aided by Buller, Leader, Charles Villiers, and a few more. I really feel astounded when I hear of Radical after Radical losing.' To this Molesworth replied: 'Your political gloom I don't share in. I think the Whigs miserable wretches, and shall rejoice when I hear their death-shriek . . . I have a firm faith in the progress of the human mind and in the steady advance of democracy, and I don't believe the Whigs can keep us back.'

He was not so optimistic about the *London and Westminster Review*. He had believed that it would be influential in promoting his own political views and standing, but it was turning out to be a liability. The worry was not just that he was losing money over it – which he was, quite a lot. The main trouble was that the contributors of articles to the *Review*, always anonymous, so often misrepresented his views. His Leeds constituents believed, just as his Cornish constituents had, that everything was written by Molesworth himself. Reluctantly he decided to resign from his position as proprietor. John Stuart Mill took over full responsibility for the management of the *London and Westminster* as well as its editorship. Politically he was as hostile to any compromising with the Whigs as was Molesworth. At a meeting in his house in November 1837, after the Whigs had declared against any reform

of the Reform Bill, Mill swore that 'the time is come when all
temporizing – all delicacy towards the Whigs – all fear of disuniting
Reformers, or of embarrassing Ministers by pressing forward reforms,
must be at an end'. He urged the Philosophical Radicals to 'assume
the precise position towards Lord Melbourne which they occupied in
the first Reformed Parliament towards Lord Grey. Let them separate
from the Ministry and go into declared opposition.'

Molesworth's scorn for the Whigs in Parliament extended to the
manner in which the Whig aristocracy spent so much time at dinner
parties and other social indulgences. Nevertheless, now that he was
in his third term in the House, he had come to realise that dining
and gossiping were essential elements in any political career. The
hospitalities of Holland House were an integral part of life for all
leading Whigs. Some Radicals said jokingly, some said spitefully,
that Mrs Grote regarded her Eccleston Street house as the Radical
Holland House. Maybe she did. But her most regular guest, Sir
William, devoted as he was to Mrs Grote, needed to shake off
the impression of being forever her protégé. He needed a London
house of his own in which to offer his own hospitalities. So when
he heard that the lease of a handsome house in the newly completed
and very fashionable Eaton Square – convenient for Westminster –
was available, he suggested to a close friend, John Temple Leader,
fellow Radical, also wealthy, that they should take it together. To
this suggestion Leader agreed.

T.P. O'Connor, in his description of the Philosophical Radical
group in the first Parliament of Queen Victoria's reign wrote of him:
'Mr Leader, who sits next to Sir William and is constantly consulting
with him – for they are bosom friends – looks still younger [than
Sir William] and, though plainer in dress, has also the appearance
of the politician who is at once Radical and rich. Mr Leader has
recently given strong proof of both the wealth and the Radicalism,
for twice in three years he has contested Westminster, one of the
most expensive constituencies.'

There seems to have been a certain amount of gossip about the
Eaton Square *ménage*. Sir William, in a letter to his mother,
undated as so many of his letters most tiresomely were, wrote in the
last paragraph 'I was amused to hear from Mrs Ward that her sister
had been desired to write from Cobham to know my direction and

Daniel Maclise's sketch of Sir William in the Eaton Square house. No.79 in
Fraser Magazine's *'Gallery of Illustrious Literary Characters'*.

whether Duppa and myself were living together. They had better
next time write for a detail of my moral and religious conduct, and
enquire if I am living with a . . . What the hell is it to them with
whom I am living?'

It was in this Eaton Square house that Daniel Maclise drew a
portrait of Molesworth for the series in *Fraser's Magazine* called
'Fraser's Gallery of Illustrious Literary Characters'. Sir William
Molesworth appeared as No. 79 in the series. The satirical character
sketch which accompanied the portrait was not signed, but is in
recognisable Thackeray style – although William Maginn wrote most
of the sketches in the series, Thackeray is known to have written
some. His Molesworth piece is less spiteful than some by Maginn's
cruel pen; but he has fun with the hypocrisy of ardent Radicals
'setting up their liberty-flag in a fine mansion in Belgrave [sic]
Square . . . They keep a French cook, and feed their less fortunate
political brethren – a generosity noble on their part, but, indeed,
necessary; for the wholesome quality of the victuals serves to keep
these Radicals from starving, and likewise greatly elevates the *morale*
of the men'.

Daniel Maclise's drawing portrays Sir William lying on a luxurious sofa, and Thackeray's sketch continues 'His limbs are enveloped in a damask robe; a Grecian cap, marvellously embroidered, ornaments his sconce; his legs are crossed in an attitude of profound meditation . . . Not politics alone engage his mind; he is a profound metaphysician; as a linguist, stupendous; as a mathematician, he has attained a depth which is more easily imagined than described . . . He reads off a page of Chinese with great ease, and the true Peking accent; Professor Whewell is a ninny compared to him in mathematics; and we have heard that he not only admires, but understands, Jeremy Bentham. By the honourable baronet's side lie the ashes of four-and-twenty cigars.' Sir William's cigar was as famous a feature as the monocle in his right eye.

Thackeray ended his sketch with a neat thrust at the Radicals: 'It would be cowardly to attack yonder peaceful and studious philosopher in the midst of his mild meditations; let us praise him, rather, as well we may, for the great and serious benefit which, every day, the kingdom is receiving from him. He, his friend Mr Leader, and the ex-member for Bath, Mr Roebuck, have done as much for Conservatism as any subjects of Her Majesty. They make more converts than Sir Robert Peel himself. For as young Gentlemen in Sparta were taught to abhor drunkenness by beholding the consequences thereof in tipsy Helots, even so the British public learneth political sobriety by witnessing the mad antics of the above trio.'

CHAPTER VI — 1838-9

IN Parliament Molesworth was becoming increasingly involved in Colonial affairs, which were hopelessly managed in a haphazard fashion, not being the particular responsibility of any one Government department. He was totally opposed to the 'Manchester School' which represented the belief of first Bentham and later Cobden; this was that the Colonies would become an ever increasing burden to the mother country and should therefore eventually be cast off. Molesworth's aim was to bring about a scientific system of colonisation by sending out suitable, responsible emigrants, then gradually introducing self-government with representative constitutions. Only that way, he believed, could Britain retain the loyalty and affection of her colonies. There had been a few schemes earlier for better colonisation – for example, the Swan River settlement of Western Australia in 1828 – but all had ended in virtual failure; and the evil of emigrant settlements being populated mainly by transported convicts continued. More hopefully, in 1834 the Australian Association had been formed, Molesworth being a founder member; and in 1838 a Transportation Committee was set up of which Molesworth was elected chairman, although he was far and away the youngest member.

Just before the new Parliament of 1837 was about to adjourn for the Christmas recess, news came of an alarming rebellion in Lower Canada. Before the adjournment, Molesworth and several other Radicals spoke out fiercely against the policy – or rather the lack of policy – that had driven the Canadians to feel that their grievances would never be redressed by constitutional non-violent agitation alone. Then during the Christmas recess, the Radicals fixed a meeting for January 4th at The Crown and Anchor in Westminster, at which Molesworth, Leader and Roebuck would make major speeches condemning the Government for its mishandling of Colonial affairs, and put forward their solution of the Canadian crisis. Edward Baines, proprietor and editor of the *Leeds Mercury*

and Molesworth's colleague in the representation of Leeds, feared
that they would speak *too* violently. He wrote a letter of warning
to Francis Place on January 2nd 1838, saying that many people who
might otherwise become their supporters would be antagonised by
over-charged invective: 'It is exceedingly desirable that Mr Leader,
Sir W. Molesworth and other speakers should be less violent and
less bitter against the Government than they were during the late
debates in the House of Commons; for I assure you that their tone
has considerably prejudiced the cause they so ably and so justly
espouse, in the minds of very many people in the country, as well
as in London.'

Francis Place replied to this letter after the meeting was over:
'I, as you know, have seen and conducted many public meetings,
yet few that I have seen have equalled that of today in numbers,
enthusiasms and perseverance. Never before did I hear, and never
did I expect to hear, such a speech as was made by my old friend
Roebuck, and never did I see such effects produced by any speech.'

On the reassembling of Parliament later in January, Lord John
Russell brought into the Commons a Bill for the suspension of
the existing constitution of Canada. Mr Grote opposed the Bill;
and later in the evening he presented a petition from John Arthur
Roebuck (who was no longer a Member, having lost his seat at Bath)
praying to be heard at the Bar on behalf of the House of Assembly
of Lower Canada – of which he had been the agent in England
during 1835. The request was granted, and Roebuck described
Canada's long struggle for the right to administer her own internal
concerns without interference from the Foreign Office in London.
He spoke earnestly, poignantly and persuasively – but failed to move
Lord John and his clique. The Bill for the suspension of the existing
constitution of Canada was passed; and Lord Durham was appointed
to go out as Lord High Commissioner and Governor-General with
special powers.

Lord Durham, a Liberal with strong leanings towards Radicalism
(indeed, the Radicals hoped that he might join their group and
become its leader) left England in May, accompanied by Charles
Buller as his secretary and Chief Commissioner of Crown Lands, also
by Edward Gibbon Wakefield in an unspecified official capacity.
Wakefield was a colourful character who had lived down various

scandalous episodes in his early life. In 1826 he had been sentenced to three years' imprisonment for abducting a young heiress. Ten years earlier, when employed at the British Embassy at Turin, he had eloped with a Ward of Court. During his imprisonment, realising he would need to leave the country for a spell after serving his sentence, he read as many books as he could get hold of about New South Wales, and managed to obtain a series of colonial newspapers. Released, he arrived in Australia in 1831, studied the problems of transportation on the spot and worked out a plan for systematic colonisation – his system will be explained in the next chapter in relation to a proposition he made to Molesworth.

It was Wakefield and Buller who drew up Lord Durham's controversial Canadian Report during the five months they were with him in Canada. They returned to England with Durham when he resigned in dispute with Lord Melbourne, who had succeeded Lord John Russell as Prime Minister. Melbourne disliked and distrusted Durham. The completed report was handed to the Government in February 1839. Lord Durham was very sure that it would not be liked, and that the Government would attempt to bury it without comment. He therefore sent copies of the report in advance to the Press, and it was printed in *The Times* on February 8th. Controversial as it was at this time, Lord Durham's report came to be looked upon as the great charter for colonial freedom. But the hope of the Radicals that Durham would join them and become the strong leader their group so badly needed was not to be realised – Lord Durham died the following year, on July 28th 1840, at the age of forty-eight.

IT may well have been that Molesworth's concern for the colonies was inherited, so to speak, since his family had a long-standing connection with Jamaica. Hender Molesworth, grandson of the John Molesworth who bought Pencarrow in Elizabeth's reign, was a very early coloniser. He settled in St Katherine's, Jamaica, becoming President of the Island Council; then later, in the reign of Charles II, was appointed Acting-Governor of the Colony. In due course he became Governor. In 1689 he was created a baronet by William III as a reward for loyalty during the religious persecutions in Jamaica during the reign of James II. Now, two centuries later, in the year of the Durham Report on Canada, our Sir William Molesworth,

8th baronet, made a great gesture of faith in the future of another
colony, New Zealand – he sent his brother Francis, only twenty-
one years old, as an emigrant to New Zealand. It was a gesture
which showed his confidence that, were the colonies to be given
the advantage of development by healthy, educated, resourceful,
courageous emigrants, instead of by the scum of England's prisons,
they would flourish peacefully and remain loyal to their mother
country. In a speech at Devonport in February 1840, enthusiastically
received, he spoke of Francis:

My brother has the honour of being one of the intrepid men who have
departed on the arduous task of waging war with the wilderness and
rendering it productive – productive of objects of exchange with us. He
did it at my advice (much cheering). He was a young man in want of
some occupation, and unwilling to live in idleness. All occupations here
are over-stocked; in every branch of industry, in every description of trade,
in all the professions competition is excessive. 'Go then' I said 'imitate the
example of your ancestors, and make for yourself a career in a new world
of your own creation, and be assured that in seeking in this manner to
advance your own interests, you will confer a great and lasting benefit
upon your natural country'. (Immense cheering). And this advice which
I have given to him, I give to all persons who find this island too thickly
peopled.

Strange to think now that Molesworth thought Great Britain
over-populated more than 150 years ago.

It must have been a hard decision for Sir William to take.
The strong ties of upbringing and affection that bound him to
Francis, whose education he had planned and guided so carefully,
must inevitably become weaker at such a distance; and it will be
remembered that William, so proud of his handsome, quick-witted
young brother, had three years previously, when travelling with him
in Germany, said that he expected Francis would be his successor
in Parliament. Accompanying Francis on the sailing ship Oriental
on September 10th 1839, was James Bryant, one of the gardeners
at Pencarrow. His wife, who was Mary Ann Michenson Pollard of
Bodmin before their very recent marriage, was also of the party,
as well as young Molesworth tenants from Washaway village and
Tetcott property. In New Zealand, James Bryant collected plants and
specimen trees and sent them back to Sir William for Pencarrow.

There was a sad sequel to this brave, bright enterprise. After only four years in New Zealand Francis was injured by a falling tree when working on a forestry project. He returned to England for skilled medical treatment, but died as a result of the accident in 1846, when he was just twenty-eight years old. Francis is remembered in Wellington by Molesworth Street, and by a portrait hanging in the Government building with those of other of the island's pioneers. The most evocative memorial, perhaps, is the Pencarrow Lighthouse near the harbour entrance. The largest pastoral run or station in New Zealand is Molesworth in the South Island – over 700 square miles – and this was named after Francis by his friend F.A. Weld.

DURING the whole of 1838 Sir William suffered intermittent bouts of illness. In spite of this, his work at the House had been as onerous as that of any of his more robust colleagues. He had presided over the Parliamentary Committee on Transportation and had written its report. He had made two very important speeches in the House on Colonial questions, on January 23rd and March 6th. Both of these speeches run to over forty pages, crammed with facts and figures. He had worked actively as a director of the New Zealand Association to promote in practice the views which he advocated in theory. His Leeds constituents, with justice, felt *their* interests were being neglected. Molesworth, aware of this feeling when sending them a copy of the Transportation Committee's Report, apologised that through ill-health he had been prevented from 'taking so active a part in the business of Parliament as his duties towards my Leeds constituents rendered desirable'.

However, there was one good side to his being confined to the house so much that summer – he was able to start on a literary project which Mrs Grote claimed to have suggested. In her words, this was 'that he would confer a benefit on the students of political philosophy by bringing out an edition of the works of Thomas Hobbes of Malmesbury – adding thereto a preface, which should give an appreciation of various writings and speculative disquisitions of that profound thinker.'

It was a project after Sir William's own heart, a challenge to his reach of thought. During the reign of Charles II Hobbes was the philosopher most in fashion – no gentleman was held to have completed his education unless he had the thoughts of Hobbes at his tongue tip. But Hobbes was overtaken in fashionable esteem by John Locke. Although his treatises on Logic, Human Nature and Government continued to influence scholars, there was no collected edition of his Latin and English works, and separate publications had become almost impossible to find. Molesworth undertook the task of collecting and publishing what was to be the first uniform edition of 'The Entire Works of Thomas Hobbes, with a Life of the Author and View of his Philosophy', anticipating that it would form about twelve volumes, each containing from 500 to 600 pages. In September 1838 he wrote to Mr Grote to ask permission to dedicate the volumes to him; and in a separate letter to Mrs Grote he told her 'I have written this day to Mr Grote, to ask permission to dedicate the volumes to him. I wish for that permission for two reasons – first, because I shall ever feel the deepest gratitude for

Sketch at Pencarrow of Sir William the scholar. Artist unknown.

the philosophical instruction he gave me when I first knew him, which induced me to study Hobbes and similar authors, and created a taste in my mind for that style of reading; secondly, because I have a greater regard and esteem for himself and his wife than for any other people in this wicked world . . . It will not be much less than a four years' work, and in that time I may produce something not very bad in the shape of a 'life', etc. . . in the political world there seems to me to be nothing of any interest . . . I am afraid there is no immediate prospect of any good, and I am very tired of the wearisome broil of political life.'

IN SEPTEMBER 1838 Charles Austin and his sister Lucy came to stay at Pencarrow. Suspicions were circulating on the Radical grape-vine at this time that Lucy Austin was in love with the so eligible young baronet. Whether William shared her feelings to any degree we do not know, but a letter to Mrs Grote written during the Austins' visit shows that he was still smarting from his rejection by the Carews:

> Pencarrow, September 27th
> . . . Charles Austin & his sister came here on Monday. The former goes away in a day or two; the latter, I believe, stays. You need be in no alarm. Young ladies don't nowadays die of love, but *fall in love again*, a much more sensible course. I am, as you know, not a marrying man; I have other things to do, amongst which the most important is my edition of Hobbes. Austin & myself have been discussing this subject with great interest. He intended once to undertake it himself and has given me much useful information . . . You can't conceive how agreeable Charles Austin has made himself notwithstanding my thorough knowledge of him, he at times almost humbugs me; particularly at the present moment he has got on my weak side about Hobbes' works; and in his generous offers of assistance in reading proofs and giving advice he has almost won my heart. Still I don't like him.

Earlier in the year there had been talk that Charles Austin was hoping to marry William's sister Mary. If that were so, he had either been rejected or had himself cooled off. It is very possible that William's instinctive dislike of Charles had influenced Mary. Or, if Charles had simply been flirting with no intention of proposing,

that could be one of the reasons for William's dislike. On the
other hand, it may have been that Charles was just too pleased
with himself, too dominating. John Stuart Mill wrote of him,
'The impression he gave was that of boundless strength, together
with talents which, combined with such apparent force of will and
character, seemed capable of dominating the world.'

When Mary and Lady Molesworth were staying in Edinburgh in
January of this year, William, in one of his letters to his mother,
wrote: 'I hope Mary will get a lover – are there any in Edinburgh?';
and later, in one of his teasing letters to Mary from London:

I send you today a letter from your friend Miss Austin, whom I saw last
night at Mrs Grote and with whom I had a long flirtation. I have not seen
anything of your friend and quondam admirer Charles, he is most busily
engaged in election petitions making lots of money. My mother says you
have lots of admirers in Edinburgh, who I suppose have driven the barrister
out of your mind . . . I presume they are all Tories and will soon eradicate
the small portion of radicalism you have derived from your unfortunate
brother and make a good Christian of you. *A propos* of that subject what
think you of Mr Spring Rice persuading Lucy Austin to be baptised, he
being godfather . . . What a joke?

Write me all the news about your parties, you seem to have had some
lately. Are there many pretty girls? I never see one nowadays. Indeed I go
nowhere and live more a recluse than ever. I never dine out but frequently
have parties at home. Mrs Grote is now my only female acquaintance. She
complains of my not coming to her in the evening so I was obliged to go to
her last night.

Mrs Grote would not have approved of a marriage between Sir
William Molesworth, 8th Bart. and Miss Lucy Austin – nor of Miss
Mary Molesworth with Mr Charles Austin, QC. Highly intelligent,
delightful democrats that the Austins were, Charles an outstandingly
successful barrister – as was also his elder brother John whose wife
Sarah was a well-known translator of German and French historical
works – they were not aristocrats. Not even county gentry. They
ranked no higher than the professional bourgeoisie. And Mrs
Grote, despite her unflinchingly radical politics, held entrenched
views about birth and background. She attached tremendous
importance to 'having blood', to coming 'of good stock', and
claimed that her own family, the Lewins, was one of the oldest

in the land. Abraham Hayward, writing to Lady Eastlake when she was considering publishing a tribute to Harriet Grote after her death, declared that Monsieur Guizot never made a greater mistake than when (in his *Memoirs*) he wrote of Mrs Grote as representing the *bourgeoisie*.

MRS GROTE had suggested to Sir William that he should join her and George in a trip to Paris in November of this year, an idea that he was delighted to fall in with. After the Austins' visit to Pencarrow, he wrote to Mrs Grote on September 27th; 'I shall be at your orders about the 17th November; but remember I am to be *with you*: lodgings and or Hotel I don't care which, but I won't be separate'. But in October he had another relapse, and his doctor decreed he must abandon any such journey. His disappointment was, of course, shared, even exceeded, by that of Mrs Grote, who had been looking forward to having such a gallant young escort in Paris to parties and places that George preferred to avoid; but as always she was concerned and solicitous about his health. Other friends were also worried. Charles Austin wrote on November 6th: 'I hope you are as careless about politics as I am, and are busy in taking care of your health. I am very glad you have given up the journey to Paris . . . There are three reasons why I am anxious that you should live and not die – or, rather, kill yourself; one perhaps you will not value, even if you believe it – it is that I should be personally sorry; another that I want to see Hobbes completed and on my bookshelves; the last that you will, if so minded, and take proper steps, be of great use to Liberal principles and the Liberal party, which God grant. All this to induce you to mind your health, take exercise and live reasonably.'

William's way of taking exercise was on horse-back, and he worked in his garden whenever his health permitted. There was much to be done, he had many plans. During the eleven years of his minority he had been rarely at Pencarrow. There had been the four years in Edinburgh and the years abroad after his short time at Cambridge. The Pencarrow grounds had been maintained by the outdoor staff, but only just maintained. On his return from Italy in 1831, fired by admiration of the beautiful villa gardens of the Italian nobility, he was full of plans. The Italian garden he designed on the south side of the house was just a beginning – he visualised great tree-planting schemes for the whole estate, also orchid houses, a fern house and vineries. This was no passing enthusiasm – from early childhood he had been interested in all things botanical.

It was an interest that had been encouraged by his aunt, Miss Caroline Molesworth, who lived in Cobham, Surrey. She was a distinguished botanist and meteorologist, whose scientific papers were edited by Miss Ormerod.* She must have been delighted when William was elected a Fellow of the Royal Society in 1835, when he was only twenty-five – a very young Fellow. His nine sponsors recommended him 'from our personal knowledge as a Gentleman versed in several branches of natural Philosophy'. He used to visit Loddige's Nursery Gardens at Hackney with his aunt when he was in London, and together they spent hours at various botanical gardens. Aunt Caroline took a keen interest in his schemes for the Pencarrow grounds, and was a fount of knowledgeable advice. William chose his gardening staff with great care. When Mrs Grote heard in the autumn of 1836 that he was going to have to replace his head gardener, she wrote saying she knew of the very man – but Molesworth's reply was akin to a rebuff:

With regard to your gardener. Mine for whom I have the greatest regard is dying rapidly of a consumption. He cannot by any probability live over this winter. I am in want of a *good* one, but he must be a really *good* one, able not only to look after gardens but understand plantations etc. I don't know whether yours will do and I know how very *base* people generally are in their recommendations when they wish to get an old servant a place; his reason for quitting Lord Beauchamp's is suspicious, as a person would hardly turn off a good and trustworthy servant for so venial an offence, offence indubitably it is, but allowance may be made for the ignorance and prejudice of the lower orders. I cannot however say anything at present; the

*Miss Emily A. Ormerod was the first lady Fellow of the Royal Meteorological Society, working in the field of meteorological and phrenological observation. Her editing of Caroline Molesworth's observations on natural phenomena, taken between 1825 and 1850, was a vast undertaking not completed until 1880. Miss Molesworth died in 1872, leaving another huge collection of observations – on plant life and weather – which she had assembled over more than 40 years.

person whom I require should in every way be a superior person, and I am most anxious upon this subject. His place will be a comfortable one.

William's insistence that his new gardener must understand plantations was because he was specialising in rare conifers, personally supervising the planting of each tree. He later financed plant-collecting expeditions to the Far East and Western Australia, and the collection of specimen conifers at Pencarrow is widely renowned. From Australia William introduced some of the most rare species of *Araucaria*. The name by which this species is generally known was given to it by Charles Austin on one of his visits to Pencarrow: 'That tree,' he remarked, 'would puzzle a monkey.' And monkey-puzzle has ever since remained the name by which this most unloveable tree is known.

On the east of the lawns surrounding the house there is a great rockery built with granite stones from Bodmin Moor. This rockery has a political association. When Sir William retired from the representation of East Cornwall it was principally because the leading Whig land-owners, antagonised by his uncompromising pursuit of what they considered outrageously radical policies, had withdrawn their support. But the tenant farmers, the estate workers, and the tradesmen who served the estate and the house, wished to do something to show their loyalty and affection. When it was known that Sir William wanted a rockery, they saw it as their opportunity. Every farmer and tradesman in the neighbourhood who possessed a cart and horse used them for many weeks after the hay and corn harvests to transport great blocks of granite from Bodmin Moor to Pencarrow. It was said that between forty and fifty carts were used and that Sir William himself supervised the placing of every single granite block. He later appropriated a granite Celtic cross from the wayside and set it at the top of the rockery – maybe symbolically marking his grave to be.

A few years later Sir William made a grotto, winding deep into the rockery. Charles Austin, knowing his desire to be buried in his own grounds instead of the family vault, wrote to William on June 11th 1842:

My dear Molesworth,

Hearing that you are building for yourself (like an ancient Egyptian) a grave in your own garden [which I look upon as an innocent, if not a pleasing amusement – and much cheaper than building or improving a house] – I could not refrain from trying my hand at an Epitaph for you to be ready when you take possession. All I ask in return is that you will keep a corner for me – another for the brute Garth [William's Estramadoros Mastiff] and the fourth for the Celt [his wolfhound]:

> When I'm carried to Earth
> With Sir William and Garth
> In the hole may I be crammed –
> – For with such as they
> Whatever they say,
> May I be saved or *damned*.

A villainous parson in the neighbourhood has, I understand, written another in leonine hexameters, which I have translated freely, thus:

> Here in a hole Sir William lies;
> His soul in hell the devil fries.

It may well have been the insensitive jokey streak in Charles Austin, illustrated by this letter, that was at the root of William's dislike of him. As he told Mrs Grote in the letter quoted earlier in this chapter, he was grateful to Austin for his help with Hobbes, but 'Still I don't like him'. William's desire to be buried in his own grounds instead of the family vault was connected with the anguish of Elizabeth's death only seven years earlier – it was not something for his friends to be funny about.

CHAPTER VII — 1840-1

IN October 1840 the Grotes paid their first visit as guests of Lady Molesworth at Pencarrow. That August Sir William had written:

'My dear Mrs Grote – I am in ecstacy at finding there is a chance of your paying us a visit. Taunton is about 90 miles from here, roads excellent and the distance might be made without difficulty in a day. I will come and escort you if you like, which I would not do for anybody else. My mother will likewise be most delighted. I can't say *equally*, for there is no one to whom your society can be so delightful as to myself.'

Mrs Grote, although no doubt charmed by Sir William's gallantry in offering to escort them from Taunton, evidently replied 'no, no, *too* kind'. There is an account of their journey in her *Life of Sir William*: 'We quitted our residence at Burnham Beeches [their Buckinghamshire country house], and posted down by easy journeys all the way to Pencarrow, where we arrived, I think, in the afternoon of the fourth day. My health was so delicate that I could not bear more than eight hours travelling without suffering from headache of painful amount, even though we journeyed in a comfortable, easy post-chaise, rolling along with four horses all the way.'

The visit was a success. She described it later in a letter to her sister in Sweden: 'We passed five weeks in Cornwall, visiting chiefly at Sir William Molesworth's seat, Pencarrow, where his mother and sister live with him, and I much enjoyed the entire tranquillity and rational uniformity of our lives there. We were made much of and invited to other houses and I made a number of new acqaintances among fine folks which I found very agreeable, and which I think to follow up now that Radicalism is extinct and politics no longer absorb my energies. In fact, in our position it is undoubtedly pleasant to live rather with high-born people than with plebs, and as politics are dead I may as well revert to my natural affinities.'

A revealing letter, showing Mrs Grote to be now distancing herself from those of the Radicals she considered 'plebs', and her belief that her natural milieu was the society of 'high-born people'. It was during this October visit that Sir William confided to Mrs Grote that he had fallen in love again. It had been love at first sight when he was a guest at Carclew, the house of Sir Charles Lemon, Bart., MP for Truro. There he had met Miss Caroline Trelawny, daughter of another Cornish MP, a Tory. They met again at a ball given during William's Carclew visit, then on other occasions. Miss Trelawny showed pleasure at Sir William's attentions – but her father showed definite displeasure. He told her she must discourage Sir William's advances – he could never permit such an alliance owing to Sir William's radical politics and infidel opinions on religion. It was the Julia Carew saga all over again; and when Mrs Grote arrived at Pencarrow, 'he used to talk of this new *penchant* to me whenever we were alone, canvassing every conceivable form of proceeding calculated to bring him into the society of Miss T'.

One day they paid a morning visit to Sir Hussey and Lady Vivian at Glynn, about six miles from Pencarrow, believing the Trelawny family to be there – but they had left an hour or two before the Pencarrow party arrived. Soon after that, Mr and Mrs Grote set out in their post-chaise with Sir William on an expedition to Lands End, paying a visit to Sir Charles Lemon at Carclew *en route*. While there, Mrs Grote questioned various people about the chances of Sir William's suit. Everyone said it was hopeless – Mr Trelawny was inflexibly hostile to the alliance. Back again at Pencarrow, William kept Mrs Grote in the library until late every night, 'dwelling upon the obstacles which stood between him and his pursuit of Miss T. and tormenting me with suggestions as to the practicability of my contriving some way of promoting a meeting with her'. All Mrs Grote could do was to promise that if the Trelawnys came to town for the London season she would try to effect a meeting.

They did come, taking a house in Berkeley Square. What followed is nowhere documented except in Mrs Grote's book; so the tale must be told by a few extracts from it, allowing for her tendency to dramatise and for the fact that she was writing twenty-five years later: 'Molesworth lost no time in paying his devoirs at Berkeley Square, was politely received, allowed to join the luncheon-table, met the party at third places, laid himself out for invitations, rode with them in the Park, and after a fortnight found himself invited to a house where he was to meet Miss T. – at *dinner*. I believe Molesworth scarcely missed a day, at this period, coming to our house to 'report proceedings', and to compare his chances of success . . . He would come rushing in, sometimes, about four o'clock, before the Park lounge, calling for something to eat (having perhaps been at committee work at the House of Commons in the morning, and faint with fasting), and for some champagne; then fall to upon the refreshment, and rail, between whiles, at "his own cursed folly" in persevering against so much mortifying discouragement. One day, however, he came radiant with satisfaction. "I am to meet her tomorrow," he said, "at Sir Hussey Vivian's, at the Ordinance, and I am resolved to play a bold game, once for all." '

In the afternoon following Sir Hussey Vivian's dinner party, Mrs Grote was sitting alone in her drawing-room, 'when in came Sir William, his face flushed with emotion, and his voice tremulous and agitated . . . "What is the matter, Sir William, I beg?" He took a glance round the drawing-room to make sure that no one was within hearing, and then burst out "She is nothing but a . . . heartless coquette! and I have lavished my affections on a cold, hard girl!" '

It seemed that Sir William had been fortunate enough to take Miss T. down to dinner, had 'engaged her in conversation having a certain significance; persuaded himself that she regarded him with interest, possibly with favour. Buoyed up by this, Molesworth continued their conversation after dinner when the gentlemen joined the ladies; and when the Trelawnys made a move to depart, he endeavoured to place her evening wrap around the shoulders of Miss T., but that she abruptly took the shawl from his hands, and refused to permit it, or even to take his arm to the carriage'. Mrs Grote's account of Sir William's torrent of anguished confidences continued: 'He stayed a long while, expatiating on the ill fortune which attended every love-pursuit of his – eating, and drinking champagne, storming against every member of the T. family in turn, and winding up his philippic with "'. . . them all! They repudiate my attention, and pretend to think me unworthy as a suitor! I will tell you what, my dear friend, I will marry my cook, and society shall be forced to swallow *her*! and I shall be revenged on them all, by . . ." '

In spite of this tirade, it seems that he was not yet able to abandon all hope of Miss Trelawny. 'He oscillated for a while, however, between love and fury, and seemed irresolute how to act. Meanwhile, I would *not* consent to his making a formal proposal . . . I could not suffer him to incur a risk of a fresh mortifying refusal.'

Surely Sir William must have resented this assumption, by Mrs Grote, that he would not act without *her* consent? Her account goes on to say: 'As a final move, I took an opportunity of consulting Mr Charles Buller, an intimate acquaintance of ours, of Molesworth and of the young lady. "Do you think she likes him?" I asked. "Yes, I think she does." "Well, but if that should be the case, perhaps he would do well to come boldly forward as a candidate for her hand?" "No," replied C. Buller, "and I will explain to you why not. That family are very affectionately united. The girl respects and loves her father, and depend upon it she will never marry a man whom he dislikes and disapproves of, as he does Molesworth." Sir William made one last tentative move, riding in the Park one evening alongside of Miss T. It failed in its purpose, and he took the wise, though painful determination of abandoning his pursuit.'

Mrs Grote added a footnote to this account in her *Life of Sir William Molesworth*: 'I afterwards came to know the real history of the dinner at Sir Hussey Vivian's. During dinner, Mr T. noticed Sir William's earnest manner in conversing with his daughter; Mrs T. observed the disquiet brewing in her husband's mind and in consequence felt uneasy in her turn. So, when the ladies retired, she administered an emphatic *avis* to her daughter, enjoining her to give no encouragement to Sir William's attentions, *for* that it would displease Mr T. extremely. Moved by the parental admonition, she accordingly gave him the rebuff.'

A dutiful daughter indeed. Not spirited enough, surely, to be the wife of William Molesworth.

THIS second humiliation as a suitor, added to the political
frustration caused by the Radicals' parliamentary disintegration, may
well have been why Molesworth seriously considered a proposition
put to him by Edward Gibbon Wakefield. It was a project that
would take him far away from England for many years; and little
short of despair, surely, can have made him listen, over several
months, to Wakefield's enthusiastic persuasions. Briefly, the project
was to send a colonising expedition to New South Wales, headed
by Molesworth 'accompanied by your old friend E. Duppa and
my brother Arthur. There you would plant the settlement of
Molesworth, leading out some thousands of people, and arrange
its municipal government. Then, as a member of the General
Council of Government for the Islands, you would give the tone
and character of the general legislation. You would be more than
Governor, who is an officer dependant on the breath of the office
at home and sure to be impeded if he try to do well.'

Molesworth had been in full agreement with the plan which
Wakefield had published when he first returned from Australia,
a plan for 'systematic colonisation'. This suggested that occupied
land in a new colony should not be granted promiscuouly, but
should be parcelled out on a regular system and sold at an adequate
price. Funds so raised should be used to promote emigration, the
emigrants being carefully selected with a preference for the young,
with an equal number of each sex, and with emigrants representative
of all classes, skills and occupations. But it is astonishing that
Molesworth should consider *himself* becoming an emigrant. Only
the previous year he had sent his brother Francis to New Zealand.
Could he now abandon all the responsibilities of his family and
estate to his mother, sister and youngest brother Arscott, only
twenty-two years old? Could he abandon his gardens and hot-
houses, his intellectual pursuits and his editing of Hobbes which was
less than half finished? Would he not miss the stimulating sparring
of political friends, and was not his life-style and his manner of
dressing that of a fastidious elegant? Beyond all that, there was
what surely was an insuperable objection – his so vulnerable health.
How could he contemplate living in a country at least four long sea
months away from skilled medical care?

Nevertheless, unbelievable though it seems, he did seriously ponder over Wakefield's suggestion for a quite considerable time. This is shown by a number of letters to Wakefield and to Thomas Woollcombe. In his last letter to Woollcombe on the subject, undated but probably in January 1841, he wrote:

The more I reflect upon Wakefield's project, the stronger appear the objections to it which we discussed at Plymouth. I have no doubt of the success of the colony, but in a personal point of view I don't think the honour gained will be very great or sufficient to repay the privations. I do not feel that either my *health* or *character* qualify me to be the *popular leader* of an expedition. I do not see what position I should hold, or what I should have to do . . . My chief uses would be first in this country as a great *decoy duck* to tempt emigrants; secondly in the colony as a sort of *pidgeon* whom every one will feel he has a right to pluck, from whom everything will be expected, and whom everyone will abuse if anything goes wrong, taking care at the same time to attribute all success to their own personal exertions. Besides this there is too great an inclination on the part of Wakefield for stage-effects, and too much will depend upon them to satisfy me; for my feelings are revolted by such a course of proceeding. And lastly I can't put reliance in Wakefield, because he has too many projects afloat. This is the summary of my last letter to Wakefield in reply to one which I now enclose to you . . . I told him your project of a company of which I should be governor; the only feasible plan, but to which again there seems to me grave personal objections . . . I should like to go to New South Wales with powers that the Colonial Office won't give; because that would be to terminate a task I had commenced, and would not seem to change me from an Englishman into a colonist, as Wakefield would advise me to let it appear. The topics mentioned in your letter will receive my best consideration. You are perfectly right in not abandoning a certainty for an uncertainty. I must say that the obstacles to Wakefield's plan seem to me unsurmountable, but I shall wait till I meet him in town to come to an absolute decision in the negative.

In none of Molesworth's letters to Woollcombe, nor in those written to Wakefield, does he mention having sent Francis to New Zealand nor his responsibilities to his family and estates. He and Woollcombe *must* have discussed these at some of their meetings, but in his letters it was chiefly the implications to his political career that he considers. This last letter on the Wakefield project to Woollcombe ends 'I am clearly rising in public opinion here, and if I have [firmness?] to pursue for the next ten years the course which I have already pursued, I shall have the opportunity of distinguishing myself, and by that time a change probably will take place in the aspect of political affairs. I feel disgusted at present it is true but on mature reflection I think that feeling is not justified.'

So the flame of political ambition was rekindling. He was telling himself that 'in the next ten years' he might be in the position he desired above all others, that of Secretary of State for the Colonies.

NEVERTHELESS, when a General Election was announced for June 1841, Molesworth decided not to stand again. Another spell of ill health may have had much to do with his decision; but also he was aware that his Leeds constituents were not all in favour of the policies he had been pursuing. For instance, during the time in 1840 of critical tension in Europe, he had held a peace meeting in Leeds at which he had spoken out strongly against Russia and advocated an alliance with France. France, more than any other European nation, he declared, wanted to check the Russian aggression upon Turkey: 'To go to war with France would be playing the game of Russia'. An alliance with France? Leeds did not like the suggestion. It was twenty-five years since the battle of Waterloo, but the man in the Yorkshire street, unlike society in the London salons, still regarded France as 'the enemy'.

After much thought, Molesworth took the decision to leave politics, at least for a while, and have an uninterrupted period during which he could work on his editing of Hobbes. George Grote would also have liked to leave politics and give undivided attention to work on his *magnum opus*, his history of Greece; but he had not yet retired from the City banking house, Prescott, Grote and Co., of which he was a partner, so at the 1841 General Election he stood again for the City of London. In Parliament he continued to work for the reforms he believed to be so essential for the country. Nevertheless the Grote social orientation was changing. Mrs Grote had lost her political fervour and dropped some of the radical friends who had frequented her Eccleston Street parties. She was now unashamedly, indeed blissfully, moving in the kind of aristocratic Whig circles that in her more radical days she and George had felt it their duty to scorn. As she wrote in her *Personal Life of George Grote*, 'We even went so far as to accept friendly overtures from Lord and Lady Holland, and to commence intercourse with Holland House; whither Grote would never have consented to go in past times'. How like Mrs Grote to imply that it was the Grotes who were condescending to the Hollands.

The Grotes' first visit to Holland House was the cause of many a quip in radical circles. Charles Buller, who was happily gregarious in all circles and was a frequent guest at Holland House, was, according to John Stuart Mill's autobiography, 'entrusted with the delicate task of negotiating an invitation to the Grotes to dine at Holland House, and was reported to have said "There should be some memorial . . . of the very most arduous negotiations ever entrusted to human diplomacy" '. Sydney Smith was also recruited to add his persuasions; and on May 11th 1837, Mrs Grote wrote to her sister-in-law, Mrs Charlotte Lewin, at Barn House, Eltham: 'I have just seen Sydney Smith, and agreed to dine with Lord and Lady Holland at that dear old pile in Kensington to-morrow with him. They had made a great point of it, employing both Sydney Smith and Charles Buller as ambassadors, so that I think my dignity quite safe in accepting their advances, and all the world knows such society is not to be had in London as at their assemblies. George finds Lord Holland's conversation exceedingly agreeable. He really is a liberal minded man and a scholar.'

The other guests at that Holland House dinner were: Lord Melbourne (then Prime Minister); Lord Duncannon (afterwards Ld. Lieutenant of Ireland); Lord Cottenham (then Chancellor) and Lady Cottenham; Marquis and Marchioness of Normanby; Mr and Mrs Edward John Stanley; Charles Buller; Mr Allen (Lord Holland's resident librarian); Mr John Ponsonby and Sir Edward Lytton Bulwer. Monsieur Guizot (the French Ambassador), the Duchess of Somerset, General Alva (the Spanish Ambassador) and some others joined the circle after dinner, assembled in the time-honoured library upstairs.

Mrs Grote's account of the evening ended with what she must have felt to be an exoneration from any accusation of infidelity to Radicalism: 'This evening passed at Holland House made a deep impression on our imagination, and I, at least, felt sincerely grateful for the opportunity afforded us of realizing the scene of past celebrated histories.' Then she added a throw-away line: 'We also were present at the Queen's Ball at Buckingham Palace, and this, too, without any twinges of conscience on his [Mr Grote's] part.' Even when Lord Melbourne's Whig Government was replaced in 1841 by Sir Robert Peel and his Tories, Mrs Grote recorded that it 'excited no sensible feeling of regret on our part'. This was indeed a sea-change. Who would have thought the Grotes, of all people, would accept so unconcernedly the premiership of Sir Robert Peel, considered then to be enemy of everything for which the Radicals had fought?

MRS GROTE, however, was a complicated character, her reasoning seldom cut and dried. There were layers to her character of which few people, with the exception of William Molesworth, were aware. When in August 1842 she spent a week with the Sydney Smiths in Somerset, accompanied by the novelist Mrs Anne Jameson – George Grote was 'detained by other duties' – Sydney Smith discovered a layer unsuspected by those who knew her only in London. After the visit, he wrote to Sir Roderick Murchison: 'We have had Mrs Grote here; Grotius could not come. The basis of her character is rural, and she was intended for a country clergyman's wife; but, for whatever she was intended, she is an extraordinarily clever woman, and we all liked her very much.'

Mrs Grote a country clergyman's wife? – a surprising suggestion. Surely her downright criticisms of people, her occasional slang and unpredictable behaviour, her eccentric manner of dressing – those white stockings and red shoes, those challenging hats – all this does not fit in with one's image of the gentle helpmeet of the incumbent of a country parish. But that the 'good stock' Mrs Grote prided herself upon came from sound rural roots is borne out by M.C.M. Simpson in her *Many Memories of Many People*. Mrs Simpson was a daughter of Nassau Senior, lawyer and economist, Master of the High Court of Chancery, who was involved with the drafting of the Poor Law Act against which Thomas Carlyle stormed with the full blast of his most bitter invective. From childhood she had known Mrs Grote as a close family friend, and her memories illuminate a little known side of Mrs Grote's character:

She was especially proud of her business talents, and, in order to set her husband free to work at his History, she undertook the chief management of their property. In a letter to me from their estate, Long Bennington, in Lincolnshire, she describes her diligent supervision . . . 'We have been ever since [we arrived] hard at work hearing grievances at every turn, dealing with demands for repairs and improvements, and persecuted by unrelenting bad weather. I have been from 3 to 4 hours on horseback, most days under umbrella and cloak, taking surveys of our various dominions, which lie 3 miles apart in some cases, the ground being too wet to allow of my walking, except on Tuesday, when I passed 3 hrs in walking through glorious wheatfields, mangolds, rich pastures studded with beasts, and the like. For a little estate of this character, it is incredible what a quantity of matter arises for adjustments as between landlord and tenant, stewards and tenants inclusive . . . We are putting a new wheel on our watermill, at a cost of £150, begad!

This involvement in the management of country property was another bond between Harriet Grote and William Molesworth. They could talk husbandry together as well as politics and love affairs.

CHAPTER VIII — 1841-4

FOR two years after Molesworth retired at the dissolution of Parliament in June 1841, he lived quietly at Pencarrow. He had appointed a literary assistant, Mr Edward Grubbe, and had now reached a point in his editing of the works of Hobbes when he could feel that the end was within his grasp. In 1842 he had supervised the making of a mile-long drive from Washaway village to Pencarrow House, passing through woodlands and an ancient fortified encampment – and had planted its borders with rhododendrons, hydrangeas, and camellias, backed by conifers that have now long since reached forest growth. He had tended his orchid and fern houses, two large vineries and a cucumber house. Heated pits had been built for melon-growing and forcing beans in the spring. Three long rows of potato pits had been dug, which were also used for early turnips and radishes. It had been a long, useful period of healing tranquillity; and he now felt, towards the end of summer 1843, the need to be diverted by some stimulating company. A letter from Mrs Grote came just at the right moment, saying that she and George were planning a little tour of the West Country. 'Come to Pencarrow, of course,' William commanded – and set about asking a few other guests to make an intellectually lively party.

The Grotes spent a few nights with the Sydney Smiths at Combe Florey, then two more at Ilfracombe, whence 'one more day's journeying by the coastal road took us to Pencarrow where we found Sir William in good health, with more than usual appetite for conversation after a considerable lull in his social exertions'. They were welcomed by Lady Molesworth and Mary; and the guests already there were Charles Austin, Monckton Milnes and a Miss Fanny Howarth who was judged by Mrs Grote to be 'an attractive young lady' – we know nothing else about her. Mr Grubbe was approved by Mrs Grote as 'a lawyer of no ordinary stamp'. She wrote of the party in her *Life* of Sir William as being extremely lively. Even Mr Grote was in a more sociable mood than usual:

He had shaken off the feeling of mortification which hung over the closing period of his political career . . . and was well disposed to engage in the intellectual sport now going on. Our host played his part to admiration, whilst the ladies, on their side, found the topics neither heavy nor tedious, though often profound and learned, and the daily dinner-hour ever found us eager to renew the friendly fray of the morning – Mr Grubbe, a modest and intelligent person, forming a sort of 'chorus', or arbitrator, among the talkers.

One notes a slight condescension on Mrs Grote's part to 'the ladies', while allowing that they were able to keep their end up. She herself, of course, was no lady when it came to intellectual conversation, and was always able to give as good as she got. A brief break in this happy house-party was made after about a fortnight when Mr Grote, Charles Austin, and Mr Grubbe left Pencarrow for London with the sole purpose of voting for Mr James Pattison, the Liberal candidate in a by-election for the City of London. That George Grote should undertake a return journey of some 500 horse-drawn miles just to poll in a by-election, attests to the constancy of his political dedication even in the twilight of the Radical decline. It seems to contradict Mrs Grote's assertion (quoted in the last chapter) that the replacement of Lord Melbourne's Whig Government by that of Sir Robert Peel and his Tories 'excited no sensible feeling of regret on our part'. But it must be taken into account that most of the Radicals, including Molesworth, considered Melbourne's *laissez-faire* pragmatism, making concessions now to the Right, now to the Left, trimming to the wind most likely to keep the Whigs in office, to be no better for the country than Peel's entrenched conservatism.

After the house-party had finally dispersed, Sir William was able to settle down again for four undisturbed winter months working in his library; and by the early spring of 1844 the first two volumes of Hobbes were ready to take to Longman's the publishers. At the time of his retirement from Parliament he had given up the house in Eaton Square that he shared with John Temple Leader and taken the lease of a much smaller house in Lowndes Square to serve as a foothold in London for occasional visits. Now, on March 18th, he left Pencarrow, arranging for his mother and Mary to follow on April 2nd for the London season – but not to Lowndes Square.

For them he had rented 6 Chester Street, Belgrave Square. Clearly he preferred that they should have a separate establishment where they could do their own entertaining. At his age, now thirty-four years, it would be frustrating for his household to be run, as it inevitably would be, by his mother, with William having to act as host when guests of her generation were being entertained. What he sadly lacked at his own house, of course, was a hostess – in other words a wife.

It was now three years since his second love-affair ended in humiliation, but his pride would not allow him to show any interest in the marriageable young ladies he would meet, daughters of his mother's friends, at 6 Chester Street. He does not seem to have done much, either, to introduce eligible young gentlemen to Mary. Now twenty-eight years old, she was long past the débutante age when girls were entered for the marriage stakes. Lady Molesworth must have been almost as anxious that she should find a suitable husband as that William should secure a suitable wife. No descriptions can be found of Mary's physical attractions, although one memory of her by a friend after her death was that 'she had the sweetest and most fascinating speaking voice it was ever my lot to listen to – in her younger days she was a drawing-room reader, and the "At Home" cards of the day often bore upon them "to hear Miss Mary Molesworth read" '. There is no portrait of her as a young girl; but a charming one by Da Monte, painted when she was forty-three, shows that she certainly inherited from her mother some of the legendary comeliness of the Humes of Edinburgh.

Before Lady Molesworth and Mary left Pencarrow for London in that April of 1844, William wrote to his sister from 1 Lowndes Square:

I found the outside of my house new painted and looking quite clean, and the inside exceedingly dirty. Whereat I pitched into Black [house-steward-cum-butler] and gave him it right and left. My house resembles so many of the female sex, fair without, but foul within . . . Had a long talk with Grote, chiefly about Aristotle's politics. He said his wife would return [from Paris] about April 13th; and last of all proposed a game of billiards with me! I declined. They have a billiard table in one of their upstairs rooms. I went away, satisfied I had misspent the evening with a pack of fools . . . Sunday I called upon the Garwoods and saw the fair Eugenie. It was rather a stiff and stupid visit and I was glad when a new visitor was announced and I could retire.

William was evidently in an unhappy mood, and Mrs Grote was not in Town to shake him out of his depression with her robust rebukes. His next letter to Mary begins with an account of visiting Loddige's Nursery Gardens at Hackney with Woollcombe and finishes: 'My stay here will be short. The weather is too fine for London. I feel somewhat like a fish out of water, and without any regular occupation. I amused myself by reading mathematics, which however I can do better in Cornwall.' He was regretting having retired from Parliament, missing the stimulation of being at the heart of what was happening. He was bereft of a sense of purpose.

Although he had decided to cut short his stay in London, he made arrangements for Lady Molesworth's and Mary's enjoyment of the season. For instance, two days after his arrival at Lowndes Square, he noted in his diary: 'Agreed with Pearce for a new cab for four years certain at £36.15.0. per annum to be ready for the 21st April. A new cab phaeton from June for five years certain at £65 per annum.' There follow notes of political friends calling upon him – Cobden and Bright amongst them – and a visit to Knight's Nurseries to choose seven species of azaleas for Pencarrow. Then on April 1st, 'Went to Longman's and made the following arrangement with him. Hobbes works to be sold at 10s. per volume, to be accounted for at $7\frac{1}{2}$, less commission 10 per cent. The boarding to be charged at 7d. per volume.' On April 4th he is at Knight's Nurseries again: 'Bought 7 plants, total £17.5.6.' They must have been very rare species at nearly £2.10.0. each.

WILLIAM'S diary for 1844 is the earliest of his personal diaries to have survived at Pencarrow – small, leather-bound volumes, with little space for more than the noting of engagements with occasional comments on people and events; also monthly noting of expenses. At the beginning of the March 1844 section Sir William wrote two addresses:

Mrs Grote, Hotel Mommorenci, Boulevard des Italiennes
Mrs West, 29 Half Moon Street.

Mrs Grote in Paris would be demanding a lively correspondence with her dear Sir William – long letters to keep her in touch with London gossip and to confide more personal matters such as *affaires de coeur*. No doubt he did write to her, but it is clear from later developments that in none of his letters can he have mentioned his new acquaintance – Mrs Temple West of Half Moon Street.

Andalusia Grant West was the young widow of Temple West, Esq., of Mathon Lodge, Worcestershire. By all accounts she was comely, vivacious – and socially ambitious. Perhaps too merry a widow? Maybe. But scarcity of facts always breeds a swarm of theories, and so little was known about her early life that a great deal of talk went around. There was inevitably something intriguing about an attractive young widow living alone in her own establishment in Half Moon Street – that short street of five-storey houses, little balconies at their drawing-room windows, leading from Piccadilly to Curzon Street, close to Shepherd Market. Half Moon Street has always traditionally been a street of expensive bachelor apartments, both in life and in literature, from Boswell to Bulldog Drummond. But what really made Mrs West 'doubtful' was that she was said to have been on the stage – and as a young girl had married a man three times her age. It was presumed that when the old man in due course died, he had left her a satisfactory amount of money; after all, the Half Moon Street establishment had been acquired since she became a widow, and Mrs West hired her own carriage for the season. Also, she was not without a sponsor, so to speak, in London circles. Her late husband's younger brother and his wife, Admiral Sir John and Lady West, lived in Berkeley Square – a fact that should surely have given her an impeccable entrée into society. But her own parentage was unknown, and the stage stigma stuck.

It is not known where or exactly when Sir William first met Mrs Temple West, nor whether it was after their very first meeting that he noted 29 Half Moon Street in his diary. That he experienced a *coup de foudre* across a crowded drawing-room seems very likely, since he introduced her to his mother as soon as she and Mary arrived in London. Four days later, on April 6th, his diary notes: 'Took a box at Drury Lane to hear Duprex in *William Tell* – my mother, Mary and Mrs T. West went with me'; and on the 18th, 'To the Italian Opera to hear Gina Pornasea in *Sommerside* with Lablau and Fornachi. The latter a decided failure. Mrs West, my

Every description of Carriages & Harness, both for Home and Foreign Use

COACH MAKERS

By Appointment

To Her Majesty the Queen Dowager

H.I.M. THE EMPEROR OF THE BRAZILS
AND
H.M.C.M. THE KING OF THE NETHERLANDS.

No 103 Long Acre. LONDON.

Account from Pearce the Coachmakers of Longacre, from whom Sir William hired carriages for the London season for himself and his mother.

mother and Mary were of the party.' On the 30th he took Mary and Mrs West to the exhibition of flowers in the Botanical Gardens in Regent's Park: 'The weather was cold from an easterly wind' – there follows a long list of plants seen.

There is clear evidence that William's decision to cut short his time in London had now been reversed. On April 25th he signed an agreement with Pearce the Coachmakers, 103 Long Acre, for hire of a cabriolet for five years. Dashing two-wheeled one-horse cabriolets were the fashionable turn-outs for young men-about-town – no question that William could be hiring one for his mother and Mary. Next, the dandy in him propelled him to London's most esteemed tailor, Stultz, to order '1 frock coat, 2 morning waistcoats, 2 white ditto'; and to Pilke for '1 pair dress trousers, 2 pairs morning trousers'. On April 25th Mr Woollcombe came to London with the estimates for repairs and alterations at Pencarrow, totalling £4,000. Sir William, flushed by his new vision of a rose-coloured future, not only approved the estimates but decided that Pencarrow should have yet further improvements, and signed a contract with Mitchell for the increased sum of £4,720.

Mary returned to Pencarrow for a short spell at this time – probably at William's request – to make sure that there was no delay in starting the repair work. A letter from him, undated, tells her of an afternoon spent with Mrs West alone at her house in Half Moon Street:

My dear Mary,

I have just returned from Mrs West's with whom I have been sitting for the last hour and a half. She is looking very well and enquired after you. She wants to know the name of a fern with delicate foliage I gave her. It is in the fern house and may be known by its stalk being as black as ebony. I remember it well, having often remarked the beauty of the foliage and the peculiar black of the stalk. It will be about the fourth or fifth pot from the door leading to the Heath House. You can send a specimen of it between two pieces of pasteboard per post.

She was very glad to see me and hoped I would call again soon, as very few of her friends were in town and she found it dull.

Yours, W.M.

Clearly, Mrs West had guessed that the way to win William was by showing a great interest in plants and botanical gardens. Mary, for her part, must have realised that William was once more urgently in love – and that this time the tables would be turned. Disapproval of the alliance would come, not from the lady's family, but from his.

MRS GROTE, like Mary keenly sensitive to William's moods, must have been aware of what was happening; and he, aware that he had been neglecting his dear friend and hitherto close confidante, made amends by inviting her to the Opera to hear *Zampa* ('which I did not think much of'); and also spent another evening at her house. This was at a time when Mrs West was out of town for about two weeks, during which William's diary notes various evening parties that suggest he was not only doing his duty by Mrs Grote, but also by his mother's friends: 'At Lady E. Hope Vere's (stupid)'; a raffle at Mrs Gibson's, a call upon Mrs Tollemachan; 'Went to the Caledonian Ball, which was very stupid'. Mrs West was not there. But by May 21st Mrs West is once more in the picture: 'Musical party at Chorley's. Met Mrs West and Mendelssohn. The music was beautiful.' On June 1st there was a musical party at the Garwoods, to which William took his close friend Edward Duppa and introduced him to Mrs West. Two days later there was a splendid evening at his mother's house in Chester Street: 'Madame Duren played. Mrs West sang beautifully; the whole went off with nice people. Thence I went to Sir Wm. Clay's, where I amused myself much.' And although he was not in bed until half-past-three in the morning, he was up again early and in high spirits, writing a long, teasing letter to Mary, to be delivered to Chester Street by hand:

You ought to be well pleased with the success of your party last night. You had plenty of nice and some superior people, whose society, such as Babbage, Austin, Grote etc. was honourable to you. You had a Lord and several Ladies to gratify your aristocratic leanings, and many pretty girls and women to adorn your rooms. Madame Dalken played admirably, though you were frequently the least attentive of her listeners, and I was delighted with the piano. Mr Holmes is certainly a very good natured person and sings well, and you must acknowledge that Mrs West did her best. You will allow that I behaved excessively well. I spoke to every person I knew, and to many I did not. I was the pink of politeness to Lady Elizabeth Hopeton, conducted her to tea, talked to her daughter who is a sweet girl, and one of the prettiest in the room, and seemed for want of better, to be by no means disinclined to be friends with me. I escorted Lady Vivian to tea, and handed her to her carriage. Lord Vivian was more affectionate to me than ever and his wife was equally polite, proposing me to visit them in Wales . . . You seemed to me to have admirers enough and the tenderness of Mill excited, it is said, the astonishment and jealousy of Austin. I did not go near Mrs Grote, and intentionally; as she can do without me, I can do without her.

This mention of Mrs Grote indicates some huffiness between her and William. Maybe, during that evening he spent at her house on May 20th, she had in her tactless way expressed concern at his attentions to Mrs West. She may even have made some downright derogatory remark about her, at which William would have made an equally hard-hitting return. If indeed she had then suspected he had fallen in love, his vivacious, debonair, flirtatious behaviour at the party (so unlike the stiff stand-offishness about which she used to chide him) must have confirmed her suspicions. It was the behaviour of a man not only in love, but confident that he is loved in return. His letter to Mary continues:

Having engaged myself to dance with Miss Meir, to her I was most attentive, danced with her, took her down to supper, and every person except the lady herself thought me in love with her. She confided to me all her sorrow, her engagement to Mr Smythe, his extravagant demonstrations of love, and his subsequent infamous conduct. I gave her some good advice in very plain English – I really feel for the poor girl, whose great beauty more than any other fault has harmed her . . . Having finished with her I next took to that funny girl, Miss Wightman, who the moment I came in the room, came up to me, and declared to the astonishment of Sir A. Maclean that she intended to dance with me – I did so and then we sat down and talked and I gave her a lecture upon marriage and the duties of the married state. Then I commenced the most extraordinary flirtation with a very odd person, to the excessive amusement of those who observed it . . . she called me across the room, told me to come and sit alongside her, and then she cross-examined me about myself. She first inquired whether I was a roué to which I answered her I was more a libertine and debauchee without prejudices or principles, so she had better take care of herself – we talked away. I handed her about the room, told her her daughter was very handsome, handed her down to supper. Then I found her daughter, who joked her on our flirtation which I acknowledged, I saw her to her carriage and then went home myself about half past three.

William followed up this letter to Mary by himself calling at Chester Street to thank his mother for a delightful evening. In the afternoon he escorted Mrs West to the exhibition at the Botanical Gardens, Regent's Park – this time without Mary. Regent's Park, always a romantic milieu, together with the *great* interest Mrs West will have made sure of showing in the botanical exhibition, must have brought him to the brink of a proposal. Just one more meeting, at an evening party at Mrs Gibson's on June 8th, and his mind was made up. Next day the diary records: 'Determined to propose to Mrs West, and informed my mother of my intention to do so'. There is a note of defiance in that entry, an expectation of opposition. He was not going to consult his mother, but to inform her. Next day, June 10th: 'Dined with the Wightmans, went to the Polish Ball and proposed to Mrs West'. That Mrs West accepted forthwith, without any pretty protestations about needing 'time to think it over', is shown by their fixing the marriage date there and then for just four weeks ahead.

CHAPTER IX — 1844 cont.

THERE was no public announcement of the engagement. Lady Molesworth, of course, was the first to be informed on the morning after the Polish Ball. This happened to be the day on which Francis Molesworth arrived from New Zealand. Two days later, on April 13th, Mrs West introduced her fiancé to her brother-in-law and his wife, Admiral Sir John and Lady West, whom William had not previously met. That evening William took a box at the Opera for *Don Giovanni*, to which he and Andalusia went alone. This was in defiance of social etiquette, and must have excited whispered comment among others in the Opera House. Even formally betrothed couples were not expected to appear in public places unchaperoned, most especially in the evening. If Andalusia West had been a young girl, her parents would certainly not have permitted it.

Her parents, in fact, at this important time in Andalusia's life seem to have been kept in the background, although they lived in London. It was not until the day after *Don Giovanni* that William's diary records: 'Introduced to Mr and Mrs Carstairs'. He does not record whether the meeting took place at the Carstairs' home – perhaps it was at Half Moon Street. That afternoon he took Andalusia to the Horticultural Gardens once more, this time accompanied by Mary and Francis. The injury Francis had sustained in New Zealand, although it was eventually the cause of his death, was not one that kept him in bed at this time.

Three days later Lady Molesworth gave a little dinner party for the betrothed couple, at which Mr Pendarves and Mr Grote were the only guests outside the family. Was Mrs Grote invited but refused? We do not know. All we do know about her reaction to the engagement is from her *Life of Sir William Molesworth*, published ten years after his death. Her account fascinatingly illuminates her feelings, but it cannot be taken as factually accurate. It begins with an error. She writes, 'Upon our return from Paris towards the end of April, almost the earliest news that now came to me was that, during my absence, Sir William Molesworth had formed an engagement to marry a lady of the name of West, a widow.' 'During my absence' is a nice touch, suggesting indignation that he should have taken such a decision without her permission. But Mrs Grote's memory misled her when writing that news of the engagement was circulating towards the end of April, and that it had taken place while the Grotes were in Paris: Sir William did not propose to Mrs West until June 10th. Also, his diaries tell of two evenings he spent with Mrs Grote in May, one at the Opera and one at her house; and again she was at Lady Molesworth's party on June 3rd, as we know from William's letter to Mary after the party. However, it is possible that gossip was already circulating when she returned from Paris; and allowing for inaccuracies, Mrs Grote's account is revealing, both as to her own feelings and those of the Molesworth family. It continues:

The relatives of Sir William speedily imparted their extreme dissatisfaction to me, on account of the disparity which, it seemed, existed between Mrs West and himself in respect of birth and connexions. On learning the humble antecedents of the lady, it was but natural that I should participate, to a certain extent, in the feeling of regret so deeply entertained by his family. However, shortly after the receipt of this news, Molesworth came in person to tell me how it had come about. What passed between us at this interview there is no need to relate – enough that I expressed the most anxious wish that his intended marriage might bring him happiness, adding a sincere desire to contract and maintain friendly relations with the lady, whose acquaintance I professed myself ready to form without delay. Accordingly, Mr Grote and myself, accompanied by Sir William, paid an early visit to Mrs West, at her own residence in London. Pending the completion of the preparations for their union, Molesworth continued to frequent our house as usual, and we sometimes drove out together for an hour or two, in my carriage or his, as was our wont, when our talk would often run upon the prospects connected with his married life, his probable occupations, his modified social habits, and so forth.

What did Mrs Grote mean by 'his modified social habits'? Far from being modified, the danger lay in them being dramatically stepped up . . . Society was saying that it was Andalusia West's ambition to be a great London hostess, entertaining the élite of political circles and the international *beau monde*. Sir William's delicate constitution, it was feared, would not stand the pace.

THE WEDDING was to be on July 19th, exactly one month after their engagement. The brevity of the engagement period was not unusual. Long betrothals were not in fashion at that time. Even young couples, affianced with the blessing of their parents, were often married within a month – presumably to give them no time to change their minds. Preparations for the quiet wedding of a widow would not be elaborate, but nevertheless there was much to be done beforehand. Most urgently, Sir William had to travel to Cornwall to see what stage the restoration work at Pencarrow had reached, whether it would be in a fit state to receive his bride. He left Paddington with Maclean at two o'clock on June 24th by the newly opened Great Western Railway to Exeter, arrived there at 9.30 p.m., and slept at an hotel. It seems likely that before he left Exeter by the 5 a.m. mail next morning he booked accommodation at the hotel for his wedding night. The mail coach reached Bodmin at 11.30, where he hired a post-chaise for the last five miles to Pencarrow.

At Pencarrow he found it would be impossible for them to live there immediately after the wedding. The work under way was extensive: new roof, new plaster to the outside walls, the old Elizabethan part pulled down and rebuilt, every room in the house but two to be re-papered. The interior alterations were to include the addition of an alcove to the music room. Fine panelling from the old mansion house at Tetcott was to be used for the music room walls and those of the entrance hall, which was to be made into a second library. To plan and supervise this interior work, Sir William had engaged the architect George Wightwick, partner with John Foulston of Plymouth, a well-known West Country firm whose buildings in Stonehouse and Devonport were particularly admired. A decorative cast-iron stove by the Plymouth firm of S. Hearden was to be installed in the inner hall for much-needed warmth.

William wrote to Mary: 'Pencarrow most uncomfortable, fit only for Miss Dietz and Ailsa, who concern themselves with killing the disturbed rats. I had to reside in an oblong ten feet by four in my room, the rest being filled with sofas and chairs.' Miss Dietz was Lady Molesworth's personal maid. Presumably she had been left in charge of the staff at Pencarrow instead of accompanying Lady Molesworth to London. Few lady's maids would consider the tackling of rats as part of their duties, but the devotion of Miss Dietz to Lady Molesworth equalled that of Maclean's to his master. After his first uncomfortable night, William went to judge the possibility of living temporarily at Costislost, a Molesworth property within a short distance, whose tenant was John Lakeman, steward of the Pencarrow estates. It was but a small farmhouse, so some of Mr Lakeman's family may have had to be found temporary accommodation elsewhere. Whatever arrangements were made, according to William's diary he 'found it would do very well for our residence till we can inhabit Pencarrow. Wrote accordingly to Mrs West'. Did he begin his letter 'Dear Mrs West', or 'Dear Andalusia'? Or, more recklessly by some term of endearment? No letters between them, either before or after their marriage, survive. To Mary, William wrote that he was bringing her 'a beautiful spike of Stanhofen Wardic, two of which of equal beauty came out today at Pencarrow and made a splendid appearance.' Next day, June 29th, he 'left Bodmin per Mail at 1 o'clock. Reached Exeter at 8 o'clock; left Exeter at 25 mins to ten o'clock and arrived in London at 10 mins to 4 o'clock.' That would be June 30th. Altogether, he had spent twenty-two hours and two nights journeying for his three days at Pencarrow.

He would, of course, have apprised the staff there, and at Costislost, of the approaching marriage; and the exciting news would certainly have passed through them to the tenantry and local tradespeople. But it did not reach the local press until Friday, July 5th, when the Bodmin *West Briton*, carried a paragraph gleaned from a London newspaper, under the headline 'Sir W. Molesworth': 'The *Sun* of Tuesday says that a matrimonial alliance is said to be on the *tapis* between Sir William Molesworth, Bart. of Pencarrow, late MP for East Cornwall, and the accomplished relict of a wealthy commoner. The ceremony is expected to take place the week after next.' The *Sun* was being careful in reporting that the 'matrimonial alliance' was 'on the *tapis*', just in case it was only a rumour – the Molesworths were still not making any formal announcement. Even the *Satirist*, the *Private Eye* of that time, was cautious: on July

7th, only three days before the wedding, it published the news as a rumour, not as hard fact:

'Sir William Molesworth is, we believe, about to undergo a *radical* change, and to relinquish his *liberal* principles; it being his rumoured intention to lead to the hymenial altar a lady celebrated for her musical talents and *other* accomplishments.'

The denigrating implication of the '*other*' was probably a shot in the dark; but the known fact that Mrs West had at one time been 'on the stage' was sufficient for a scandal-rag to imply that her eleven years of widowhood had not been solitary.

ON SIR WILLIAM'S return from his brief visit to Pencarrow, there were only eight days left before the wedding and still much to arrange. The only social engagement noted in the diary was for July 2nd, when he took a box at the Opera to see Moriani in *Lucie de Lammermoor* – 'Mrs West and Miss Cash went with me.' That is the first and only reference to Miss Cash, and it seems probable that Andalusia had been advised, this time, to invite someone suitable to chaperone her. After her appearance at the Opera alone with Sir William two nights after their engagement, Lady West may very well have hinted to her that it was not *comme il faut*.

On July 7th the marriage settlement was drawn up. It stated that Mrs Temple West, having become owner of Mathon Lodge in the Parish of Mathon, Worcestershire, with freehold lands, it now became the property of Sir William Molesworth. It made a settlement for Andalusia of £1,000 a year. The signatories were: John Temple West of Berkeley Square (Andalusia's brother-in-law, the Admiral); the Revd Hugh Molesworth of St Ervan (a first cousin of Sir William); the Revd Gilbert West of West Monkton in the County of Somerset; Thomas Woollcombe of Devonport. When a year later the Mathon estate was sold, 'the total settlement of the Estate paid to Sir William Molesworth, in August 1845, in right of his wife (late Mrs Temple West) was £10,500.0.0.' In 1844 the pound sterling equalled at least 20.5 times in purchasing value that of 1990. Therefore the addition to Sir William's fortune from the Mathon Estate amounted in today's terms to a not inconsiderable £215,250; and Andalusia's settlement gave her pin-money of £20,500 a year.

Only two days after the signing of the marriage settlement was the day of the wedding, July 9th. Sir William's diary gives only brief details: 'Married at St George's Hanover Square (about ten o'clock) to Andalusia Grant West. Breakfasted with Sir John and Lady West; left town by the two o'clock train and arrived at Exeter about ten o'clock in the evening where we spent the night.'

The witnesses' signatures to the marriage certificate were those of James Bruce Carstairs, Harriett West (Lady West), Mary Molesworth (Lady Molesworth, now the Dowager); Annie Twiss (wife of Sir Travers Twiss of Park Place); and Thomas Woollcombe. Andalusia's mother, Mrs Carstairs, was most surely at the wedding. Most surely Mrs Grote was not – for in retrospect she wrote: 'Mr Grote and I offered to attend the ceremony, but Sir William declined to accept the compliment implied in the proposal, saying that no one out of the circle of the family was to be present.' No wonder the Grote offer was declined (and sharply, one suspects), proposed as it was with the implication that their presence would be a compliment – would confer a social cachet upon a marriage that Society in general considered unsuitable.

After the wedding night at Exeter, Sir William and his bride travelled next morning to Bodmin – either by the mail coach or by hired post-chaise. Molesworth's own carriage from Pencarrow would be waiting at Bodmin coach headquarters, The Royal Hotel, to take them the last five miles to Costislost. Sir William's diary for July 10th simply records: 'Arrived at Costislost, and found every arrangement for our residence there satisfactory'. It then records the previous day's expenses:

Journey to Cornwall, July 9th and 10th	£23. 8.0.
Maclean's board	3.10.0.
Sundries	8.16.0.

On another page it records the marriage costs:

Marriage licence	£ 2.12.0.
Clerk	1. 0.0.
Marriage, clergyman and church fee	6. 0.0.

IN LONDON after the wedding the *Satirist* commented: 'Sir William Molesworth has travelled farther than newly-married folk generally do. He is, we hear, passing his honeymoon in the pleasant valleys and shady recesses of Andalusia.' Fortunately it is most unlikely that the now Dowager Lady Molesworth was a subscriber to the *Satirist*. But no doubt its comment will have been repeated with appreciation around the gentlemen's clubs, and may very possibly have reached the ears of Mr Grote, if not those of his wife.

PART TWO

1844 – 1855

THE YEARS WITH ANDALUSIA

When Sir William Molesworth's marriage became known, there was a disposition among what is termed Society to regard it with aversion, not to say disdain. 'The Town' did not like the marriage; but Molesworth, well aware of the prevalent sentiment, said, 'I will make them like it.'

Mrs Grote, The Philosophical Radicals

Lord Derby, in one of his speeches, likened a statesman to a barque, which trims its sails and alters its course with each changing wind and varying breeze. This is not my notion of a statesman. I liken a true statesman and upright politician to a steam vessel which pursues its steady course against storms and waves in defiance of adverse gales and opposing tides, and straight forward reaches its destined port.

Sir William Molesworth in House of Commons speech
June 1st 1852

CHAPTER X — 1844 cont.

WHEN the Molesworth carriage brought Sir William and his bride from Bodmin to Costislost on the day after the wedding, it may possibly have made a detour at Washaway village to go by the mile-long drive he had made just two years previously through the woods to Pencarrow. He would surely wish Andalusia to have a glimpse of the Georgian mansion-house of which she was to be mistress before taking her to Costislost, which was but a modest farmhouse. Of seventeenth century origin, Costislost was partly remodelled in the eighteenth century, then extended in the early 1800s; but it still had few amenities such as indoor sanitation. As with all Cornish farmhouses, one entered by the kitchen – there was no drive up to a main entrance. When the Molesworth carriage arrived with the bridal couple, it must have drawn up at the stable buildings, from where they would need to walk through the yard to the kitchen door. Nevertheless, Sir William noted happily in his diary that they 'found every arrangement for our residence there satisfactory.'

Next day they went to see how the restoration work was getting on at Pencarrow. Progress had evidently been made since the chaos William had found on his flying visit before the marriage, because four days later 'Hugh lunched with us at Pencarrow'. Hugh was the elder son of the Revd. William Molesworth, rector of St Breocke – the uncle who had been so upset by William's radical politics and lack of religious belief. Hugh had followed his father in taking holy orders; and it was he who, in the event of William having no son or surviving brother, would inherit the baronetcy, Pencarrow, and all the other Molesworth properties in Cornwall and Devon.

The odds were in Hugh's favour. Andalusia's first marriage of eleven years had been childless. This did not mean that she was incapable of child-bearing – there could be other reasons, including the advanced age of Temple West. But she was now in her thirty-sixth year, which meant she had not many child-bearing

years ahead. Historically, male Molesworths died young; therefore
a family of several children was desirable to ensure the survival of
a son into manhood, marriage and the follow-through to the next
generation. William's father, Sir Arscott Molesworth died at the age
of thirty-three, having sired five children. Now William himself was
thirty-four, and the likelihood of his marriage being infructuous
(Mrs Grote's word) added to the family's dismay at his choice of a
wife. William's brother Arscott had died two years before when only
twenty-eight; and Francis might well not survive William. Indeed,
he died two years after his return from New Zealand, also at the
age of twenty-eight.

The Dowager Lady Molesworth, Mary and Francis had remained
in London after the wedding, and Mary was recruited to supervise
adjustments at William's Lowndes Square house to change it from
being the residence of a bachelor. There was also the transfer of
Andalusia's possessions from Half Moon Street to be arranged.
Soon after arriving at Costislost, William wrote to Mary: 'There
is a miniature of Andalusia in one of the boxes sent from Half
Moon Street to Lowndes Square, Black [his butler] may open the
boxes to look for it.' At the beginning of September, William and
Andalusia themselves travelled to London from Costislost to put in
hand major work at Lowndes Square. Thomas Doubiggins and Son
of 23 Mount Street, Grosvenor Square, were commissioned to do the
interior painting, wall-papering, construct new cupboards, supply
fresh carpets and soft-furnishings. Tactfully, William's mother and
Mary took the opportunity, while William and Andalusia were in
London, to go to Pencarrow and pack up their personal possessions,
the accumulation of so many years. From now on they would only be
occasional visitors. For them it was an abrupt uprooting, the sudden
snapping of an era.

By the last days of September, William and Andalusia were back
at Costislost again, and William was writing happy letters to Mary,
telling her of new plans he was making for the garden and grounds
at Pencarrow, including a four-acre walled kitchen garden and new
stable buildings surrounding a great courtyard. The stabling was not
fully completed until 1852. In one of his letters he tells Mary: 'I am
putting up on the sundial a little instrument called a Dipleioscope
for the purpose of ascertaining the exact time of noon-day. It is

an invention of the celebrated clockmaker, Mr Dent [of Pall Mall], who has sent down a person to put it up.' William, although meticulously careful over small expenditures, spared no expense in anything to do with his garden, greenhouses and grounds. The letter continues:

> I find myself in better health than I ever remember having been before, and can walk well. I gave Bran [a dog] to Duppa, who wishes much to have a child of Brenda, whom he gave to me. Thor has in consequence taken up his abode at Costislost, where he has captivated Andalusia. He walks into her dressing room every morning, plays all kinds of antics with her. Steals her pocket-handkerchief and makes her little dog jealous. Andalusia is not very well, and must take care of herself, not take too much exercise, eat nourishing food and drink port-wine, so says Tickle.
>
> Give my best love to my aunt; tell her that the thistles she sent me are thriving . . . Have you seen anything of Mrs Grote? I have not heard from her since I last wrote. Andalusia desires me to send her love to you and hopes to hear from you soon . . . and with our united loves to my mother and Francis.
>
> Your aff. brother, W.M.

This very happy letter surely includes a hint that wonderful news may soon follow . . . Andalusia's indisposition and the doctor's instructions for her diet and exercise suggest the beginning of pregnancy. If indeed Andalusia were pregnant, miscarriage must sadly have followed. William's question at the end of this letter about Mrs Grote shows that he had been in correspondence with her; and Mrs Grote in her *Life of Sir William Molesworth*, wrote that after the marriage 'one or two familiar letters had been exchanged between Molesworth and myself.' Only one of his to her has survived, dated Costislost, October 1844:

Dear Mrs Grote,

I am much obliged to you for your kind letter of enquiry. I had intended to have written to you before, but I put it off from day to day, having very little to write about. I am leading a very tranquil life here, chiefly occupied in going daily to Pencarrow to inspect the works, and to see how things get on, returning here to dinner, and going to bed early, fatigued with being so much in the open air.

My wife and myself get on admirably: I am perfectly satisfied with my choice, and that I have selected a sensible, amiable and agreeable woman with whom I shall live most happily. In short I am more than ever persuaded that I am a wise and prudent man.

Perhaps he felt it would be tactful not to tell her how ecstatically happy he now was. His description of Andalusia as 'a sensible, amiable and agreeable woman' could be a tongue-in-the-cheek response to warnings from Mrs Grote with regard to Andalusia's temperament. Tactfulness was not one of the virtues that Mrs Grote herself laid claim to. Rather she took great pride in being forthright – nay more, downright. William, knowing her so well, was able, as long as her opinions were expressed to him personally, to brush them off good-humouredly. But a little later, something Mrs Grote had said to someone else regarding Andalusia filtered back to him. This proved to be the catalyst that utterly destroyed their so close, confidential and affectionate friendship of the past twelve years. In her *Life* Mrs Grote wrote that it was to her and Mr Grote's unspeakable surprise that 'Mr Grote received from Sir William a communication to the following effect: "As I am informed that your wife has thought fit to indulge in ill-natured remarks about my marriage, I shall feel obliged by your intimating to Mrs Grote my wish to receive no more letters from her."

'To this curt missive', Mrs Grote related, 'there was only one answer to be given. Mr Grote therefore wrote to Sir William in this strain: "I have been painfully surprised on reading this letter which you have addressed to me. You will hear no more from Mrs Grote, with whom all intercourse will of necessity cease; and I must beg, that in this cessation of intercourse you will consider me as included. In justice to Mrs Grote I permit myself to add, from my own observation, that she has pursued a line of conduct in reference to the subject in question wholly opposite to that with which you charge her. I am, etc. George Grote." '

And this, according to Mrs Grote, 'abruptly terminated a connexion extending over a period of nearly twelve years; the value of which had, it is true, been greatly appreciated by the party most benefited, whilst it had been throughout maintained on my side, with a steadfast regard to Sir William's best interests. From this day we never met again.' Her 'disciple' had turned and hissed at his benefactor – what ingratitude.

IX *Andalusia Grant Carstairs, aged 15 years. Portrait by Sir William*
Ross at the time of her entering the Royal Academy of Music.

X *Sir William in the garden at Pencarrow;*
Andalusia in the drawing-room.
Water-colour portraits by A.E. Chalon
in the year of their marriage, 1844.

Naturally Mrs Grote set out to absolve herself from all blame for the rupture. She claimed to have been misquoted and cited Henry Warburton and Joseph Parkes as the misquoters. In August, the month after the Molesworth wedding, they had stayed with others at a small house-party in the Grotes' Buckinghamshire retreat at Burnham Beeches. This is Mrs Grote's version of what happened:

The recent marriage was spoken of, and with undisguised reprobation; but I took up the other side of the question, and defended the step, declaring that, after all, I believed Molesworth knew what sort of wife he wanted better than we did, and that I augured well of the future, etc. The guests manifested by their manner some astonishment at my taking the tone of apology in reference to this subject, and it presently dropped; Mr Grote saying nothing one way or the other.

As the party returned to London, Mr Warburton broke out into expressions of surprise at my strange mode of viewing Molesworth's marriage. 'Surely,' he said, 'Mrs Grote cannot be sincere in what she said yesterday. It is not possible that a woman of her sense and penetration *should* take such a view!' To which apostrophe on the part of Warburton, Mr Parkes replied, 'I agree with you that Mrs Grote can hardly believe what she expressed with her lips; but her long and faithful friendship for Sir William impels her, as I imagine, to defend the marriage against all attacks.' Mr Parkes related this dialogue to me a few weeks after it took place, but I maintained the opinion I had put forward, on principle, though *he* affected to be incredulous on the subject.

Joseph Parkes and Henry Warburton were both members of the original group of Philosophical Radicals, and it might be supposed that Radicals would not consider it deplorable for one of their group, though a baronet, to marry a lady who was believed to be 'of humble origin' – that therefore it was the contrast in character and temperament that they believed boded ill. Certainly that contrast was a factor; but it has to be said that most Radicals, certainly those who were Members of Parliament, while sincere in their desire to improve the conditions of the poor, to provide more educational opportunities and give them more influence, through the ballot, on the way the country was governed, nevertheless did not advocate a mingling of the classes. As for Mrs Grote, she fervently believed that aristocratic blood should not be diluted. In horse-breeding language, she regarded *pur sang* as essential to the stability of the country.

Lord John Russell – not a Radical, but a Liberal – wrote in an essay on marriage: 'It is very well to say that love levels all ranks. Rank has its revenge. Even love, strong as he is, cannot long hold by the anchor of beauty. A thousand ties of similar friendships, or of similar occupations, of similar habits, and even of similar amusements, are necessary to connect the man and woman who are chained to each other for life.'

Andalusia did not have the benefit of similar habits and background to those of William, and they were certainly not of similar temperament. She loved music, people and parties, was merry and out-going, tireless in the pursuit of pleasure, extravagant in her love of beautiful clothes and jewels. Some people said she had a soft caressing manner; others perceived beneath the surface sweetness a determined, driving ambition – ambition for herself to be a leading society hostess and for William to be a leading statesman. Joseph Parkes wrote in a letter to Richard Cobden that Andalusia had 'declared she would raise him into the Cab[inet] and a Peerage'. The nagging fear of his close family was that the pace of social life with Andalusia, combined with the strain of politics if she were to persuade him to stand for Parliament again, would be too great for his delicate health to withstand.

CHAPTER XI — *Andalusia before William*

AT this point in Sir William's story, it is necessary to explore as far as possible the early life of Andalusia Grant Carstairs, about which so little was known by his family and friends at the time of the marriage – or, indeed, ever after.

On the south wall of Egloshayle Church, three miles from Pencarrow, a marble tablet bears this inscription:

In memory of James Bruce Carstairs, Esq., the last surviving member of the family of Sir James Bruce, Bart. of Kinross. N.B. He died at Pencarrow on the 10th September 1845, aged 75. This tablet is erected by his affectionate daughter, Andalusia Grant Molesworth.

That the coffin containing James Bruce Carstairs was received into the Molesworth family vault at Egloshayle is shown by an account at Pencarrow:

'Bruce Carstairs funeral, James Bovey's account,
Funeral   £33.7.4.
Vault opening £10 Marble monument   £16.2.4.
            (and fixing)
Engraving 208 letters at 9 pence a letter   £17.4.0.'

This was the vault into which Sir William, after his sister Elizabeth's funeral, determined that he himself would not be consigned.

THUS Andalusia stated on marble, for all to read, that she was descended from a baronet as well as being married to one; and with the help of Burke's Peerage a *possible* link can be traced through the female line connecting James Bruce Carstairs with the baronetcy that was created on April 21 1668 for Sir William Bruce. One of Sir William Bruce's daughters married Sir John Carstairs of Kilconquhan; and the descendants of their son James Carstairs carried on the line of the Carstairs family towards the end of the eighteenth century. It could be that a son or a grandson of his was Andalusia's father.*

Next question – why was she christened Andalusia Grant? We know that her mother's forename was Andalusia, because one of the signatories on the certificate of her daughter's marriage to Temple West was that of Andalusia Carstairs. Maybe her maiden surname had been Grant. Bearing in mind her daughter's clear soprano singing voice and vivacious manner, could her family have been of Spanish extraction? Had she been named after the Spanish province from which they originated? All is speculation. There is nothing to tell whether Mrs Carstairs went with her husband to Pencarrow in that summer of his death. It could be that she had died previously and Andalusia had dutifully invited her widowed father to make his home at Pencarrow. That he had not been there very long before his death is suggested by the receipt of a bill from Knobel, Hamilton & Co., 2 King Street, St James's to B. Carstairs, Esq.:

> '1845 May 15
> June 28
> August 28 . . . Port and Sherry, £10.6.0.'

However tenuous the Bruce baronetcy connection, there is reason to believe that James Bruce Carstairs, although poor, was a well educated man. When he entered his daughter for the Royal Academy of Music, he secured her recommendation for examination by Sir John Murray, Bart., KGC. Andalusia passed the examination on June 27th 1824, and the registration gives her age as fifteen years – indicating that she was born in 1809; just one year before William Molesworth.

Records at the Royal Academy of Music show that her original application was made from an address in Downing Street,

---

*In 1876, twenty-one years after Sir William died, Andalusia made an abortive attempt to trace her father's direct descent from Sir James Bruce, Bart. She corresponded with David Marshall, Lochleven Place, Kinross, but he was unable to find any direct link. Then, nearly ten years later, in 1885, she tried again, corresponding with R.R. Hobart, 51 Northumberland Street, Edinburgh, without success. This was when she was in ill health, less than three years before she died. Was she perhaps thinking of her obituaries? – wanting finally to prove to the Molesworths and Society that she was not of humble birth?

Westminster (no number given); but when she entered the Academy at the beginning of the Michaelmas Term she gave her address as 41 Hart Street, Bloomsbury. Hart Street is now renamed Bloomsbury Way and runs from New Oxford Street to the south side of Bloomsbury Square. In the year Andalusia entered the Academy the street was being renumbered; but in the London Street Directory there is no record of any property in Hart Street owned by a Carstairs, so it must be concluded that they were living in rented accommodation. Most of the Hart Street houses were owned by professional people – physicians, solicitors, architects. Andalusia's father could have been an assistant or clerk to one of them – perhaps tutor or writing master to a family. The RAM register gives no clue to his profession; there is a blank in the column 'Business of Father' – not even the very usual 'gentleman' or 'No occupation'; and, perplexingly, he signed the register James Carstairs Grant, instead of James Bruce Carstairs. Maybe this was to keep the name of Bruce uncontaminated by any connection with *professional* music. Andalusia, probably instructed by her father, adopted the professional name of Miss Grant at Academy concerts and then at all public and stage performances.

The Royal Academy of Music had been founded, with George IV as patron, just the year before Andalusia entered. It opened on March 24th 1823, and one of the original students to register, on April 23rd, was Charles Dickens' sister Fanny. Her nomination was obtained through the Dickens' family friend Tomkinson, a piano-maker of 77 Dean Street, Soho. Fanny spent four years at the Academy, and she and Andalusia were close friends. Many years later, Fanny's famous brother was a frequent guest at Molesworth dinner-parties. The first of 'Miss Grant's' appearances at Academy concerts was on June 5th 1826 at the Concert Rooms, Hanover Square. That same year she won a prize for singing and honourable mention for Italian. On June 2nd the following year she made her *début* on the public stage at the Theatre Royal, Covent Garden, on the occasion of Madame Pasta's first appearance at an English theatre on her return from the Continent. Other singers included Madame Vestris and the most acclaimed tenor of the time, John Braham. The programme stated that 'the celebrated Master Liszt' was at the piano forte. Next morning *The Times* reported 'A Miss

Grant made we believe a first appearance, and gave the aria *'Parto;*
ma tu ben mia' with a delicious sweetness and fullness of tone that
called down a universal encore.'

The *Morning Post* was even more enthusiastic: 'Miss Grant sang
one of Mozart's pieces with the greatest effect, which was rapturously
encored; her voice is remarkably powerful and sweet, aided by science
and taste; and she may be considered to have made, what is termed,
a complete *hit.'*

This successful *début* led to Andalusia being cast as Diana
Vernon, leading lady in *Rob Roy Macgregor*, a popular opera
based on Walter Scott's novel *Rob Roy*. It opened at the Drury
Lane Theatre on October 6th 1827. Next day, the *Morning Post*'s
music critic was dubious about 'the practice of introducing female
singers on the stage as soon as they have acquired a certain share of
vocal power, without the least attention being paid to the various
other qualifications of dramatic art. . . . We do not believe the
friends of Miss Grant have exercised a sound discretion in bringing
her at once before a metropolitan audience. She is very young, timid
and wholly uninstructed in the business of the stage. Her voice is
one of pure and somewhat brilliant quality, but deficient in power
downwards. . . . She sang the ballad 'A Highland Lad' with much
spirit, and was encored. She is unquestionably a present acquisition
to the Operatic Department of the theatre, and promises hereafter
to become more so.'

The Times critic was much of the same mind: 'Miss Grant
is, as an actress, perfectly inexperienced, and we would almost
say, untutored, but her powers as a vocalist have been evidently
cultivated with care, and with no ordinary degree of success. . . .
Her style of singing is extremely scientific – too much so, perhaps,
for the simple Scottish melodies which are attached to the character
of Diana Vernon, but which would enable her to execute with spirit
and effect music of a more lofty nature. . . . Her two first songs
were loudly encored, and her success was as great as her most
sanguine friends could desire. When time and study shall have
removed (as they speedily do so) her awkwardness of gesture and
indistinctness of utterance, which are solely to be attributed to youth
and inexperience, she will prove an acquisition of no common value
to the operatic corps.'

The *Evening Standard* review gave the only description we have of Andalusia's physical appearance when a young girl; 'She is exceedingly tall and delicately proportioned. Her features though small, are not without expression.' *Rob Roy Macgregor* was repeated and then followed by an operatic version of *Guy Mannering* at Drury Lane, with Miss Grant in the character of Lucy Bertram, Miss Paton as Julia Mannering, John Braham as Henry Bertram. *The Times* reported 'Though this was only Miss Grant's third appearance on the stage, yet we could perceive a visible improvement in her demeanor, as well as in her mode of speaking. She has acquired more confidence of manner, and a more decisive style of elocution . . . Miss Grant's articulation in singing is very perfect. We do not lose a syllable in a stanza – a practice contrary, and certainly preferable, to that of some great public favourites who give us notes in abundance, but do not seem to think it necessary to trouble us with *words*.'

The following month, on November 29th, Miss Grant was cast as Estelle, a Savoyard girl in the opera *Isidore de Merida*. *The Times* reported that 'the duet between her and Mr Braham was heard with much pleasure. The piece was announced for repetition amidst expressions of the most unmixed applause'. The *Morning Post* reported that 'among the audience we noted the following fashionables: Her Royal Highness the Duchess of Kent and the Princess Victoria, Prince Esterhazy, Dukes of Wellington and Devonshire, Earl of Belfast, Lord and Lady Wharncliffe, Lord Granville Somerset, Lord John Russell, Sir F. Burdett, Sir B. East etc. etc.'

It was less than six months since the eighteen-year-old Andalusia had made her *début* at the Theatre Royal, Covent Garden, yet now she was singing duets with John Braham before an élite audience which included the future Queen Victoria. And two months later, on January 28th 1828, she made a stage appearance with the celebrated actor Macready in *Edward the Black Prince*. This drama was billed to 'combine melodrama, opera and farce.' It was *not* a success. In fact it was a flop. *The Times* condemned it as 'a parcel of unintelligent trash . . . an historical play in which there is no trace of history.' The *Standard* reported it to have been 'ill received and must be speedily consigned to the same tomb in which all Mr

Reynold's dramatic efforts have been safely deposited'. This critic did, however, praise two of the cast: 'Miss Grant as Agnes, the attendant of Helena, acted with modesty and propriety. One of her airs was encored. It was the only encore of the evening. Macready's acting was in his most powerful manner.' Wisely, after this, Miss Grant during the next three months appeared, not in drama, but exclusively at Mr Bishop's Concerts at the King's Theatre, Drury Lane. A brilliant career as an international soprano, *not* as an actress, was predicted for her.

A NAME on the list of subscribers to the Royal Academy of Music from the year of its inception is that of Andalusia's future husband: 'Temple West, Esq., subscriber (First Class) of One Hundred Guineas.' His name is also on the list of subscribers to the Royal Academy Concerts in 1826, at which Miss Grant made her first public appearances, and it seems likely that it was at one of these that her slender young form and clear soprano voice first caused his elderly heart to beat faster. Temple West was also a patron of the Assembly Room concerts at Bath, which he attended regularly from his Worcestershire home during their season. So it may well have been he who suggested that John Braham bring Miss Grant with him for an important 'Grand Performance of Sacred Music' in the Bath Assembly Rooms on Christmas Eve, 1830.

Temple West was the eldest son of Lieut-General Temple West of the Grenadier Guards, by the daughter of Pitt Drake, Esq. A younger brother who became Sir John West, CBE, Admiral of the Fleet, was born in 1774; so it can be assumed that Temple was born circa 1770. He was the owner of Mathon Lodge, the West family home, standing in its own grounds, Mathon Park, near the Malvern Hills. The village of Mathon has long since become a suburb of Malvern, and Mathon Lodge just a house in Harcourt Road, West Malvern. Temple West was an enthusiastic amateur singer and, according to the *Bath and Cheltenham Gazette*, 'learned singing under the instruction of the celebrated Mr Bartleman and was known and distinguished for possessing a voice of superior richness and power and for the considerable taste and skill in the management of it.' This newspaper also reports Mr Temple West's daily attendance in the Pump Room 'to listen to the gratifying performance of the very excellent instrumental band belonging to it'; and that 'when residing in London, the Concert of Ancient Music and the long-established Catch-Club of noblemen and gentlemen at the Thatched House Tavern were rarely without his personal presence at their meetings'. The Thatched House Tavern in St James's Street had a famous Great Room with an immense dining-table, and was a prestigious meeting-place for the Dilettante Society, the Literary Club and such-like societies.

Why had not this cultivated, convivial, music-loving and land-owning gentleman, now about sixty years of age, acquired a wife to preside over his *ménage* at Mathon Lodge and provide him with an heir? Perhaps he had loved and courted in vain. Perhaps his looks were against him. Perhaps some feature made him unloveable – an unfortunate nose, or the kind of hair that Lady Stanley, writing of a friend's fiancé, described as being so stiff that one could not put it in a locket, only set it in a toothbrush. Lacking a portrait, we can but conjecture. At his death the obituaries dwelt on his 'highly honourable character', his 'very respectable connections', his being well-known for his 'truly social and convivial qualities' – but nowhere is he described as handsome, of distinguished bearing, or any other of the flatteries that the writers of obituaries are not usually parsimonious in bestowing upon their deceased subjects. One thought occurs before leaving the subject of Mr Temple West's appearance: is it unkind to suggest that a gentleman possessed of 'a voice of superior richness and power' is traditionally inclined to be portly?

To return to that Grand Performance of Sacred Music at the Bath Assembly Rooms on Christmas Eve, 1830, the *Bath and Cheltenham Gazette* declared: 'We never recollect having heard Braham in better voice' . . . His duet with Miss Grant, 'Behold and See', completely electrified the audience. Miss Grant's performance of the whole of the solo pieces allotted to her was sweet and beautiful in the extreme.' In the programme, among the names of the chorus singers, was that of Mr West. Could this have been Temple West? If not, he will certainly have been in the audience, and will certainly have agreed that Miss Grant was 'sweet and beautiful in the extreme'. This occasion would give him the opportunity to become acquainted with her. Maybe he offered to be her guide to places of architectural and historic interest in Bath and the surrounding country.

Andalusia remained in Bath for the first three months of 1831, appearing in concerts of sacred music at the Octagon Chapel, also at Assembly Room and Pump Room concerts. Her last appearance at the Pump Room was on March 23rd in a 'Grand Concert in aid of Funds for the Prolongation of the Pump Room Music.' The impressive list of patrons of this concert, headed by the Countess of Belmore, included Temple West, Esq., and it was upon Andalusia's return to London after this concert that she announced her betrothal. Even if the decision to accept Temple West had been made on an impulse she had time to withdraw, since the wedding did not take place until two months later, on June 2nd 1831, at fashionable St George's, Hanover Square.

WHY did Andalusia marry a man three times her age? It was customary for girls earning a pittance on the stage and living in cheap lodgings to have a 'protector'; indeed it was accepted tradition. Considered fair game by men-about-town and randy young aristocrats, it was safer to have an elderly rich man as a steady protector – safer still to opt out of the profession by accepting an elderly rich man as a husband. But opera and concert singers were in a superior, less vulnerable, category than actresses and dancers; and in any case Andalusia, living with her parents in Bloomsbury, close to Drury Lane, would be under their vigilance, would certainly not be allowed to have a 'protector' to dine and wine her after the opera and see her home – or elsewhere. Nor can Andalusia have felt obliged to make an early marriage for money. Her parents might be impoverished gentlefolk, but her brilliant early successes as a singer meant she could be sure of future engagements, with fees rising with her rising fame. Could she not wait until some handsome young Galahad was at her feet? It is possible, of course, that she had fallen in love with one such, then been jilted – and accepted Temple West on the rebound. But there is another explanation which may be suggested in the light of Andalusia's later life – social ambition. To marry into the county gentry could be the first rung on the ladder – worth taking if the county gentleman be of an age suggesting that his demise would come while she was still young enough to climb to a higher rung.

Once they were married, Temple West withdrew his young bride from the limelight. No gentleman would permit his wife to appear in opera or public concerts. To sing at the occasional musical evening in the drawing-room of a fashionable friend would be different; he would be very proud of her then. How much of the year they spent at Mathon Lodge, whether they ever went to London, is not known. Certainly they often stayed in Bath during the season there, which was from October to April – the names of Mr and Mrs Temple West can be found in the 'Fashionable News and Arrivals' column in the *Bath Chronicle*. Mr West did not own a house there – his name cannot be found in the Street Directory at Bath Library. Like many others, he will have taken apartments for the fashionable concerts and other elegant occasions. In 1839 they were staying at Oxford Row, Walcot, in the City of Bath, when the *Bath Chronicle* reported:

'April 13th, in this city, of apoplexy, Temple West of Mathon Lodge, Worcestershire; a gentleman well known in the fashionable circles of London, Bath and elsewhere; of very respectable connections and highly honourable character; the very unexpected demise of this worthy gentleman has occasioned considerable feelings of regret to many who were in the habit of associating with him, as well as to his family connections.'

'Considerable feelings of regret' may not have been experienced by Andalusia once she recovered from the shock of the apoplectic fit – even if it was not publicly distressful by taking place in the Pump Room. After the solemnity of the funeral and all the legal business, she could rejoice in a feeling of freedom – freedom while still young, also freedom in the monetary sense. In his Will, Temple West had left 'to my dear Wife all my real and personal Estate, Goods, Chattels and Effects as to what nature so ever for all and their absolute use.' This meant that Andalusia could rent Mathon Lodge and with the income from the estate set up her own establishment in Mayfair, hire her own carriage for the season, have her clothes made by fashionable dressmakers. For the first year as widow, of course, she would have to observe the strict mourning that etiquette decreed. It is therefore unlikely that she took up residence in Half Moon Street before the summer season of 1840. It seems she did consider starting her singing career again. The *Boase Dictionary of Biography* (not an impeccably reliable source) states that Miss Grant's last appearance was as Hymen in *As You Like It* at Drury Lane in 1841. If *Boase* is correct, it is likely that Admiral Sir John West, who lived in Belgrave Square, advised his sister-in-law that if she wished to circulate in the best society she should not renew her professional career.It would ruin her chance of a good second marriage.

After five years of widowhood, Andalusia certainly achieved a good second marriage. Much as it displeased Sir William Molesworth's relatives and friends, it must have greatly pleased – and relieved – the Admiral and his Lady.

CHAPTER XII — 1845-6

ON November 14th 1844, Sir William's diary records the move to Pencarrow from Costislost, 'having lived there most agreeably for a period of more than four months'. Another entry, shortly after the move, has a sweet flavour of domestic felicity:

'Weighed Lady Molesworth, 148 lbs.

Self, 155 lbs.'

William, tall and slight – not an ounce of fat on him – was only half a stone heavier than Andalusia, who was also tall, but not so slight as when she made her *début* at the Drury Lane Theatre.

At the beginning of December they were invited to a house-party at Whitiford, where they spent two nights . . . 'An agreeable party most of whom my wife invited to Pencarrow utterly regardless of the means of accommodating them.' Andalusia was commencing rather over-enthusiastically upon her role as hostess. That this was the role she had mapped out for herself was the general belief of Molesworth's friends; but perhaps only Mrs Grote knew that William himself was just as determined that his wife should shine in élite circles. In her *Life* of him she later wrote: 'When Sir William Molesworth's marriage became known, there arose a disposition among what is termed Society to regard it with aversion, not to say disdain. "The Town" did not like the marriage; but Molesworth, well aware of the prevalent sentiment, said "I will make them like it." ' There had also been, it will be remembered, his outburst to Mrs Grote after the humiliating rejection of his second suit: 'I tell you what, my dear friend, I will marry my cook, and society shall be forced to swallow her – and I shall be even on them all.' Now at least he was not marrying his cook.

It must not be presumed therefore, as many did, that his subsequent relinquishment of a peaceful, studious life at Pencarrow, the happy hours tending his gardens and hot-houses, was entirely to please Andalusia. For one thing, with Andalusia, quiet hours would not now be part of the Pencarrow programme; and in any case, after

three years out of Parliament, his health regained, he will have felt
the pull of politics once more. The causes for which he had fought so
idealistically during his twelve years in Parliament were still not won
. . . colonial self-government, the ending of transportation, national
education, religious equality, free trade. So it was that in the very
early spring of 1845 they moved to London. They wanted to be in
good time to make sure that the refurbishment at 1 Lowndes Square
was completed, and everything ready for entertaining by the start of
the season.

When the round of parties began, the very atmosphere of the
fashionable drawing-rooms to which they were invited must have
put the scent of politics in Sir William's nostrils as seductively as
the scent of gardenias and ladies' perfume. For at that time *haut ton*
entertaining and politics were inextricably mixed; indeed, success in
the first was necessary for success in the other. Slingsby Duncombe,
the Member of Parliament for Finsbury, was a great diner-out; and
a passage in his *Life and Correspondence* underlines the importance
of dinners:

> There are few persons holding any position in society who do not
> appreciate the dinner party as a promoter of power, charity, business
> and pleasure. The statesman by it seduces his opponents and strengthens
> his supporters; there is not an establishment of a beneficial nature in the
> country that does not rely on its attraction as a sure means of support;
> men in every department of commerce trust to it for maintaining a good
> business connexion; and the individual in the upper ranks who desires to
> live well, either as patron or client, must realise it by the number and
> excellence of his prandial invitations.

Andalusia fully appreciated the importance of prandial invitations.
No record remains of the dinner guests at Lowndes Square during
this her first season as Lady Molesworth, and Sir William's diary for
1845 is missing. However, there is an indication that entertaining
began soon after their arrival from Cornwall: a bill dated March 1845
from the wine merchants Knobel and Tuckwell totals £164.17.11.
one item being twelve dozen champagne. Another wine merchant,
Knobel Hamilton and Co. of 2 King Street, St James's, let a bill for
£378.1.2. run up from March 1845 to August 1846. The time-span
of this account is uncharacteristic, as Molesworth was a stickler for

Sir William Molesworth Bt. (London) Clines 1845

BOUGHT of LAMBERT & RAWLINGS.
Goldsmiths, Jewellers & Silversmiths
TO THEIR MAJESTIES
and Her Royal Highness
THE DUCHESS OF KENT.
10, 11 & 12, Coventry Street.
1176

	£	S.	D.

1845				
Apl 9. Repairing & polishing ivory box			7	6
Repairing Card Case			4	6
22 Silver mounted dogs collar with Padlock & bells		2	2	—
x Repairing and cleaning coral Bracelet			4	—
x Morocco Case for do.			12	—
26 Repairing Mosaic Box			4	—
18 Shell table forks		22	15	—
18 — spoons		21	15	—
12 — desert do.		8	15	—
12 — forks		9	10	—
12 — Teaspoons		5	10	—
2 — sauce ladles		2	10	—
2 Chased Salt Cellars		6	10	—
Engraving crest & motto		3	5	—
Chased Silver Tea Kettle		23	—	—
May 6 2 Shell Salt ladles		1	—	—
Engraving crest & motto			2	—
30 Repairing Scent bottle			1	6
July 29. Gold Necklace		8	10	—
	£	116	17	6
Old S'd		2	5	—
	£	114	12	6

Lambert & Rawling's account for table-silver and other household valuables.
Includes a gold necklace and a silver dog-collar.

prompt settling; but since this account is not marked 'account rendered', it seems that Knobel Hamilton had simply not sent it in. An account from Thomas Doubuggins and Co. for 'further work at No. 1 Lowndes Square' for £1,075.16.0. was paid forthwith.

Soon after they had settled into Lowndes Square, Molesworth let it be known he would be interested in standing for Parliament if a by-election should occur. At this time the possible repeal of the Corn Laws was the dominating concern of all parties. The disastrous potato disease in Ireland which was bringing starvation to an always under-nourished peasantry, coupled with the failure of the cereal crops in some parts of England, were causing clamorous demands for duty-free food from abroad. Sir Robert Peel, now in his third year of office, was suspected of swinging towards repeal against the inbred inclination of his Tory government. Hitherto even the Whigs had been against repeal. Most of them being landowners, they felt it would be a bad thing – cheap corn from abroad would mean losing their economic predominance, and the country would be run in the interest of the new urban and manufacturing communities, predominantly middle and lower class. To most of the aristocracy, repeal of the Corn Laws was an issue almost as revolutionary as the Reform Bill had been.

This was the sensitive political atmosphere when a vacancy occurred in the constituency of Southwark, South London, caused by the death of Benjamin Wood. Molesworth offered himself as the Radical candidate and was adopted. In his address to the constituency, dated August 14th 1845, he declared himself to be in favour of repeal, saying that during the nine years he had previously been in Parliament, he had consistently advocated the principles of free trade, and had in fact been one of the first in the House of Commons to speak out for total repeal of the Corn Laws. If elected, he would actively promote measures calculated to extend commerce by removing the fetters of Protection. Then he set forth his other political faiths: extension of the ballot, triennial parliaments, abolition of the property qualifications for Members of Parliament, reform of the House of Lords, universal education, religious emancipation, colonial self-government and justice for Ireland.

A gayer note to Molesworth's election campaign was supplied by

Andalusia, who established herself in his Committee Rooms at the Bridge Hotel, Southwark and was a lively attraction beside him on the hustings in her so beautiful clothes. He also, as always, being exquisitely dressed, they were hardly what people had imagined radicals looked like.* There were two other candidates: Jeremy Pilcher, Conservative; and Edward Miall, Liberal. Unexpectedly, it was Molesworth's editing of the writings of Hobbes that Miall used for his most blistering attacks, on the grounds that the philosopher had possessed evil, infidel tendencies. Few of the voters of Southwark knew who Hobbes was, nor anything about his work; but among the few were some Nonconformist ministers who concentrated their energies against the union of Church and State – Miall himself was the editor of a weekly newspaper *The Nonconformist*. They knew that Hobbes had believed in the supremacy of the State over the Church, and had written that the preservation of social order depended upon the assumption of the civil power to wield all sanctions, supernatural as well as natural, against the pretensions of any clergy, whether Catholic, Anglican or Presbyterian. It was easy for Mr Miall to mislead the electors of Southwark into linking Hobbes with 'infidel', a word which they did understand; and wherever Molesworth went in the constituency he was met by cries of 'No 'Obbes'.

Molesworth's reaction was to send the volumes he had completed of Hobbes's writings in English to each committee room in the constituency, challenging those who called Hobbes an infidel to find one word in the least degree hostile to Christianity. Then on the day before the election, he made on the hustings a long speech which was virtually a concentrated discourse, not only upon Hobbes of Malmesbury, but also on Gibbon, Copernicus, Galileo, Bacon, Descartes, Locke, Newton, Franklin, Priestley, down to the philosophers, scientists and geologists of the day. Very, very few of the good people of Southwark can have understood what he was talking about, and surely many, many of them must have drifted

*The *Edinburgh Weekly Herald*, Oct. 27th 1855, in an obituary of Sir William Molesworth wrote: 'He was indeed somewhat of an exquisite in his dress, but he did not care whether his dress harmonised, or was incongruous with the merely external associations of his political creed. He could advocate the extension of the franchise, or vote by ballot without throwing off his gloves, or without donning a fustian jacket.'

away before he at last reached the climax with a ringing challenge to Mr Miall:

In all ages, and amongst all nations, infidelity has ever been the war-cry which the base, the ignorant, the intolerant and the canting tribes have raised against the great, the noble and the generous spirits of the human race. That cry you, Mr Miall, have attempted to raise against the works which I have edited. I now again solemnly call on you, before the electors of Southwark whom you wish to represent in Parliament, to make good your assertion. If you shrink from the attempt, or fail as fail you will, then I accuse you before your fellow-citizens of having brought this charge against me for base electioneering purposes. I brand you as a calumniator, and appeal to the poll of tomorrow.

The poll of tomorrow, September 13th, responded to his fervent though incomprehensible oratory. Or was it that the voters of Southwark responded, as did those of Leeds, to the pull, unacknowledged but instinctive, of an aristocrat over a man of the middle class? The result was: Sir William Molesworth 1,943; Jeremiah Pilcher, Esq. 1,182; Edward Miall, Esq. 352.

Molesworth's re-entry into Parliament was honoured by his being the subject of *Punch's Portrait Gallery* in the issue of October 4th 1845, when one of the topics of the day was whether Oliver Cromwell should have a statue in London. An excellent cartoon likeness of Sir William, emphasising his meticulous dandyism, monocle at his right eye, was captioned: 'The question whether "Should Cromwell have a statue?" suggested to us, "Shall Molesworth have a Portrait?" We immediately answered the question in the affirmative; and here he is!'

At the dinner given to celebrate Molesworth's return for Southwark, he began his speech by expressing his appreciation that Sir Robert Peel was considering renouncing the doctrine of Protection. Another controversial issue high-lighted by the Irish potato famine was that of emigration to the colonies – great numbers of Irish peasants were emigrating as the only way to avoid starvation. This enabled Molesworth to bring into his speech the cause upon which he had concentrated so much of his energies during his previous years in Parliament – colonial self-government. The colonies should not be valued just as a means of extending the British Empire

Cartoon by John Doyle in Punch, *October 4th, 1845, after Sir William's victory in the Southwark election.*

ever increasing part they play in developing commerce and increasing wealth:

We have planted colonies in every portion of the globe; men of our race are rapidly spreading themselves over the vast northern continent of America, are menacing the Spanish colonies of Central America, and already grasp in their imagination the provinces of the south. During the last half-century the previously unknown lands of the southern hemisphere have been invaded by Englishmen; flourishing communities are springing up in Australia; emigrants are settled on the shores of New Zealand, and at no remote period an Anglo-Saxon people will rule as sovereigns throughout the islands of the Southern Sea.

Well, that does have a ring of simple unashamed Empire building,

of 'wider still and wider shall thy bounds be set'; but Molesworth
went on to insist that free representative institutions should be
granted to each new colony as soon as it ceased to need the care
and protection of the mother country . . . 'England is indebted
for the position she now holds amongst the nations of the earth
to her free institutions – to her ships, colonies and commerce. And
by these means, and with unfettered trade, she will long be able
to maintain that position.' The system Molesworth advocated was
that the Imperial authority should precisely define the legislation
to be under direct imperial control, then everything else should
be regulated by the colonies' own elected government. This, he
believed, would result in a contented and loyal colonial empire,
'bound to Great Britain by the strong ties of race, language, interest
and affection'. These ties would hold fast by their original roots
if planted by the quality and commitment of the right kind of
emigrants from the mother country.

In 1842, during the Colonial Secretaryship of Lord Stanley, a
start had been made in granting representative institutions in the
Australian colonies; an Act had been passed which created for New
South Wales a single legislative chamber, two-thirds elected and
one-third nominated by the Crown. For Molesworth this was not
going far enough. He was opposed to *any* nominated element in
a so-called representative chamber. What would it be like, he had
asked, were the British Government able to nominate 220 members
of the House of Commons? Furthermore, he believed that colonial
freedom from English officialdom should extend to religious liberty
. . . the Empire had millions of subjects belonging to almost every
great religion in the world – Protestant, Roman Catholic, Jewish,
Mohammedan, Hindu, Parsee, Buddhist. Religious liberty should
be upheld in every British colony.

COLONIAL matters, however, were not to the fore in the
autumn session of 1845 when Molesworth took his seat as Member
for Southwark. Parliament was over-ridingly concerned with the
question of the Corn Laws. After a disastrously wet summer, the
cry throughout the country was for repeal, the demand for cheap
food from abroad was becoming ever more compelling. By December
Sir Robert Peel could waver no longer. At a Cabinet Council on

December 2nd he declared himself in favour of ultimate repeal. He was unable to carry Lord Stanley and Lord Buccleuch with him, so he tendered his resignation to the Queen on December 20th. Lord John Russell, Leader of the Opposition, was unable to form an alternative Administration – and after a Parliamentary eclipse of a little more than two weeks, Peel was restored to the Premiership on December 20th, supported by all his former colleagues except Lord Stanley.

In the meantime the political temperature had been heightened by a leader in *The Times* on December 4th – just two days after the Cabinet meeting at which Peel had declared himself in favour of *ultimate* repeal – which stated:

'Parliament is to be summoned for the first week in January, and the Royal speech will recommend an immediate consideration of the Corn Laws, preparatory to their total repeal. By the end of January at the latest the produce of all countries will enter the British market on the absolute equality with our own.'

This misleading 'leak' from the Cabinet meeting, indicating that there had been an unanimous Cabinet decision in favour of total repeal, caused intense speculation as to how *The Times* had obtained its exclusive information. One report going the gossip rounds and for some time widely believed was that Sydney Herbert, War Secretary in the Cabinet, had talked of it to the Hon. Mrs Norton, with whom he had a close friendship at the time – and that Mrs Norton, separated from her husband and known to be short of money, had sold the information to Delane, editor of *The Times*, with whom she was socially acquainted. This was the second scandal in which the beautiful Caroline Norton had been involved. In 1836 there had been the notorious adultery case brought by her husband, citing Lord Melbourne (then Prime Minister) as co-respondent. She had been proved innocent in that case; and now the suspicion of her involvement in this Cabinet leak was found to be groundless – but the slur tended to stick, as slurs do. It was revived with cruelly sharp identification by George Meredith many years later in his novel *Diana of the Crossways* – for Diana read Caroline. Central to the novel's plot was a Cabinet leak proved to be sold to *The Times* by Diana. Ostracised by society, she is supported throughout by an older friend, Lady Dunstane, a character Meredith based recognisably on Lady Duff

Gordon, who was Caroline Norton's staunch friend throughout the scandals.

Lady Duff Gordon was also a friend of the Molesworths, being Charles Austin's niece, Lucie, daughter of his older brother John, friend of James Stuart Mill and Jeremy Bentham. Lucie had been brought up in scholarly, radical circles; and she and Sir William had a mutual interest in German literature, Lucie's mother being a gifted translator of German writers. Strikingly beautiful, Lucie had married Sir Alexander Duff Gordon, 3rd Bart. in 1840 when she was nineteen. They were among the earliest dinner guests at Lowndes Square when the Molesworths returned from Cornwall after the Christmas recess, at the height of the Cabinet leak scandal.

Eventually, Sir Robert Peel introduced his Corn Law and Customs Bill on January 22nd 1846. It proposed the total repeal of the corn duties, although the ports were not to be completely opened until 1849. In spite of the resistance of many of his former followers, he succeeded in getting the Bill passed through the Lords by June 25th. Molesworth had spoken at length, strongly in favour of the Bill, when it was debated on March 19th. His position in Parliament was ambivalent as to party. When he was returned for Southwark there were too few Radical members in the House to form a party, so he had sat with the Whigs – although his opinion of Lord John Russell was one of scornful impatience. He greatly admired Sir Robert Peel as a person and a politician – but to join the Tory party was unthinkable.

Ironically, on the same night that Peel's Corn Law Bill received the assent of the Lords, Peel was defeated in the Commons at the second reading of his Irish Coercion Bill – a combination of Whigs and Protectionists succeeded in its rejection by a majority of seventy-three votes. Four days later, Peel announced his resignation of office in what Molesworth noted in his diary as 'a remarkable speech, wherein he stated his views as to the manner in which the country should be governed, and advised a course of liberal policy which his successor will find it somewhat difficult to carry out. My opinion is that he will return to power within a year or two.' This was not to be. Peel remained in opposition for the next four years attached to no party; but as guardian of the policy of free trade he was the mainstay of the Whig Government. On June 29th 1850, he was thrown from his horse on Constitution Hill, and died from his injuries on July 2nd.

CHAPTER XIII — 1846

FOR that first Parliamentary session of 1846 in which Sir Robert Peel introduced his Corn Law and Customs Bill, the Molesworths had travelled from Pencarrow early in the New Year. They needed time before the House sat on January 22nd to settle into Lowndes Square and arrange their personal affairs – the expenses of which were noted in Sir William's diary. For instance, an Opera Box was booked in advance for fifteen nights from April to July at a cost of £157.10.0., and a pair of horses hired at £23.2.0. per month. William bought a diamond bracelet, price £65, as a birthday present for Andalusia. She was evidently doing much extravagant shopping for herself, exceeding her £1,000 a year settlement, for on February 2nd the diary notes: loan to Andalusia, £75; Madame Devy [the fashionable *haute couturière*] £172.13.0. – followed by a further £45.16.9. and an order for a purple velvet gown of unknown cost.

For himself, William ordered a great-coat to be made, of course, by Stultz of Clifford Street. The name of Stultz crops up in many memoirs and fashionable novels of the Regency and later. The dandy hero of Bulwer Lytton's *Pelham* set a new style by insisting that Stultz make his suits without padding. All the best tailors, like all exclusive dressmakers and famous chefs, were at this time foreigners. Besides Stultz, there were Staub, Delcroix and Nugée. They were refugees from the countries Napoleon had over-run, and some of them made immense fortunes in England – despite the long credit they gave their aristocratic clients. Paradoxically, England's reputation for supremacy in bespoke tailoring, still held today, originally stemmed from the skill of these refugee foreigners.

Amongst the Molesworth bills this January was £3.17.6. from Truefitt and Hill of Old Bond Street, gentlemen's hairdressers by Royal Appointment. Andalusia may have insisted upon William having his rather straggly locks re-styled *à la mode*; or the bill could have been for Andalusia herself, since Truefitt and Hill had recently opened a ladies' salon, the first in Mayfair, with assistants dressed

Sir William Molesworth.

NO CONNECTION WITH ANY OTHER HOUSE.

ORIGINALLY ESTABLISHED 1819.

H.P. TRUEFITT,

Hair Dresser to the Royal Family

"20 & 21" BURLINGTON ARCADE.

POST OFFICE ORDERS TO BE MADE PAYABLE TO HENRY TRUEFITT.

July 20th 1848

1846·/47/48

Bill Del.   £ 4 . 4 . 0

Attendance   . 2 . 6

Floral Extract   . 12 . 0
                 ────────────
                £ 4 . 18 . 6

Account from H.P. Truefitt of Burlington Arcade, Hairdressers to the Royal Family.

119

like ladies' maids in black with white caps. They operated at marble shampooing basins with plugged outlets and a slop-pail beneath. They also attended clients in their own homes, so the account could have been for coiffuring Andalusia at Lowndes Square. Teeth also had to be attended to – by Mr Clarke, the Molesworths' dentist. Andalusia had a tooth drawn 'and bore the operation with great fortitude' – no anaesthetic nor injection, of course. Considerable fees for the attendance of Holmes, Andalusia's doctor, were also recorded in the diary.

Once entertaining began at Lowndes Square, there was not only the outlay on food, wine, fruit and flowers, but also on the hire of a French cook. One small economy was to give dinners on two successive nights, since the French cook then charged one fee for the two (around 5 gns.) – and most of the flowers and fruit, perhaps some of the sweet courses, would last over. Important social engagements began with the levée on February 24th, and on March 22nd they dined with the Lord Mayor in the Egyptian Hall at the Mansion House with Her Majesty's Ministers . . . 'Andalusia looked very handsome and made great friends with the Attorney General for Ireland who sat next to her.' Perhaps to show his pleasure in her success, William 'bought a diamond and emerald bracelet for Andalusia, price £262.10.0. from Howell and James.' Or perhaps she had been a little disappointed by the £65 diamond bracelet he had given to her on her birthday? Andalusia's appetite for jewellery, and most particularly for bracelets, was expensive. That month, another Howell and James account for £362.4.0 was settled. It was not itemised, so could have been for house furnishings as well as Andalusia's adornment.

Howell and James of 9 Regent Street (now called Lower Regent Street) was the most highly esteemed shop of the day. There the great and the wealthy bought furnishings, jewellery, ceramics, silver, plate and glass. There was an *haute couture* salon and a wine department. Coachmen and footmen waiting for their ladies were given free beer and cheese in the basement. It was Howell and James who precipitated the collapse in 1849 of the gorgeous Lady Blessington's splendid *ménage* at Gore House, Kensington, by foreclosing on their account for furnishing it thirteen years earlier. Long credit indeed; but suppliers always gave titled clients a lot of rope before the noose was tightened. Dukes could postpone paying forever, because they could not legally be sued. Molesworth was an exceptional aristocrat in always settling his bills promptly. This may have been partly his radical conscience not wishing to exploit his position at the expense of tradesmen; but it was also a discipline imposed early in life by his Scottish mother. At Pencarrow there are bundles and bundles of receipts from the 1830s onward, not only from fashionable London shops, tailors, caterers, wine merchants etc., but also small tradesmen's bills as trifling as those of chimney sweeps, carriers, newsagents, farriers, coal merchants – not an 'account rendered' amongst them.

For the first months of this spring, Andalusia confined her entertaining to little dinners for about ten people. A typical guest list was that of June 7th: Lord and Lady Vivian, the Earl of Lovelace, Miss Quentin Dick, Monkton Milnes, Sir John and Lady Easthope (Sir John was the proprietor of the *Morning Chronicle* and MP for Leicester), Sir Edward Bulwer Lytton (long-established as a novelist, not at this time in Parliament) and Lady Morgan, who was a very near neighbour of the Molesworths. She and her husband (who had died in 1843) left Ireland in 1838 to settle permanently in London; and the account in her *Memoirs* of the house they bought, 11 William Street – the very short street leading from Lowndes Square to Knightsbridge – shows how recent was this part of Thomas Cubitt's Belgravia development: 'I am just returned from looking at such a charming maisonette in William Street, which will meet our taste, and not exceed our means; no houses opposite, and all looks rather wild and rude (a thing that would be a field if it could), and a low wall round it; but then there is to be a pretty square . . .'

This pretty square-to-be was in due course named Lowndes Square; and the Molesworth's house was at the north-east corner of the Square – a five-storey terrace house, considerably larger than the Morgans' 'charming maisonette'. Lady Morgan was insatiably sociable, a reveller in gossip; she adored the aristocracy in spite of declaring herself to be a radical. She will doubtless have been an early caller on her new neighbour, Sir William Molesworth's bride, about whom there was so much talk. There are frequent references in Sir William's diary to 'Evening at Lady Morgan's' – she held a regular salon, and was successful in attracting well-known authors, journalists and a sprinkling of politicians, who never failed to be rewarded with some amusing contretemps or outrageous statement to pass on at their next dinner party. This successful hostess was of considerably more humble origin than Andalusia. Born in Dublin in the 1770s (she never divulged her exact age), she was Sydney, daughter of Robert Owenson, who was a third-rate actor and theatre manager frequently in prison for debt. She became a governess, started writing books, and became famous in 1806 with her third novel *The Wild Irish Girl*. Her marriage to Dr Charles Morgan took place at the Irish castle of Lord and Lady Abercorn, who had befriended Sydney Owenson in her governess days. Morgan was their family physician, and was knighted on the wedding day. According to Lady Morgan's biographer, Hepworth Dixon, 'It was an act of courtesy to Lord Abercorn on the part of the Vice-Regent to confer knighthood on his family physician, who had done nothing to deserve it on public grounds. Morgan himself cared nothing about it.'

But Miss Owenson, since she had been taken up by the Abercorns, had very grand ideas about the rank into which she should marry.

IN 1816 the Morgans visited Paris, and the book entitled *France* which Lady Morgan wrote about the state of France under the new regime ran through four editions in England, two in France, four in America. Sales were stimulated by an attack in the Tory *Quarterly Review* upon Lady Morgan's liberal opinions by John Wilson Croker, Secretary to the Admiralty. A frequent criticism of *France* – and of some of her novels – was the inconsistency of Lady Morgan's fervour for republicanism and her undisguised worship of the aristocracy. Well, in Sir William Molesworth, Bart., she could delight in an aristocrat who was also an outspoken radical. Andalusia, for her part, could appreciate that this literary celebrity with her successful salon was no rival in either birth or beauty. Contemporary descriptions agree that Lady Morgan was hardly more than four feet high, with a spine not quite straight and eyes which her biographer maintained 'though not perfectly straight were remarkably large, beautifully blue, lustrous and electrical!' Did she ever come face to face with Mrs Grote's 'carriage-lamp eyes'? As the season advanced, Lady Morgan was a less frequent guest at 1 Lowndes Square. Perhaps her 'curiosity value' diminished as Andalusia's acquaintances widened –

became too wide sometimes for Sir William's liking. For example, on April 6th they had a dinner party, followed by an evening's music . . . 'crowded party, Andalusia having invited many more people than she was aware of. Fischer sang delightfully. No tea.' Had Sir William banned tea being served after all the music for fear the guests would linger on interminably?

Invitations were now pouring in for all kinds of occasions, and Andalusia was rejoicing in the rhythm of the fashionable year. On May 1st they went to the Private View of the Royal Academy to see their portraits by Alfred Edward Chalon. Painted soon after their marriage, these two charming water-colour portraits now hang at Pencarrow. William, seated in the garden, looks youthfully romantic in pale blue breeches, silver-frogged jacket, lace cuffs, high cravat; his favourite dog Garth is beside him. Andalusia, in the drawing-room with her little boudoir dog, looks more staid than one imagines her – Chalon has portrayed her as a comely married lady of position and place: charcoal grey gown with lace collar, cuffs and apron, two gold and turquoise bracelets, handsome diamond ring. A reproduction of this portrait appeared as the frontispiece to the 1857 edition of *The Keepsake*, one of the fashionable anthologies known as the Annuals. It was accompanied by a flattering poem by Henry F. Chorley.

A month after the Royal Academy Private View they went to the Polish Ball. This was a sentimental occasion for them, it having been at the Polish Ball two years before that they had become engaged. But sadly William's diary records that the ball was 'not worth attending. A piece of glass fell on my wife's shoulder and cut it.' He was beginning to find the pace of social life exhausting. A dinner party two days after the Polish Ball at Lady Pocock's was noted as being 'stupid'. Andalusia went on after that dinner to Lady Aylmer's but William went to the House of Commons. It was usual for there to be several engagements in one evening, and he was not always able to excuse himself. For instance, there was the evening they 'dined with Colonel and Mrs Chaloner, then went to a musical party at Mrs Gibson's, then to a ball at Mrs Matheson's, then myself to the House.' Mrs Milner Gibson, wife of a Liberal MP, lived on the corner of Wilton Crescent, very near the Molesworths in Lowndes Square. She held a regular salon frequented by well-known people in literature, the arts, radical politics and the legal profession – always with a sprinkling of interesting foreigners, and always with a substantial supper. Grander and more challenging were Lady Ashburton's soirées at Bath House, Piccadilly. Daughter of the 6th Earl of Sandwich, Lady Ashburton's standing as a hostess was supreme. Charles Greville described her as 'the most conspicuous woman in the society of the present day'. Not beautiful, but of commanding presence, her quick intelligence and dagger-sharp wit were backed by a wide knowledge on many subjects – it was said one heard the best talk in London at Bath House, free from conventions, stimulating, no holds barred – Lady Ashburton imposed her own social laws. Among the frequenters of Bath House was Charles Buller, whose devotion to Lady Ashburton was thought by some to be the reason why he never married. Thomas Carlyle was another who was almost daily drawn to her shrine. Only one soirée at Bath House is noted in William's 1846 diary, and that without comment. Neither he nor Andalusia would shine, hardly hold their own, in the quick cut and witty thrust of Lady Ashburton's gatherings.

Wisely, Andalusia concentrated on her wide knowledge of music to give distinction to her evenings. The Lowndes Square dinner parties were usually followed by music, sometimes a professional singer or pianist being engaged. More ambitiously, on June 18th, her guests were invited to a drawing-room concert. The diary notes: 'Concert at home. Great crowd. Villiers, Cobden, Buller. Singers, Miss Hawes, Mlle Corbusier, Pickets and F. Lablanche. Everything went off well.' There were evidently lavish refreshments following the concert, because Gunter's bill at the end of the month was £63.18.0. Gunter was caterer for all the most fashionable balls and parties – also for *fêtes champêtres* and race-meetings out of town. His premises and tea-room were at No. 7, on the east side of Berkeley Square. It was the only place of refreshment in London where it was perfectly correct for a lady to be seen alone with a gentleman in the afternoon. Gunter's ices were famous, made by a secret recipe. In hot summer weather, it was the custom for ladies to recline in their elegant landaus under the trees on the *opposite* side of Berkeley Square, while waiters scurried to and fro with trays of ices.

When Parliament went into recess at the end of July, the

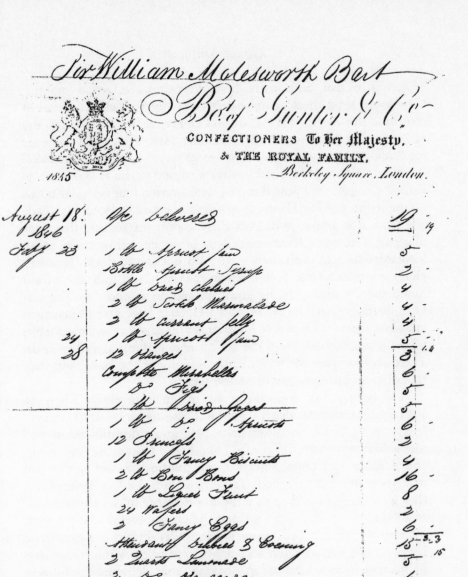

Sir William Molesworth Bart

Bot of Gunter & Co.

CONFECTIONERS To Her Majesty,
& THE ROYAL FAMILY,
Berkeley Square, London.

1845

August 18 1846	Ho delivered	19	19
Feby 23	1 lb Apricot Jam	5	
	Bottle Apricot Syrup	2	
	1 lb dried Cherries	4	
	2 lb Scotch Marmalade	4	
	2 lb Currant Jelly	4	
24	1 lb Apricot Jam	5	1.4
28	12 Oranges	3	
	Compote Mirabelles	6	
	Do Figs	5	
	1 lb Dried Pears	5	
	1 lb Do Apricots	6	
	12 Pruneaux	2	
	1 lb Fancy Biscuits	4	
	2 lb Bon Bons	16	
	1 lb Liqueur Fruit	8	
	24 Wafers	2	
	2 Fancy Eggs	6	
	Attendance delivered & Evening	15	3.3 15
	3 Quarts Lemonade	5	
	3 Do Orangeade	6	
	3 Do Cherry Water	6	
	3 lb Pound Cakes	8	
	Plum Cake	2	
	Seed Do	3	

Part of a very long account from Gunter, the famous caterer and confectioner of Berkeley Square. The Molesworths also hired French cooks for their dinner parties through Gunter.

125

Molesworths had been away from Pencarrow for seven months, not having been there at the Easter recess. Nevertheless, instead of returning this August they set out for Le Havre, from where they did not return to Pencarrow until September 25th. They left Folkestone for Boulogne on August 3rd, 'both of us very sick; went to the Hotel du Nord. Not a good hotel.' After a second night at Boulogne to gather strength, they posted to Le Havre, staying four nights at hotels on the journey. At Le Havre, they stayed at Frascati's Hotel for a little less than five weeks. William's diary comments suggest that time dragged – he must have yearned to be at Pencarrow, busy about his garden and grounds, happy with his horses and dogs: 'Frascati's Hotel is situated close to the sea so that we could walk out of our rooms merely with a drying gown on and go at once into the sea. Our apartments are small. Frascati's Hotel a large and ill-managed establishment; on the whole however we managed to make ourselves tolerably comfortable, and the sea air and bathing agreed with us. There are no agreeable walks in the vicinity of the hotel, our only walks being into the town or on the pier.'

Very boring. At least there was a small diversion when an acquaintance named Benzi, who was staying at a nearby town, 'got a paroquet for Andalusia price 50s., and a beautiful white and rose coloured cockatoo price 25s.' She had a passion for cage birds, and William had bought her a 5 gn. bullfinch earlier in the year to replace one that had died. These new birds, perfect darlings that they were, soon proved to be a bit of a nuisance in the Molesworths' small apartments at Frascati's Hotel. After two weeks, a rather costly solution was determined upon; Maclean was sent in the steamer to London with the cockatoo and parrot, returning within three days by steamer from Southampton, 'having safely delivered the birds to Dr Blake's for safe keeping'.

The Molesworths left Le Havre on September 14th for Dieppe, where they stayed the night and 'Ordered three bonnets from Mme Poignèe, No. 12 rue d l'Ecu'. Next day they went on to Boulogne for another two nights before taking the steamer to Folkestone, thence to London for three nights, Exeter one night and Pencarrow on September 25th.

There is no record of the travelling expenses, which must have been great owing to all the hotels they stayed at *en route*.

Sir William noted:
    'Expense of living one month at Frascati Hotel:
Lodgings – two small bedrooms, sitting-room
and servants room   £504.
Wine £71.   Lights £11.
Breakfast, dinners etc.   £399.
TOTAL: £985'

AFTER their return from France there was only a short time at
Pencarrow before it was back to London for the Autumn session; and
although they were home again at the beginning of December, it
was not to tranquillity *à deux*. Tranquillity was not what Andalusia
enjoyed. A succession of visitors had been invited, the first on
December 5th. More guests arrived on the 10th, including William's
mother and sister, just before heavy snow set in the next day. The
winter of 1846-'7 was a severe one in all parts of the country, and
Cornwall did not escape from the frost and snow. This did not
however deter the hospitalities at Pencarrow. A carriage with five
guests got through on the 14th, and another five guests next day.
The snow continued, so entertainment was confined to the house,
and it must have been a relief when a slight thaw allowed most
of the guests to get away on the 17th. On December 21st thirteen
guests arrived for the Christmas week, not departing until the 30th.
The Dowager and Mary remained until January 21st, when they left
to stay with the Revd William Molesworth at St Breoke Rectory.
Three days later, William and Andalusia set out for London again
by mail-coach from Bodmin, staying the night at Exeter. There
William managed to fit in a visit to Prince's Nursery Gardens,
where he ordered a plant of camellia to be delivered to Pencarrow.
They then took the express train to Paddington. William's time at
Pencarrow was becoming a matter of just a few weeks in the year
– weeks seldom free from guests.

CHAPTER XIV — 1847

WHEN Parliament re-assembled in that bitter cold winter of 1847, it was the already tragic situation in Ireland, made even more desperate by unprecedented blizzard conditions, that was the dominating subject. On February 15th Molesworth spoke in the debate on Lord George Bentinck's proposal that sixteen million pounds should be spent on building railways in Ireland as a way of employing workers destituted by the famine. Molesworth, always in favour of any railway initiative, supported the proposal. It was a long debate and he did not get home until four o'clock in the morning. His speech had not been a success – 'I was nervous, not being very well'. Next day, after Lord George Bentinck's closing speech which Molesworth considered a very poor one, the Bill was defeated. Although Molesworth was aware of the start of a feverish cold, he had the following evening to preside at a conversazione at the Southwark Literary Institute, 'accompanied by Andalusia and Mary – evening v. cold and attendance not v. good'. Next day, not surprisingly, his cold was worse and he retired to bed, excusing himself from a party given by his mother the following evening. He had to stay in bed for some time, but there were no serious developments and he was back in the House in early March, making a long speech on Irish Poor Law.

The Easter recess was approaching, and on March 29th William went to Loddiges' Nurseries to choose some unusual plants to take with them to Pencarrow. But the weather was still very wintry, and in his vulnerable state of health the long journey was too great a risk. Also Pencarrow, like all big country houses, was cold, very cold, even in a normal winter – in spite of that cast-iron stove William had installed in the inner hall. Andalusia decreed that Brighton was the answer. So, accompanied by Mary, they went by express train on March 31st and stayed four days in the Bedford Hotel – 'one of the best I know', wrote William. Its comforts were very necessary, for outside it was snowing. People were beginning to feel that this dreadful winter would never end. The four days in Brighton for the three of them cost £41.1.0, including the railway fare, and William gave Andalusia a loan of £25. Maybe this was for her to make some special purchase for the State Opening of the Italian Opera at Covent Garden on April 6th, which they were going to attend with a large party on their return to London.

The talk in musical circles that season was of Jenny Lind, hailed by the Press as 'The Swedish Nightingale'. Her reception into London Society was due to the patronage of Mr and Mrs George Grote. Mrs Grote's youngest sister, Frances Eliza von Koch, was married to a Swede and lived in Stockholm. She had enlisted Harriet Grote to resolve a dispute which had caused Jenny Lind to forfeit an engagement at Drury Lane. Lady Eastlake (wife of the President of the Royal Academy) wrote in the sketch of Mrs Grote she published after her death an account of 'the generous reception and patronage which Mr and Mrs Grote extended to Mlle Lind . . . they received her in their own residence in Eccleston Street, at the door of which the benevolent hostess stood to welcome her, with no less a celebrity at her side than Felix Mendelssohn, then on his second visit to England, and about to bring out his Elijah at Exeter Hall.' Jenny Lind made her London *début* that May at Her Majesty's Theatre in the part of Alice in *Robert le Diable*. Lady Eastlake's account continues:

I went to Box 48 as usual, and took with me Fanny Kemble and Sir Charles Lemon. Mrs Grote's maternal care for Jenny Lind never relaxed. Parties were arranged for her at the Grotes' house in Eccleston Street, and rest and quiet were provided for her in their country house at Burnham Beeches. She was chaperoned to great entertainments in and near London, and Mrs Grote even extended to her the aegis of her protection on a professional tour of the West of England.

Lady Eastlake did not mention that Mrs Grote included 'Lines to Jenny Lind Golschmidt, May 1859' in her *Collected Papers in Prose and Verse, 1842-1862*. Few people were aware that Mrs Grote occasionally broke into lyrical verse.

The West of England tour did not include a visit to Pencarrow. How ironical that Mrs Grote, passionately fond of music (herself, we are told, no mean performer on the piano, rather less admirable on the violin-cello), self-appointed chaperon of Jenny Lind, should have looked down on Andalusia for having been a professional singer. There must have been times during the year of the Swedish Nightingale when Andalusia felt that if 'Miss Grant' had continued her singing career beyond its brilliant *début*, her fame would have equalled, or even surpassed, that of Mrs Grote's dazzling protégée. The Molesworths, of course, had their box at the Opera, and Andalusia attended with different guests every week. It is inconceivable that the Molesworths should not occasionally have encountered the Grotes in the vestibule or the Crush Bar. Civilities will have been exchanged, but no such chance encounter was used as an opportunity to bury the hatchet and revive the old affectionate friendship. Henry Fothergill Chorley, music critic of the *Athenaeum* and a close friend of the Molesworths was, according to Henry G. Hewlett, 'alone during the "Lind Fever" of 1847 in raising a single voice of protest against the "chorus of idolatry" which ignored the existence of any defects in the public favourite, and forbade the discussion of any other claims than hers. This brought upon him, to adopt his own words, "such ignominy as belongs to the idiotic slanderer".'

Perhaps Andalusia had told Chorley that she considered Jenny Lind's vocal powers over-rated.

How and when Chorley became acquainted with the Molesworths is not known; but he conceived an early admiration for Sir William amounting almost to hero-worship, and boasted that the Molesworths' door was open to him at all hours. The son of a Liverpool lace-manufacturer, he came to London burning with social and literary ambitions. He wrote some unsuccessful novels and dramas, but achieved some success in writing libretti for composers and translating foreign libretti. It was his post as music critic of the *Athenaeum* that established him in literary as well as musical circles. He took no interest in politics; and music, ironically, was the one intellectual pursuit that Sir William, his hero, had no taste for. Certainly, before his marriage he had taken an Opera Box in the season for his mother and Mary; and after his marriage, of course, it was a necessity for Andalusia. But he himself found opera irritatingly boring. Chorley wrote in his *Memoirs*: 'Without an atom of taste for music, or care about the drama above melodrama, Sir William endured both in indulgence to other persons, but not very willingly.

It is comical to recall how, after the first performance of *Le Prophète*,
he never again entered his own opera box; driven thence, he said
(and, I suspect, not averse to the excuse), by the psalmody of the
Three Anabaptistes!'

Of course Sir William had other excuses than the Three
Anabaptistes for not always joining Andalusia's parties in their
Opera Box. There are diary notes: 'Too tired to go to the Opera';
'The production of *Norma* on June 17 said to be splendid, but I
remained at home and read papers with regard to Portugal'; and on
another day simply 'Too busy to go to the Opera'.

He was aking a very active part in House of Commons debates,
and the strain of preparing and making speeches, the hours at
committee meetings, and above all the late night sittings which
often followed dinner parties and other social engagements the same
evening, was beginning to over-tax his physique. One especially
long speech was in a debate upon transportation on June 3rd
1847. Abolition of transportation to the colonies was ever at the
forefront of his political aims; and this speech, though in itself it
brought about no halt to the evil, was respected for the clarity of
its exposition and his far-reaching study of the subject. An earlier
debate in which he took an important part in April of this year was
a debate upon increasing the grant for national education. The grant
had stood at a miserly £30,000 a year since it was first made in the
reformed Parliament of 1833. It was divided between the National
and British School Associations and was allocated for the erection
of school buildings. The Whig Government now proposed that a
grant of £100,000 should be made for general educational purposes.
In the course of a long debate, twice adjourned, it emerged that
it was proposed that the grant should not be given to Roman
Catholic schools. Strangely, Lord Ashley (later Lord Shaftesbury), so
honoured in British social history for his Christian charitable works,
was associated with this piece of religious intolerance. Aligning
himself with the Wesleyan Methodists, he intimated to Lord John
Russell, on behalf of the Methodists, that if Roman Catholics had
any share in the grant, they would decline to participate in it.
Lord John, never a fighter, gave way; and some members of his
Cabinet, nervous of intense Catholic wrath at the exclusion of
their schools from the grant, devised a devious way to make this

exclusion seem to be of the Catholics' own choice. They proposed that the grant should be restricted to schools using the whole of the authorised version of the Bible in their classes, well knowing that this would exclude all Catholic schools. Molesworth was outraged at the meanness of this proposal, and on April 22nd made a powerful speech giving notice of a Resolution. This he moved on April 27th, condemning the Government's proposal as not only a grievous injustice to the Roman Catholics but as a downright insult. They would be sacrificed to please the Wesleyans. His speech ended by making a further point:

'It is acknowledged on all hands that ignorance is the parent of vice and crime and that education is the remedy. But does vice, does crime cease to be noxious to the State when it is the vice and crime of Roman Catholics?'

Lord John Russell, dilatory as ever, tried to postpone the matter, promising to make up the injustice at some future time. Sir William retorted: 'The time to do justice is now!' – and appealed to the House to acquit themselves like men, to lead and not to follow or be dragged at the heels of a popular prejudice in the hope of catching a popular vote. The Government eventually gave way and made a firm promise that the Minute should be so framed as to enable Roman Catholic schools to receive the grant. This being assured, Molesworth withdrew his motion.

Mrs Millicent Fawcett wrote of Sir William that 'No man ever had less affinity with Roman Catholics than he, but no man was more instant in assault upon any attempt to put Roman Catholics under disabilities and injustice.' Her phrase 'instant in assault upon' nicely suggests Sir William's impulsive springing into attack, or into defence, of any cause about which he felt strongly – as does that retort of his to Lord John Russell: 'The time to do justice is now!' In spite of his own agnosticism, he was always ready to give land for the building of churches and chapels of any denomination. For example, he gave the land for Methodist chapels to be built on at both the nearby villages of Washaway and Egloshayle. There is no doubt that he recognised the importance for stability in country life of firmly based, practising Christianity whatever might be the denomination. In his own opinion, the most firmly based was that of the Church of England. This is revealed in a speech he made in

1853, two years before his death. He was speaking about the Clergy Reserves in Canada, and said that he preferred the doctrine and disciplines of the Church of England to those of any other religious denomination.

There was another aspect of religious discrimination that Molesworth was eager to attack – discrimination against the Jews. The Corporation Act that made the taking of the sacrament obligatory for all who held municipal office had been repealed in 1828; but Jews, being unable to take the oath 'on the true faith of a Christian', continued to be excluded from Parliament. Disraeli was there because his father, Isaac D'Israeli, had presciently had his children baptised into the Church of England. He himself retained his own strict adherence to practising Judaism. Molesworth, together with some other believers in religious liberty, decided to make an urgent issue of anti-Jewish discrimination by nominating Jewish candidates for important constituencies. Baron Lionel de Rothschild agreed to stand for the City of London in 1847, although he well knew that if elected he would not be allowed to take his seat in the House. Charles Greville, the diarist, was probably expressing the view of most of his contemporaries when he wrote that Rothschild's candidature was 'a great piece of impertinence, when he knows he can't take his seat'. Molesworth's speech on July 18th in support of Rothschild's candidature needs to be quoted at some length for it is particularly interesting in his recognition of the imperial importance of religious liberty:

In his [Rothschild's] election a great principle is practically involved, important to the whole of the human race, the principle of religious liberty and equality among men. If you, the electors of this great city, the commercial metropolis of the universe, who number among your citizens more wealthy, careful, energetic and reflecting men than any other community on the face of the earth, if you select as one of the representatives of your vast interests a gentleman professing the ancient and venerable creed of Jews, you will thereby protest emphatically against all bigotry and intolerance. You will proclaim in the most impressive manner, to all nations of the earth, civilized and uncivilized, your opinion in favour of religious liberty and equality. You will do an act which will win for you honour, gratitude and renown from all liberal and enlightened men. I cannot understand religious bigotry in the present age. I can understand the fierce intolerance of our rude forefathers, to whose uninformed minds the idea of a religion different from their own was inconceivable. But I cannot understand those feelings among us, who are the sovereigns of a hundred millions of human beings whose religions are different from our own – among us, who are brought by commerce in daily and friendly intercourse not only with the Jews of Palestine and the Mohammedans of Asia Minor, but with the Hindoos of India and the innumerable creeds of Eastern Asia, and who find among them equally upright, honourable and excellent men.

By returning Baron Rothschild you will protest against any distinction drawn between your fellow-citizens on the score of religion. As electors of the most important constituency in the Empire, you will set an example to other constituencies; you will tell them that in selecting their representatives they ought to choose the best and fittest men without reference to sect or creed. And who can deny that a Rothschild is a fitting representative of the bankers and merchant princes of England? I say this, not in homage to his wealth, but as an advocate of a great principle which is involved in this election.

The constituents of the City of London returned Baron de Rothschild with an immense majority over his opponent, Lord John Manners. Roebuck tried to persuade him to present himself at the table and bring the question of the oath to an issue; but Rothschild, believing the Government would take some action, delayed. His confidence was unfounded, the Ministers procrastinated. Three years after his election Rothschild at last decided, in July 1850, to make his claim to take his seat. The officials refused to swear him in on the Old Testament and he refused to take the oath 'on the true faith of a Christian', so he was excluded from the House. It was not until eleven years after his first election that Rothschild took his seat, in July 1858, the long antagonism of the House of Lords having been overcome on the third reading of a Bill admitting Jews to sit in Parliament.

A.I. Dasent, commenting on the exclusivity of mid-nineteenth century aristocratic circles from which 'the plutocracy' was cold-shouldered, wrote that the brilliantly talented Rothschilds were the exceptions, occupying a position unique in the realms of high finance. For other financiers, 'the mere possession of a colossal fortune constituted no passport to those gilded salons so lovingly described by Disraeli in *Lothair*'.

CHAPTER XV — 1847 cont.

TO RETURN to that summer of 1847 when Molesworth was playing an increasingly prominent part in Parliament, at the same time Andalusia's ambitions were escalating. The scale of entertaining she now envisaged required a larger, more splendid residence. Lowndes Square was a 'good address', being just within the bounds of Belgravia; but its five-storied terraced houses are modest compared with most of those in that so fashionable residential district created by Thomas Cubitt on the Duke of Westminster's land west of Buckingham Palace. Cubitt had begun his development in 1827 when he laid out Belgrave Square, one of the largest, most handsome squares in London. In the following year he began the even more lordly Eaton Square and Eaton Place. His architect was George Basevi, talented pupil of Sir John Soane. Basevi's brilliant career was cut short in 1845 by falling to his death from the western bell tower of Ely Cathedral. He was buried there in Bishop Alcock's Chapel, where there is a tablet to his memory.

In the early Spring of 1847 the Molesworths had heard that No. 87, Eaton Place, a corner house and therefore even larger than the other Eaton Place houses, was available; and on April 27th Sir William signed an agreement with Cubitt to take it on lease or purchase, including the lease of No. 1, Lyall Mews. The size and splendour of 87 Eaton Place is described in the auctioneers' particulars for its sale after Andalusia's death in 1888:

The late Lady Molesworth's Town House, No. 87 Eaton Place, built by Cubitt on the Duke of Westminster's Estate, with excellent stabling in Lyall Mews. This FASHIONABLE TOWN HOUSE, for many years occupied by the Right Honourable Sir William Molesworth and subsequently by Lady Molesworth, is most aristocratically placed. Singularly bright and cheerful and admirably arranged for THE SEASON RESIDENCE AND RECEPTIONS OF A FAMILY OF DISTINCTION. On the First Floor, THE NOBLE SUITE OF WITHDRAWING ROOMS are respectively 43 ft. by 16 ft. 8 ins., with bay, and 26 ft. by 14 ft. 8 ins. The Walls and Ceilings elaborately decorated in white and gold, the Panels being enriched with floriated and emblematical designs in gold, and the Ceilings supported by richly-gilt and fluted columns. There is a pretty Alcove and Greenhouse to the back window, the front windows opening on to a Balcony and Jardiniere.

The 'greenhouse' was an addition of Sir William's, as is shown by a Cubitt bill for 'Building Conservatory, £40; fountain and plumbing for it £25.5.0.' Another bill before they moved in for 'works at Eaton Place' was £1,266.15.9. Whatever improvements or extravagances these further 'works' consisted of, the conservatory was a necessity for the happiness of Sir William. It would be a small compensation for being away from Pencarrow so much of the year. He would be able to nurture rare species in it, and would have a good excuse for spending hours at Loddige's Nurseries in Hackney choosing plants. He could plan to bring favourite ferns and hot-house climbers from Pencarrow. Also, another boon, it would be an excellent place for Andalusia's beloved cage birds.

At No. 1 Lyall Mews there was stabling for three horses, and Cubitt's bill for work there was: Bathroom over stables, £25.5.8; Harness Room and Stables: making good ceilings, plastering, scouring floors, repairing woodwork, painting etc. £5.12.9. Thomas Cubitt, although by now a man of very considerable wealth and reputation, was accustomed to comply with his clients' particular fancies and fusses – even those of less monied clients than Sir William Molesworth as, for example, Lady Morgan. In her *Memoirs* she relates: 'I saw Mr Cubitt yesterday, a good, little complying man; he has yielded to all my suggestions; will knock down walls between the rooms, build balconies and a terrace, and is to give me a tree to plant in my bit of a garden (four feet by two) though I heard him say to Sir Charles, "She shall have it, but it will not grow in so confined a place." Mr Cubitt was quite mistaken. The tree was planted (a plane tree). It grew and throve from the first day. It is now a fine piece of timber, standing higher than the chimneys.'

Clearly, Lady Morgan and Sir William, with his love of trees, had an affinity beyond the attractions of aristocratic radicalism. Her description of Thomas Cubitt as 'a good little complying man' is amusingly similar to that of Queen Victoria when his reconstruction

THE

VALUABLE GROUND LEASE

OF THE

FASHIONABLE TOWN HOUSE,

For many years occupied by the *RIGHT HONOURABLE SIR WILLIAM
MOLESWORTH,* and subsequently of *LADY MOLESWORTH,*

Most aristocratically placed, being

No. 87, EATON PLACE,

AT THE CORNER OF CHESHAM STREET,

Singularly bright and cheerful, and admirably arranged for

𝕿𝖍𝖊 𝕾𝖊𝖆𝖘𝖔𝖓 𝕽𝖊𝖘𝖎𝖉𝖊𝖓𝖈𝖊 𝖆𝖓𝖉 𝕽𝖊𝖈𝖊𝖕𝖙𝖎𝖔𝖓𝖘 𝖔𝖋 𝖆 𝕱𝖆𝖒𝖎𝖑𝖞 𝖔𝖋 𝖉𝖎𝖘𝖙𝖎𝖓𝖈𝖙𝖎𝖔𝖓.

IT CONTAINS

ON THE FOURTH FLOOR—

FIVE SECONDARY BED CHAMBERS, and Passage.

ON THE THIRD FLOOR—

Large FRONT and BACK BED ROOMS, Landing, W.C., and TWO Smaller BED ROOMS.

ON THE SECOND FLOOR—

Access to which is obtained by the GRAND STAIRCASE as well as from the Secondary
Stairs, a fine Large Principal BED ROOM with Alcove Recess and Cupboards, DRESSING
ROOM communicating, TWO other BED CHAMBERS, and Large Landing.

ON THE FIRST FLOOR—

THE NOBLE SUITE OF WITHDRAWING ROOMS

(being respectively 43ft. by 16ft. 8in. with bay, and 20ft. by 14ft. 8in.),

*The Walls and ceilings elaborately decorated in white and gold, the
Panels being enriched with floriated and emblematical designs in gold, and
the Ceilings supported by richly-gilt and fluted columns. There is a pretty
Alcove, and Greenhouse to back window, the front windows opening on to
balcony and jardinière.*

*A page from the auctioneer's particulars of 87 Eaton Place when the lease
was for sale after Andalusia's death in 1888.*

137

of Osborne House to Prince Albert's Italian Renaissance style design was completed in 1851. The Queen was delighted. 'Mr Cubitt has done it admirably. He is such an honest, kind, good man.'

THE builders' work at 87 Eaton Place meant that it would be some time before the Molesworths would be able to move in. Sir William leased his Lowndes Square house on May 28th for the remainder of his term at a premium of £500, but it was agreed the date of letting should commence after they left London in August – Andalusia's dinners and musical evenings would continue at Lowndes Square throughout the season.

The name of William Makepeace Thackeray made its first appearance on the guest list on June 9th. Sir William and Thackeray had met as long ago as 1832 at Polvellan, when they were both helping Charles Buller in his election campaign. Since then their paths had seldom crossed, Thackeray not being in any sense a political animal. There had, of course, been that time when Thackeray had written for *Fraser's Magazine* the sketch of Molesworth luxuriating in the Eaton Square house he shared with Leader. Now, in this summer of 1847, Thackeray was at the height of his fame. Instalments of *Vanity Fair* had been appearing since the beginning of the year, and he had become a social lion, unashamedly revelling in his invitations from the aristocracy. He was not a brilliant dinner-table talker. According to Lady Dorothy Neville, 'he was inclined to be satiric and severe. On one occasion I recollect his administrating a terrible verbal castigation to an unfortunate individual who had incurred his displeasure.' But he was a novelist, and as such was a keen observer of human beings. He would be intrigued by the contrast of his host and his hostess, would try to determine what lay beneath Andalusia's so beguiling out-going charm, would try to detect where her seemingly shallow surface sparkle met William's intellectual depths. Or maybe never met.

Character analysing apart, there is sure evidence that what Thackeray enjoyed to the full was the extravagant excellence of the Molesworth menus. He wrote to Mrs Brookfield on July 10 1848: 'I was a little late for the magnificent entertainment of my titled friends Sir William and Lady Molesworth on Saturday, and indeed the first course had been removed when I made my appearance.

The banquet was sumptuous in the extreme, and the company of
the most select order . . . Fancy my happiness in the company of
persons so *distinguished*. A delightful concert followed the dinner
and the whole concluded with a sumptuous supper: nor did the
party separate until a late hour.'

Understandably the Molesworth entertainment bills were high.
That month alone, the hire of a French cook cost £44.0.0, and
a Gunter bill was £51.9.0. Then there was the wine, the flowers,
the candles and of course Andalusia's lovely gowns and many costly
jewels. Their dinner parties, when not followed by a concert and
supper, were often extended by everyone moving on to gatherings
in another house, sometimes to several other houses. For instance,
on June 30th this year the Molesworths gave a dinner for twelve and
afterwards went to Mrs Milner Gibson's evening salon, then on to
Lady Duff Gordon.

Among the guests most frequently at 1 Lowndes Square this
summer were Lord and Lady Lovelace. Lady Lovelace was Ada
Augusta, the only legal child of Lord Byron. Sir William had
met her mother, Lady Byron, when he was first in Parliament.
It seems the introduction had been through his physician, Dr
John Elliotson, who attended him frequently and had become
a personal friend, his professional visits merging into long
philosophical conversations. He was a well-known physician,
much in the news although not so fashionably in vogue as
Dr Quin, the first homoeopathic physician in England. Quin
was a great diner-out, in spite of having been denounced as a
quack when he first set up in private practice. Dr Elliotson was
most talked about because of his deep interest in hypnotism –
which was viewed by his colleagues at University College Hospital
with some displeasure. He had founded a small mesmeric hospital
where he had cured *tic douleureux* and carried out various minor
operations under anaesthesia induced by magnetic passes. Charles
Dickens became an affectionate friend of Dr Elliotson, as well
as a patient. Thackeray was another well-known patient, and
his dedication of *Pendennis* to Dr Elliotson reveals his deep
gratitude to him, and also the essential goodness of the
physician:

To Dr John Elliotson.

Thirteen months ago, when it seemed likely that this story had come to a close, a kind friend brought you to my bedside, whence, in all probability, I never should have risen but for your constant watchfulness and skill. I like to recall your great goodness and kindness (as well as many acts of others, showing quite a surprising friendship and sympathy) at that time, when kindness and friendship were most needed and welcome. And as you would take no other fee but thanks, let me record them here in behalf of me and mine, and subscribe myself,

Yours most sincerely and gratefully, W.M. Thackeray.

Thackeray was not a rich man; but, even from wealthy Sir William, Elliotson was reluctant to take fees . . . 'Dr Elliotson and I are great friends', William wrote to his mother. 'He came four times to see me when I was ill and would only take one sovereign, as he said he likes to converse with me.' Under Dr Elliotson's guidance, William tried mesmerism on his brother Francis for half an hour twice a day – 'Francis found it did him good'. And Molesworth's political friend J.A. Roebuck, the Radical member for Bath, gained permanent relief from a stress-related illness after a five day course which Dr Elliotson directed.

Dr Elliotson's introduction of Sir William to Lady Byron was perceptive. She was a woman of considerable intellect, and was deeply interested in Elliotson's theories. She was also actively concerned in promoting progressive education for the poor, and set up an industrial training school in Ealing Grove. William Frend, who established the first of all Sunday Schools at Madingley, near Cambridge, was one of her mainly Unitarian idealistic circle. After Sir William's first meeting with Lady Byron he wrote to his sister: 'I like her much; she is a calm, dignified and *very* clever person; expresses herself remarkably well and clearly, rather stern in manners. We got on very well, as she is almost a Radical and we talked on education. You know I like theory but do not care much about practice, and you will laugh at my inspecting several dozen dirty urchins.'

Molesworth's dedication to the cause for national education and improving the lot of the poor did not include experiencing any personal knowledge of the nitty gritty of poverty. Indeed, he had no experience of any children, either dirty or clean, since he had none of his own nor any nephews or nieces.

Much as Molesworth admired Lady Byron's intellectual depth and interests, he was even more impressed when he met her daughter, Ada Countess of Lovelace. That was before his marriage; and Lady Lovelace was at the Molesworths' very first London dinner party, when her friend Charles Babbage, inventor of the calculating machine and principal founder of the Astronomical Society and the Statistical Society, was also a guest. Augusta Ada Byron, the only legitimate child of Lord Byron, had married Lord Lovelace in 1835 when she was nineteen years old. He not only adored her, but admired and encouraged her intellectual interests, allowing her to absorb herself in books concerning mathematics, philosophy, astronomy and science. He himself was a studious, autocratic aristocrat, practising his self-taught talents as engineer and architect – he designed one of their country houses, Ashley Combe, in Somerset. They were a pair after William's own heart, and the Molesworths dined often at the Lovelaces' London house, 10 St James's Square. There the guests most often represented a mixture of science and fashion; Charles Babbage was one of the most frequent. Albany Fonblanque of *The Examiner* wrote that Lady Lovelace 'eagerly sought the acquaintance of all who were distinguished in science, art and literature'.

Her own most concentrated work was that of translating into English the notes of the Italian military engineer L.F. Menabrea (which he wrote in French) about Babbage's Analytical Engine: *Notices sur la Machine Analytique*. When Lady Lovelace showed her manuscript to Babbage he was most impressed, and suggested she should add some notes of her own to Menabrea's *Notices*. Her notes eventually extended to three times the length of the original work, and Lady Lovelace's absorption in this *magnum opus* could be likened to William Molesworth's editing of the complete works of Hobbes. They also shared an approximately similar attitude to religion. Ada liked to think that the intellectual, the moral and the religious were interlinked together in a harmonious whole. She once summed this up in a letter, with much underlining, to Bulwer Lytton: 'Pray do not conceive that I am a mere conglomeration of *logic* and of lines and triangles! Oh dear no! I am *religiously, sceptical*, and conscientiously *unbelieving*'. Very Molesworth.

By 1850 Lady Lovelace and William were going on little trips together, the kind of expeditions that Andalusia would find boring, but for which Ada Augusta was the perfect companion. Diary entries that summer include driving her in his carriage to Kew Gardens one day, on another to the Agriculture Exhibition at Chiswick, yet another to William's favourite nursery garden, Loddiges's at Hackney, where they chose some interesting plants together. They made an especial expedition to Syon House to see Victoria Regina in bloom – 'rather disappointed, flowers large and white, leaves remarkable on the lower side'. Unfortunately he ceased to keep a personal diary after 1850 (that is to say, no personal diaries after 1850 have survived) so it is impossible to know whether the friendship with Ada Countess of Lovelace blossomed beyond the sharing of botanical, mathematical, scientific and philosophical beliefs and pleasures. There were, indeed, sadly only two more summers for the friendship to flower – Ada, who since childhood had, like William, suffered intermittent bouts of ill-health, died of cancer on November 27th 1852, at the age of thirty-six. By her own request, her coffin was laid in the Byron family vault in the village church at Hucknall Torkard in Nottinghamshire, next to that of her father.

THE summer session of 1847 ended after the young Queen Victoria prorogued Parliament for the first time in the rebuilt House of Lords – even then, thirteen years after the devastating fire that destroyed the Palace of Westminster in 1834, the rebuilding was not entirely finished. Molesworth noted in his diary on July 23rd: 'Was much struck by the manner in which she made her speech, so clear, so distinct and silver-toned her voice. Parliament dissolved by proclamation.' This, of course, was also the signal for society to dissolve, returning to their country houses or departing on visits to the Continent, leaving skeleton staffs to close their town houses and carry out the annual cleaning. For the Molesworths it meant closing the Lowndes Square house for the last time. Some of the furniture and fittings were sold to the in-coming tenant for £282. They fitted in one more visit to the opera, made some purchases to take to Pencarrow, settled outstanding bills; and it was not until August 12th that they took the 4.30 express train to Exeter, where they stayed the night. There was to be no travel abroad this summer – just a short tour of the coast of South Devon at the end of August.

Account from Town & Emmanual, manufacturers of all kinds of decorative, elaborate, and expensive items for the house.

There would be more Cubitt accounts to meet, and the enormous expense of furnishing 87 Eaton Place – the great reception rooms on the ground floor and first floor, the main bedroom suites on the second floor, nine more bedrooms on the third and fourth floors – and of course all the staff bedrooms above those. The 'domestic offices' in the basement had to be equipped. According to the Agent's particulars these consisted of: 'Spacious Kitchen, Scullery, Butler's Pantry with Plate Room, Footman's Bed Room, Servants' Hall, WCs, Wine, Coal and Beer Cellars – Area on three sides, with Servants' and Tradesmen's Entrances, Arched Vaults and Cellarage. The Secondary Staircase runs from the Basement to the top of the House, and there are WCs on each Half-landing.'

It was disappointing when they returned to London on October 12th to find the house not nearly as ready to receive them as they had hoped. They went to an hotel for two nights, and then left London 'by rail to Dover where Mrs Drummond had got us very

nice lodgings at 17 Waterloo Crescent for 4 gns. per week'. Next
day they 'walked about Dover – miserable town' – and the following
day 'Andalusia tired of Dover and determined to go to Brighton'.
Maclean was sent to Brighton to find rooms for them, and on the
21st October they moved into 'very nice lodgings at 118 Kings
Road'. Brighton proved to be just as dull and unfashionable that
month as Dover . . . 'Nothing to do but walk in the town and on
the chain pier'. William caught a cold and did not go out. It was a
relief when, Parliament being summoned to meet on October 18th,
they returned to London. There, instead of staying in an hotel, 'we
took up our residence with Moffat [George Moffat, Radical MP]
at 85 Eaton Square'. This was almost certainly the house that
Molesworth had ten years earlier shared with Leader. It seems to
have been kept on, since he left it, as a kind of Philosophical
Radical base, for the Cobdens were also there with the Moffats.
Molesworth wrote 'We left Moffat's after a most agreeable visit of
31 days, during the whole of which Mrs Cobden was staying in the
same house, whom we found both a most charming companion and
agreeable person.' The Cobdens for their part must have found the

Snuff-maker and Tobacco Merchant's account — suppliers of Sir William's
cigars. There is no evidence that he ever took snuff.

Molesworths charming and agreeable, since on November 29th Mr and Mrs Cobden arrived at Pencarrow with their two children. Sir William's incessant cigar smoking had evidently been discouraged in the Eaton Square house, since a diary note that December says: 'So inconvenient to smoke in a town house that I gave over so doing and got out of the habit of it and I find myself in better health in consequence thereof'.

CHAPTER XVI — 1848-49

THE New Year of 1848 brought the glad news to Pencarrow that 87 Eaton Place was ready to receive them. They were anxious to have some time to settle in before the Parliamentary session began, but were thwarted by the weather. On the day that they finally decided to start the long journey, come what may, what came was another heavy snow storm – 'could not have got on without four horses. My mother and Mary left on the same day [four more horses?] and we dined together at the New London Inn, Exeter.' Brunel's railway did not complete its extension from Exeter to Plymouth until later that year, so they must have travelled by mail-coach the seventy-four miles from Bodmin to Exeter – a hazardous journey in winter conditions over bleak Bodmin Moor, changing horses at the Jamaica Inn.

Rail links from London to the Midlands and the North were in advance of those to Devon and Cornwall; and when in April of this year William and Andalusia travelled to the Duke of Devonshire's Hardwick Hall in Derbyshire most of the journey could be made by rail. This visit came about through Sir William having sent a set of his edition of Hobbes (11 volumes English, 5 volumes Latin) to the 6th Duke of Devonshire. He made the gift because Thomas Hobbes, after leaving Oxford in 1608, had become tutor to William Cavendish, later the 2nd Duke of Devonshire, and remained in the household of the Cavendish family for the rest of his life. When thanking Molesworth for 'that magnificent compilation', the 6th Duke wrote: 'I know not whether you have been to Hardwick; should it ever suit your convenience to go there, I hope you will let me know the time, and if I should not be able to receive you there myself, I hope that you would inhabit for a day or two that place, where you would find so many recollections of him whose memory you have done so much to honour.'

That letter was dated June 12th 1847; but it was not until the following year that the Molesworths decided to make the journey to

Hardwick. A note from Chatsworth House, dated April 10th 1848, says 'The Duke of Devonshire is most happy to find that Sir William and Lady Molesworth intend to go to Hardwick. He begs that a line may be sent to Mr Cottingham a day or two before to name the day that the house may be warm and ready: J. Cottingham, Esq., Hardwick, Chesterfield.' Anyone who has visited the draughty vastness of Elizabethan Hardwick since it became National Trust property will shudder to think how cold it must have been in 1848. Nigel Nicolson in his Introduction to *The National Trust Guide* relates that this 6th Duke of Devonshire was, he quotes, 'driven to habitation of the Library by a vain attempt we made to pass some evenings in the Long Gallery, although surrounded by screens and sheltered by red baize curtains'. Nicolson does not give the source of his quotation – presumably it comes from the memoirs of some unhappy guest.

The Molesworths, chilled to the bone or not, spent two nights at Hardwick, April 25th and 26th – no mention of the temperature in William's diary. They then proceeded 'with a ticket of admission' to Chatsworth. There they were shown over the extensive gardens (the Duke kept sixty men for the grounds and forty for the kitchen gardens), followed by the hot-houses of exotic plants, and then the great conservatory. This, covering an acre of ground, was designed by the Duke's head gardener, Joseph Paxton, who three years later became internationally famous as the designer of the magnificent, well-nigh miraculous, glass building for the Great Exhibition in Hyde Park. It was Paxton who conducted the Molesworths on their tour. Next day Sir William wrote in his diary:

Thought my own garden at Pencarrow superior in beauty and form. Was however much pleased with the grand conservatory. Having heard of the carriage drive through it, suspected something rather cockney. Nothing of the kind – perfectly simple, and a bit of a tropical forest enclosed in glass, the plants in the finest condition. The other hot houses were not worth looking at. The Emperor fountain was played for us. There was too much muck – however for beauty it's a wonderfully large squirt, and rises to an amazing height.

On their return from Chatsworth, the London Season was in full swing, with the demands of the social merry-go-round as compulsive as the rigours of Parliamentary duties. Among the names of dinner-guests at Eaton Place that of Thomas Babington Macaulay was now appearing. Molesworth had been acquainted with him in the House of Commons since 1833; but his admiration for Macaulay had first been excited in Edinburgh way back in 1825. William, then aged fifteen, was studying under a tutor in Edinburgh; and Macaulay, aged twenty-five, was beginning to contribute widely praised essays to the *Edinburgh Review*. In 1830 Macaulay entered Parliament as Liberal member for Calne, then in 1832 for Leeds – in which year his speech on the Reform Bill signalled him out as an outstanding orator. This was just after William had returned from Germany to celebrate his majority. He will have read Macaulay's brilliant Reform Bill speech, and it may well have influenced his decision to stand for Parliament at the next election.

From 1834-38 Macaulay was legal adviser to the Supreme Council of India, in which he influenced the choice of an English, instead of an oriental, type of education. On his return he was elected MP for Edinburgh; and very soon afterwards became Secretary of State for War, at the age of thirty-nine. That same year, 1839, he began his *History of England*. With the publication of his *Lays of Ancient Rome* in 1842, the name of Macaulay became a 'household word'; long passages from the *Lays* have been learned by heart by generations of school-children. It was astonishing that at the General Election of 1847, in spite of his literary fame, in spite of his position in the Cabinet, he was rejected by his Edinburgh constituency.

The main reason for Macaulay's rejection was his support, two years previously, for a motion to increase the grant to Maynooth College, the Irish college for the education of Roman Catholic clergy – a support which Molesworth, himself not then in Parliament, whole-heartedly admired. The Tory government of Sir Robert Peel had carried in 1845 a Bill to increase the annual grant from £9,000 to £26,000, with in addition a building grant of £30,000. This caused an outcry from the extreme Protestant 'No Popery' party. Macaulay mocked this outcry as 'the bray of Exeter Hall' and the 'war-whoop of the Orangemen', thus enraging Edinburgh's mainly Protestant constituents. At the next election Macaulay was duly rejected.

The Maynooth controversy also affected Molesworth. When he was making his speech seeking nomination for Southwark in 1845, he was asked whether, had he been in Parliament when the Maynooth Bill was presented, he would have supported it. He could have skirted round the question as being hypothetical; but it was not in his nature to prevaricate when his opinions or beliefs were questioned. Yes, he replied, he would certainly have supported the Bill. Heckled violently over this, he stood firm; and in his speech on September 10th following his nomination gave his reasons: 'Would not the refusal of this grant have been considered as tantamount to a declaration of hostility towards Ireland? Would not that have confirmed the assertion of the agitator, that there was no justice to be obtained from England? Would not that have lent force to the cry for repeal of the Union? I answer, it would. I am opposed to the repeal of the Union, no one more so; but then I say, do justice to Ireland.'

How ironical that it should be the Protestants who were responsible for rejecting Macaulay at Edinburgh – for when the first two volumes of his *History of England* were published, they were criticised for being written too much from a Protestant view point. Other critics deemed it biased from the point of view of an ardent Whig. It was said that his interpretation of history was too partisan. Maybe; but that can be seen as giving Macaulay's history its intense actuality – giving the feeling, for the reader, of being *there* amongst the people at the time of great events. Total impartiality can be very boring.

Macaulay was as eloquently sparkling at the dinner-table as he was in the House of Commons, and was a notable 'catch' for an ambitious hostess. Sydney Smith wrote to Mrs Meynal in April 1839: 'You must study Macaulay when you come to town. He is incomparably the first lion in the Metropolis; that is, he writes, talks, and speaks better than any man in England.' Macaulay's 'torrents of good talk' with 'occasional flashes of silence that make his conversation perfectly delightful', had none of the spitefulness of so many dinner-table wits of the day. In contrast, Ralph Bernal Osborne, MP, a political wit with a vituperous tongue in the House of Commons, spared no one at the dinner-table. Lady St Helier wrote of him 'He was very amusing and witty, but sometimes very brutal, and many people lived in a state of terror at his sharp tongue and cruel criticisms.' Osborne's biographer, Philip H. Bogenal, wrote 'His forte was ridicule, without which argument buries itself in vain in the sandbag fortifications of stupidity . . . For this Osborne had a perfect genius. He possessed the derisive faculty to an abnormal degree.'

Charles Dickens, whose name appears on the Molesworth guest list for the first time this summer season, was in yet another category. But no – he was not in any category. He was unique in the dining-rooms and drawing-rooms of the aristocracy . . . a man who had had no schooling since the age of twelve when he started work in a blacking factory, his father having been imprisoned for debt. Now, at the age of thirty-six he was revelling in invitations from the *haut ton*. Since the publication began in 1836 of *The Posthumous Papers of the Pickwick Club* in monthly numbers, he had published five novels, given immensely successful readings of his work, edited two monthly magazines and made a tour of the United States about which he had written a book. Perhaps his most astonishing *coup* was to have been elected to membership of the Athenaeum Club at the age of twenty-six. His acceptance into Society had begun when Samuel Rogers, that most selective and sourly critical host of intellectual wits, had invited Dickens to one of his breakfasts. Since then he had mingled in the glittering gatherings at Gore House, the coveted dinners at Holland House, the autocratic Whig gatherings at Lansdowne House. He had even been a guest at the exclusive little salon in Curzon Street of the seemingly immortal Miss Berrys. His inexperience of social *mores* had been disguised by self-confidence and unshakeable aplomb. The quick brain that had enabled him to educate himself at the British Museum in history, law and politics – and had made it possible for him to converse fluently in Italian and French – had been just as swift in acquiring knowledge of social etiquette. His unashamed personal vanity, his tendency to dress too flashily, were by most people forgiven – he was, after all, so very entertaining.

Dickens had a link with Andalusia's past life that no one else had (except Frances Countess of Waldegrave, about whom more later); his sister Fanny had been at the Royal Academy of Music at the same time as Andalusia, where they had been good friends. And it is likely that at the Molesworth dinner-table Dickens' lively conversation was more enjoyed by Andalusia than by Sir William, with whom he would have little empathy. For although Dickens was a natural radical through first-hand personal experience of poverty and depredation, he was not a political radical. He knew, and explored in research for his books, a stratum of humanity of which Sir William, despite the sincerity of his intellectual radicalism, had absolutely no personal experience – as, indeed was the case with all the members of the Philosophical Radical group in Parliament. It has to be admitted that Sir William had no desire to obtain any grass-root knowledge of the people for whose rights he fought. Did he ever read a Charles Dickens' novel? It is likely he shared the distaste of Lord Melbourne who, according to Lord David Cecil, 'put aside *Oliver Twist* after one glance, "It is all among workhouses and pick-pockets and coffin-makers", he said, "I do not *like* these things; I wish to avoid them." ' There are no records of Molesworth visiting the homes – or the hovels – of his constituents in the working-class areas of Leeds or of Southwark. One remembers the surprise he expressed in a letter to his mother that so few of the Political Unionists in Birmingham could pronounce their h's; also his joking to Mary about being introduced to Lady Byron's 'dirty urchins' at her Sunday School. Tireless in his work to end transportation, it was against the evil of polluting the colonies with a 'foul stream of criminal filth from England' that he inveighed; whereas Charles Dickens saw transportation from the point of view of those transported, some for quite trivial crimes – the inhuman conditions they had to endure for months on end in what were virtually floating prisons, packed below decks, often shackled together, half starved, suffering from dysentery and scurvy.

TOWARDS the end of the summer session of 1848 Molesworth made a very long, very carefully prepared speech on colonial expenditure and government. On the whole it was well received, by many it was admired: 'July 25th, my motion on the colonies – spoke for two and a half hours, excessively well listened to, very successful – said to be the best speech I ever made'. Four days later: 'Evening party at the Lewis's – I have been excessively complimented on account of my colonial speech.' Not everyone, however, approved of it. There were those who, perhaps not having listened attentively through all two and a half hours of his detailed analysis of the cost of the colonies to the military and naval establishments, had the impression that Molesworth was suggesting Britain should get rid of the colonies altogether. Amongst these was the Prime Minister, Lord John Russell, a traditional Whig, who regarded Molesworth as a dangerous agitator – while Molesworth regarded Lord John's cautious approach to any proposals for change as the spineless shilly-shallying of a man devoid of moral determination. The following year, 1849, in a debate on transportation, Lord John accused Molesworth of wishing to get rid of the colonial empire. To this accusation Molesworth retorted:

The noble lord has described the Colonial Empire as a glorious inheritance which we had received from our ancestors, and declared that he was determined at all risks to maintain it for ever intact. Now, I ask him how do we treat that precious inheritance? By transportation we stock it with convicts; we convert it into the moral dung-heap of Great Britain; and we tell our colonists that thieves and felons are fit to be their associates. Is this the mode and manner to inspire the inhabitants of our colonies with those feelings of affection and esteem for the mother country, without which our Colonial Empire must speedily crumble in the dust notwithstanding our numerous garrisons? If the noble Lord be sincere and earnest, as I am, in the wish to maintain that Empire intact, and hand it down great and prosperous to posterity, he will cordially unite with me in the effort to put an end to convict emigration. I maintain that we have no moral right to relieve ourselves of our criminals at the expense of the colonies, and that the desire to make a scapegoat of the colonies, by whomsoever entertained . . . is a mean and selfish feeling, of which, as citizens of this great Empire, we ought to be ashamed.

To be fair to Lord John, one can understand that his suspicion that Molesworth wished to get rid of the colonial empire had been aroused by that long speech on July 25th of the *previous* year in which Molesworth analysed the increasing financial burden of maintaining it. He had reviewed the annual naval, military and administrative cost of retaining a British presence in such relatively unimportant enclaves as Bermuda, the Cape of Good Hope, Ceylon, Hong Kong and Mauritius. He had concluded his catalogue of the military stations with the Falkland Islands, observing:

On that dreary, desolate and windy spot, where neither corn nor trees can grow, long wisely abandoned by us, we have since 1841 expended upwards of £35,000. We have a civil establishment there at the cost of

£5,000 a year; a Governor who has erected barracks and other necessary
buildings, well loop-holed for musketry; and being hard up for cash
he issued a paper currency, not, however, with the approbation of the
Colonial Office. . . . What I propose is this: to withdraw our military
protection from the Ionian States; to dispense with our stations and fleet
on the west coast of Africa; to reduce our establishments at the Cape
and the Mauritius, and to bestow upon those colonies free institutions;
to transfer Ceylon to the East India Company; to keep a sharp watch
over the expenditure for Hong Kong, Labuan and Sarawak; and to
acknowledge the claim of Buenos Aires to the Falkland Islands . . .
If this were done, there would be a reduction in military and naval
expenditure to the amount of at least a million a year for the military
stations alone.

One hundred and thirty-five years later, the British task force
sailed from Plymouth to win back the Falklands after Argentina
had invaded the Islands.

WHEN Parliament was dissolved that summer of 1848, there was
no question of continental travel – the revolution in France which
had erupted in January made it impossible. So London society
dispersed to their country houses without benefit of treatment at
the German spas, relaxation by the Italian lakes, or sea-bathing
at fashionable French resorts. On July 31st the Molesworths left
London for Pencarrow. The Great Western Railway extension from
Exeter to Plymouth had been completed earlier in the year, and
this was the first time they had travelled by rail the whole way to
Plymouth. There they stayed the night at the Royal Hotel, travelling
the long, winding roads to Bodmin by coach next day. When Mary
and Lady Molesworth (sturdier travellers than Andalusia) followed
three weeks later, they made the whole journey in one day – 'having
left London about 10 a.m. and arrived here 11 p.m.'

It was a peacefully leisured time at Pencarrow. One day they went
to Bedruthan Rocks (now called Bedruthan Steps and owned by the
National Trust), William driving Andalusia in the pony carriage.
The distance from Pencarrow to Bedruthan is about eighteen miles
which seems a long drive for a pony carriage, even though theirs
was drawn by two ponies. William had given them to Andalusia as
a present and was teaching her to drive them herself. On the way
they lunched with the Revd Hugh Molesworth, William's cousin,

Carriers conveyed goods by road from the newly opened railways to customers in towns and villages all over the West-country.

who was Rector of St Petroc Minor, Little Petherick. Hugh was now heir to the baronetcy, since both William's younger brothers had died – Arscott in 1842, Francis in 1846. The diary entry for August 30th was: 'Meeting of the Cricket Club at Boconnoc, drove my wife in the pony carriage with two outriders; dined with the Club, proposed the health of the ladies. Beautiful day.' William, one evening, went to a dinner of the Venison Club at Washaway Inn. This club was founded in the previous century when there was stag-hunting around Pencarrow, the club membership comprising most of the neighbouring gentry. Long after stag-hunting ceased, they continued to meet several times a year at Washaway Inn, dining and carousing far into the night in the Long Room where the Assizes were held and which is still there.

This happy summer-time was saddened by two deaths: 'Dog Myrtle died of old age, and was buried next to Garth on the Bank to the East of the house'. Their grave-stones still mark the place. Then on August 12th:

Poor old Conrad shot. He was broken winded and in great suffering. He had been a most useful and faithful horse. I bought him of George Leach in 1831 when he was rising five years old. Rode him frequently hunting at

Tetcott, where he served me well. Afterwards used him for many years as a Park hack; in 1844 it was on his back that I chiefly courted my wife, riding alongside of her carriage in Hyde Park, by the Serpentine drive. After that year I never rode him again, and he never went to town again.

Perhaps it was this reminder of those romantic courtship days that moved William when they returned to London that October, 'to present Andalusia with a beautiful turquoise bracelet, cost £45 – we had admired it for some time in the window of Silvani's shop.' An exquisite addition to her collection of bracelets. She was also given a November holiday in Brighton, William remaining in London where his parliamentary work was becoming increasingly arduous. He noted her hotel expenditure at Brighton: £79.7.4. with an additional £14.3.6. as spending money for the temptations of the Brighton shops – some of which were very fashionable. In particular, Hannington's, which had achieved Royal Appointment in 1820, and was considered quite the equal in 'Spa' shop prestige to that of Jolly's in Milsom Street, Bath.

TOWARDS the end of 1848 came the tragic and totally unexpected death of Charles Buller. William heard the news on November 30th: 'Extremely shocked at receiving a letter from Fleming announcing the death of Charles Buller of a low fever brought on by a slight operation, which had been performed on him. He was one of my best and oldest friends; we were at Cambridge together; we commenced political life about the same time. I had the greatest respect for his judgement, and fully expected that he would soon fill one of the highest offices in the State. He was gentle, kind and warm-hearted, liked and loved by all who knew him.' At Pencarrow there is a portrait of Charles Buller by their mutual friend Duppa.

Macaulay wrote in his diary: 'I was shocked to learn of the death of poor Charles Buller. It took me quite by surprise. I could almost cry for him . . .' And Thomas Carlyle, who had tutored Buller when he was a student in Edinburgh and had kept closely in touch with him ever since, wrote in the *Examiner*: 'A sound, penetrating intellect, full of adroit resources, and loyal by nature itself to all that was methodic, manful, true'. T.P. O'Connor remembered watching him in the House of Commons in 1837, and later described him as 'lively, almost to mischievousness; when he speaks, tearing through Tory fallacies with a merciless sense that for-shadows the style of Mr Lowe, amid a power of playful illustrations that strongly resembles the style of Sydney Smith. At this time everyone expects that Mr Buller has a great future before him, and who, looking at his bright face, his vivid manner, his gay air, can foretell for him an early death?'

For Molesworth, Buller's death not only meant the loss of his dearest friend from boyhood days, but also that of his closest colleague in Parliament, most particularly in his work for colonial self-government and the aboliton of transportation. Now Molesworth had to carry on the fight in the House virtually by himself – it was not a cause for which the other Radicals in Parliament showed much concern. Moreover the country as a whole was by no means in favour of abolition. *The Times* had always forcefully supported the system, although it was now fighting a rearguard action against the increasing influence of humanitarians and the unwillingness of the colonies to accept more convicts. On June 26th 1849 Molesworth, moving in the House for a Royal Commission to enquire into the administration of the Colonies, referred to the friend he had lost the previous year, quoting from one of Charles Buller's speeches in which he attacked the Colonial Office system:

These were the words of my late friend, Mr Charles Buller. They expressed his deliberate and unchanged convictions, and are deserved of the utmost respect; for no one had more carefully or more profoundly studied colonial questions, no one had brought greater talents to bear on those questions, no one was more anxious for the well-being of the colonies; and those who knew him well, and loved him, did fondly hope that the time would arrive when he would be placed in a position to be a benefactor to the colonies, and to make a thorough reform of the colonial system of the British Empire. But, alas! Providence has willed it otherwise.

In the year of Buller's death, a new move towards ending transportation had been taken by the issue of an edict from the Colonial Office stating that certain specified colonies, including the Cape of Good Hope and the Australian colonies, with the exception of Van Diemen's Land, should not be forced to receive convicts without the consent of their inhabitants. Despite this edict, the convict ship *Neptune* was sent to the Cape in 1849, getting round the edict by calling the convicts 'ticket-of-leave men'. Naturally, Cape Colony inhabitants considered a convict by any other name would smell as nasty. A protest was despatched with a petition that the sailing should be cancelled; but it was ignored by the Colonial Office, and *Neptune* proceeded. When she finally anchored in .Simon's Bay, the inhabitants of Cape Town and the neighbourhood prevented the convicts from landing and did their best to prevent any provisions reaching the ship. However, ships of war provided supplies of food to *Neptune* sufficient for her to remain in Simon's Bay for five months – convicts were accustomed to a near-starvation diet. *Neptune* then received orders from home to proceed to Van Diemen's Land, the Colonial Office repeating that the Home Government was making Van Diemen's Land a depot for the reception of ticket-of-leave men. Outraged, the colony formed an Anti-transportation League, the members binding themselves not to employ any male convict arriving after January 1st 1849. Petitions to Her Majesty were signed by heads of families. In the midst of the furore, *Neptune* arrived and deposited her load of convicts.

The Colonial Office justified its action by simply saying Van Diemen's Land had always been a penal colony. Molesworth declared it a tyrannical breach of faith since Sir William Denison, the Governor appointed by Mr Gladstone before he was succeeded as Colonial Secretary by Lord Grey, had, at the opening of the island's Legislative Council, announced: 'I take the earliest opportunity of laying before you the decision of Her Majesty's Government that transportation to Van Diemen's Land should be discontinued'. Arguably, Sir William Denison was jumping the gun – Her Majesty's Government had at that time made no such decision. But he was the Governor, and he had promised. Molesworth, in a speech on May 20th 1851, accused the Colonial Office of a deliberate intention to make Van Diemen's Land 'a huge cesspool, in which all the criminal filth of the British Empire was to be accumulated', and warned that 'it was in the power of the people of a colony by combination, vigour and self-reliance, to defeat the intention of the Colonial Office, and to compel it to keep faith.' He warned that an Australian League was being formed against transportation, and that persistent refusal to end it would alienate the colonies permanently. His speech concluded:

I exhort and warn the House to suffer no delay in this matter if it hold dear our Australian dependencies. For many years I have taken the deepest interest in the affairs of these colonies. I am convinced they are amongst the most valuable of our colonial possessions, the priceless jewel in the diadem of our Colonial Empire. I believe that they can easily be retained, with a little common sense and judgment on our part; that well governed they would cost us nothing, but offer us daily improving markets for our industry, fields for the employment of our labour and capital, and happy homes for our surplus population; that Australian Empire is in danger from the continuance of transportation to Van Diemen's Land; and therefore I move that 'An address be presented to Her Majesty praying for the discontinuance of transportation to Van Diemen's Land'.

The debate was brought to a premature close by a count out. But in little more than a year, on January 1st 1853, transportation to Van Diemen's Land was abolished. Two years later, the colony expunged the memory of the convict connection by changing its name. From January 1st 1855, Van Diemen's Land became Tasmania.

It was not quite the end of transportation. Western Australia, partly because it had no representative institution of its own, maintained the system long after it had been ended in all other Australian colonies. It was not until 1867 that the last convict ship was despatched to Western Australia.

I Sir William the politician.
Pencil and water-colour sketch
by Richard Dighton, 1840.

Charles Buller, MP. Portrait at
Pencarrow by Bryan E. Duppa.

XII *Andalusia, the hostess at 87 Eaton Place.*

XIII The Molesworth London house, 87 Eaton Place, Belgravia, in the 1980s, little changed since it was built by Cubitt.

The Reform Club. Members awaiting intelligence of the formation of Lord Aberdeen's Cabinet, December 1852, the Cabinet in which Molesworth was appointed First Commissioner of Works and Public Buildings. Engraving from the Illustrated London News.

XIV Sir William Molesworth, PC, MP, Secretary of State for the Colonies. 1855. By Sir J. Watson-Gordon. National Portrait Gallery.

CHAPTER XVII — 1850-52

FOR those who liked to circulate in the best society, and to be seen to circulate, the importance of spending some weeks in Paris each year was paramount. It is true that one mostly circulated there among the same acquaintances with whom one circulated in London, with whom one dined and danced, visited the opera and supped; but there were the French theatres, the Opéra Comique, the restaurants, and for wives and daughters there were the couture houses and the milliners. Above all, one needed to be known to be in Paris, to be announced to be there in the 'Movements of Society' columns, to be *seen* to be there.

Naturally Andalusia wished to be seen in Paris, and William wished her to be seen. They had to forego any visit in 1847 owing to the expense of setting up their establishment in Eaton Place. Then in 1848 there was revolution in France; and it was not until Louis Napoleon had been President for a year that the Molesworths set out from London for Paris on December 24th 1849 – breaking the tradition of Christmas at Pencarrow. Once in Paris, they were caught up in the spirit of gay extravagance that pervaded the city, William gallantly escorting Andalusia to all the occasions at which she needed to be seen, bravely footing her dressmakers' bills which were truly enormous. Lord Melbourne has been quoted by Lord David Cecil as telling the young Queen Victoria "The first time you go to Paris, the Capital of Pleasures, you should spend four thousand pounds, it is not social not to." Sir William, at the end of their visit, totalled his expenditure as £5,827.

Proof that he was determined to give this delayed Paris visit the flavour of a honeymoon is shown by a romantic note in his diary on January 3rd: 'Gave Anda a parure on condition that she should give me a lock of her hair'. A parure? – well, that could be *very* costly. According to Larousse's dictionary, it could have been a *'garniture de perles, ou de pierres, comprenant collier, pendants, bracelets, etc., un parure de diamants'*. William made no note of the price of the parure – it was not included in his summing up of total expenditure. Included were a couturier's account for £1,676.5.0. and vine leaves for the front of Andalusia's dress £70. Surely these must have been leaves spun with pure gold? Indeed, remembering that costs have to be multiplied by at least 20.5 to approximate present-day currency, some of the purchases are very puzzling. For instance, £8.5.0. for 'a bouquet of violets', and a few days later 'two bouquets of violets £23.9.0.'; then later again, just 'violets £5'. Were they fresh violets, or dressmaker's violets for the corsage or the bonnet? Andalusia wheedled another bracelet from him, 'a hair bracelet, £50'; but William's main present to her, apart from the parure, was a muff from Ledare, Rue St Honoré, costing £250. Other smaller presents together cost £18.10.0. Hire of a piano was a reasonable 25s. and he gave Andalusia £50 to spend as she pleased. In spite of all his careful accounting, at the end of the visit he noted: 'Perquisites unaccounted for by Andalusia, £95' – no doubt delicious inutilities for the boudoir. Unfortunately Andalusia was unwell during the visit. Six visits by one doctor, unnamed, cost £120. This was probably a French doctor with whom they were not satisfied, because Dr Oliffe was summoned from London at a cost of £70. An apothecary's bill was £45.10.0. and a chemist's £17.4.0. Lemonade £11.3.5.

Sir William was introduced to the President (Louis Napoleon, not yet Emperor) by Lord Normanby, the British Ambassador and writer of 'silver-fork' novels; and they met Lord and Lady Granville, Lady Sandwich and others of the many British people circulating in Paris. William called on Sir Francis Baring, MP for Portsmouth, recently appointed First Lord of the Admiralty, who was staying at 19 Place Vendôme, where they had a long conversation about the colonies. After that meeting and then another with Edward Ellice, a fellow Radical, he felt 'obliged to return to London to meet Stratfield to consult on matters affecting the colonies'. Thankful, no doubt, for the call of duty, he left Paris for Boulogne on January 7th.

Andalusia was not well enough to accompany William then, but travelled four days later – 'a bad passage from Boulogne'. Andalusia was not a good sailor, always dreaded the sea crossing, and without William to comfort and support her it must indeed have been 'a bad passage'. Of course she would have her personal maid with her, and it is likely that William left Maclean in Paris to organise the journey and serve as an escort.

THE first Parliamentary session of 1850 was one in which Molesworth played a prominent part, making three important speeches. On February 8th he spoke on the introduction by Lord John Russell of the Australian Government Bill. Molesworth's diary note on this Bill was that he 'approved of the principles but not of the manner in which Lord John applied them'. Always Molesworth pressed for the principle of colonial self-government, but Lord John's resolution proposed only that 'the Governors and Legislative of Her Majesty's Australian colonies be authorised to impose and levy duties of customs on goods, wares and merchandise imported into such colonies'. This did not go anything like far enough for Molesworth. In a long speech he argued that too many powers would still rest with the Colonial Office in London: 'Now, it is impossible for men on our side of the globe to manage the affairs of Englishmen on the other side of the globe without producing dissatisfaction . . . Therefore I infer that we ought to delegate to the colonies *all* local powers, and entitle them to pass any law affecting their local concerns.' The conclusion to his long speech was a testament to his beliefs:

In conclusion, I must assert that our true colonial policy is to have faith in our colonists, and to believe that they are as rational men as we are, and that they understand their own local affairs better than we can; therefore, I maintain that we ought to give them the uncontrolled management of their local affairs, as distinguished from imperial concerns. Then the colonists, freed from the hated tyranny of the Colonial Office, bearing true allegiance to the monarch of these realms, and willingly obeying the laws made by the Imperial Parliament, or by those authorities to whom the Imperial Parliament shall delegate a portion of its legislative powers, would be bound to the British Empire by the strong ties of race, language, interest and affection.

On February 18th he spoke on the second reading of the Australian Government Bill, conceding that it seemed a wise policy for the House to assent to the principle of the Bill, thus showing the Australian colonist that 'we are anxious as speedily as possible to give them the benefit of representative government . . . but that

all questions concerning the powers to be delegated to the colonial
authorities should be carefully considered in Committee'. His speech
ended:

Now, the colonists have no right to interfere in the management of the
local affairs of Great Britain, therefore we ought not to interfere in the
local affairs of the colonies. We are entitled to reserve to ourselves the
management of the common concerns of the empire, because imperial
power must be located somewhere for the maintenance of the unity of
the empire; and because we are the richest and most powerful portion of
the empire, and have to pay for the management of its common concerns.
In thus laying claim to imperial powers for the British Parliament, I must
add that in my opinion it would tend much to consolidate the empire if we
could admit into the Imperial Parliament representatives of the colonies,
for then the colonies would feel that they formed with the British islands
one complete body politic.

A rather startling proposition in that last sentence – and one
which, unlike nearly all the policies advocated by Molesworth in
his lifetime, never subsequently came to pass.

The Australian Government Bill dragged on. On March 22nd,
Spencer Walpole proposed an amendment which Molesworth
supported, but it was defeated by a majority of 51. Another
amendment proposed on April 19th was defeated by a majority
of 68. Then on May 6th Molesworth moved that the Australian
Government Bill should be recommitted and submitted to the
House proposing 'a constitution for New South Wales, and, with
the requisite alterations, for all the other Australian Colonies and
New Zealand'. His motion was defeated by a decisive majority of
123: Ayes 42; Noes 165. Both Gladstone and Disraeli voted in the
minority.

SPRING and early summer-time in London were the breath of life
for Andalusia – intoxicated by the elixir of fashionable pleasures,
sparkling in her success as a London hostess. For William, long
hours at the House of Commons had to be fitted in with being
host at Eaton Place dinners and musical evenings, accompanying
Andalusia to balls and receptions, to late-night suppers after the
Opera, also gay river parties and Thames-side *fêtes champêtres*. His

mornings were spent working on his speeches. And all the time there was the nagging regret that he could not be at Pencarrow at the loveliest time of the year. Early in June he decided to make a dash on his own for a few days at Pencarrow – 'in order to see the rhododendrons in flower, never having seen them in flower.' These were the rhododendrons he had planted in 1842, two years before his marriage, interspersing them with azaleas, all along the mile-long drive. He left London by the evening train to Plymouth on June 11th and arrived at Pencarrow the next day – 'much pleased with the rhododendrons and orchids'. Four days later he made the return journey in thirteen hours: 'Left Pencarrow at 10 o'clock in the morning and arrived Eaton Place at half to 11 o'clock.' He could not be away any longer because Andalusia had arranged a concert at Eaton Place for the next evening: 'artists Mario, Colette; Castleham and Angri. Amateur chorus. Went off very well . . . to bed very tired.' The following evenings there were long debates in the House. On one of these, a motion brought by J.A. Roebuck, the House did not divide until half-past three in the morning.

New names were appearing on the guest list at Eaton Place, including some of the élite of the Whig aristocracy – the Duke of Devonshire, the Marquis of Lansdowne, Lord Palmerston, the Earl of Granville, Lord and Lady Ashburton, Lord and Lady Londesborough. Other new names were those of Mr and Mrs Disraeli and the artist Edwin Landseer, not yet knighted but already painting portraits of the Queen, the Prince Consort and their children. Another new guest was Mr Ford. Was this Richard Ford? The question is relevant because Richard Ford, whose second wife had died the year before, was to marry next year his third wife, Mary Molesworth. At Mary's age, now thirty-five years, this was considered a very suitable match, approved by 'the world' and by both families, the Molesworths and the Fords.

Richard Ford was chiefly known as the author of *A Handbook for Travellers in Spain*, published in 1845 by John Murray in his famous travel guide series. In that year Abraham Hayward, after staying with the Fords near Exeter, wrote to Lady Chatterton: 'I left London more than three weeks ago, and the only conversable people I have met are Sir William and Lady Molesworth far down in Cornwall, and the Fords at Exeter [this was when Richard Ford's

*Whist party at the Ford's house on Nov. 12th, 1856. At the table are Lady
Zetland (Mary Ford's close friend), Mary and Richard Ford, and a
Miss Barclay.*

second wife was still alive]. He has at last finished his handbook,
which is full of pleasant and instructive matter, but very thick and
closely printed.' Lady Duff Gordon was more enthusiastic: 'The
most amusing book this year is Ford's *Handbook of Spain* – one of
the Red Murrays. It is written in a style between Burton's *Anatomy
of Melancholy* and any work by the immortal Sancho Panza, had he
ever written a book; so quaint, so lively and such knowledge of the
country.'

The Ford family was intellectually distinguished. Richard Ford
was a frequent contributor to the *Quarterly* and other monthly
reviews. His son by his first wife was Sir Clare Ford, Ambassador
to the Spanish Court. Richard's younger brother, James, was a
Prebendary of Exeter, wrote poetry and published a translation of
the *Divine Comedia*. the two brothers, James and Richard, were
nicknamed 'Sacred and Profane Ford' by the Nassau Senior family
– the Fords and the Seniors had been friends for several generations.
Mr Senior's daughter, Mrs M.C.M. Simpson, wrote of Richard Ford:
'Although somewhat cynical, a most agreeable companion . . .
slight, dark, Spanish looking, with delicate features. He was full
of wit and fun and very sociable. There were no dinner-parties
more agreeable than his. He was cultivated, as the French say,

down to the end of his finger nails, an accomplished draughtsman and connoisseur.' Disappointingly Mrs Simpson, writing in the late 1890s, did not include in her memoirs anything at all about Richard Ford's marriage to Mary Molesworth – nor, in fact, anything about either of his other two wives.

The Fords' London house was 17 Park Street, Grosvenor Square. In 1834 Richard had bought an Elizabethan cottage called Heavitree House near Exeter, with about twelve acres, which he gradually rebuilt and enlarged. He laid out terraces and gardens with Moorish-patterned flower-borders and planted pines from the Pincian and cypresses from Xenia. This enthusiasm for designing his garden and importing unusual species from other countries was something he had in common with William Molesworth, his new brother-in-law, an affinity to balance against their opposition in politics. The Fords were all deeply entrenched Tories.

All the Senior family, such close friends of the Fords, were equally intimate with the Grotes. Mrs Simpson wrote: 'We lived in the same circle, both in London and in Paris. It often struck me that Queen Elizabeth lived again in Mrs Grote. They both had extraordinary and versatile abilities, strong affections, a great power of ruling, and withal, not a little vanity. I think one liked Mrs Grote all the better for this vanity; it seemed to render her more individual, more human, and to temper the awe she would otherwise have inspired. She had sufficient reason to estimate highly her moral and intellectual qualities, but I believe she set more value on her small foot and Vandyke hand than on any other of her gifts.'

Mrs Simpson continued her recollections of Mrs Grote 'hostessing dinners and musical parties, even dances for young people' and ended, 'Mrs Grote revelled in a love affair, and always sided with the young' – a comment most surely confirmed by Mrs Grote's intimate participation in Sir William's early love affairs.

Considering the friendship between the Grotes and the Fords it might have been expected, or at least hoped, that Mary Molesworth's marriage to Richard Ford would bring about a renewal of friendship between Mary and Mrs Grote, broken so abruptly by William's marriage. But there is no evidence of any *rapprochement*. Perhaps this is not surprising, really, remembering that, according to Mrs Grote, William specifically asked his sister and Lady Molesworth not to receive the Grotes any more. William's wishes were law unto his family, and 'any more' meant never.

At the General Election in the year following Mary's marriage, Molesworth was again returned for the borough of Southwark. In his speech at the opening of his campaign on June 1st 1852, he said he believed that the policies on colonial self-government that he had so long advocated were gaining ground in the House of Commons among enlightened men of all parties. On the sensitive question of parliamentary reform, he stoutly expressed extreme radical goals – the extension of the ballot, a redistribution of seats, the abolition of the property qualification for Members of Parliament – 'the wider the basis on which the Constitution rests, the firmer will it be.' In addition, he defended the income-tax, supported national education, renewed his support for the Maynooth grant and declared himself in favour of all principles of religious toleration. This was at the time when the assumption by the Roman Catholic Church of religious titles in the United Kingdom had led to loud and lewd 'No Popery!' agitation by the populace and to the passing in Parliament of the Ecclesiastical Titles Act. Molesworth concluded his speech with a scorching attack on Lord Derby, the Prime Minister. This was the Lord Derby who had reimposed transportation upon Australia, who for six years had, in Molesworth's opinion, misgoverned the colonies and was responsible for the rebellion in Canada, and who

. . . sowed the seeds of our costly wars in South Africa, and caused the hideous demoralisation of Van Diemen's Land. He was wrong-headed, obstinate, ignorant, rash, reckless and careless of consequences . . . a Free Trader in the towns; a Protectionist in the counties; pro-Maynooth in Ireland, anti-Maynooth in England and Scotland; saying one thing one day, retracting it the next, repeating it the third, equivocating about it the fourth. A political jockey, riding a losing horse, hoping to win by a cross; a thimble-rigger, gammoning clowns and chaw-bacons with the peas of Protection, which will never be found under any one of his thimbles; a truckler to the bigotry he means to betray; the leader of men who have no convictions, whose only rule of political conduct is success, the end and aim of whose existence are the gratification of personal ambition; men long eager for power, surprised at obtaining it, unscrupulous as to the means of retaining it; recreant Protectionists; dishonest Free Traders, hiding insincerity under the mask of intolerance; too pusillanimous to stick by their colours, and not courageous enough to take up a new position . . . Lord Derby, in one of his speeches, likened a statesman to a barque, which trims its sails and alters its course with each changing wind and varying breeze. This is not my notion of a statesman. I liken a true statesman and upright politician to a steam vessel which pursues its steady course amidst storms and waves in defiance of adverse gales and opposing tides, and straightforward reaches its destined port.

Considering Lord Derby was leader of the Liberals, the party to which Molesworth now nominally belonged, this was strong stuff, indicative of his determination to fight his own independent crusades. It was certainly not a speech that would gain him a place in any Cabinet under Lord Derby.

The result of the General Election of 1852 had been a small Liberal majority, which enabled Lord Derby's Cabinet to hold office until December 18th, when they were defeated on the Budget by a majority of nineteen. A coalition government was inevitable since all parties were losing their identity. *The Times* summed up the situation on December 22nd: 'Whig traditions, indeed, hover about a few Whig families; but the very names of Pitt, Fox and Peel have no living significance or representation. It is a matter of common remark that there are now many Conservatives more Radical than professed Reformers, many Whigs more Tory than the professed Conservatives, and many Reformers more so than either. In such a state of things it becomes impossible to govern by parties; and nothing suits the people to be governed and the measures to be passed so well as a good coalition.'

The Queen called upon the Earl of Aberdeen to form a Government. There were, of course, many claimants for Cabinet office; and as the editor of *The Times*, John Delane, was known to be an intimate friend of Lord Aberdeen, many prospective Ministers tried to enlist his influence. One of these was Molesworth. At last, he felt, there was a possibility of achieving the office he would dearly love to hold, and for which his whole parliamentary experience had prepared him – that of Secretary of State for the Colonies. He wrote to Delane: 'I must say that I consider that I should make a great sacrifice in accepting any office except that of Secretary of State for the Colonies.' Delane admired Molesworth's abilities and the determination with which he pursued his belief in self-government for the colonies, and was willing to use his influence with Lord Aberdeen. However it was not the Colonial Office that Lord Aberdeen offered Molesworth, but that of First Commissioner of Works. Molesworth accepted – at least he would be a member of the Cabinet.

Henry Reeve wrote in his journals 'The Cabinet was wisely completed by the admission of Sir William Molesworth as a representative of advanced Liberal opinion. The place first offered was the War Office without the Cabinet, but he resolutely declined it. I endeavoured to persuade him to accept, but he gave some valid reasons for the resolution; and we endeavoured (with Delane) to persuade Ld. Aberdeen to put him in the Cabinet, which he consented to do, even though Cardwell, the President of the Board of Trade, was still excluded.'

And Greville noted in his *Memoirs* on May 30th 1853: 'Granville [then Foreign Secretary] tells me that of the whole Cabinet he thinks Aberdeen has the most pluck, Gladstone a great deal, and Graham the one who has least. He speaks very well of Molesworth, sensible, courageous and conciliatory, but quite independent and plain-spoken in his opinions.'

Sir William wrote to his mother telling her of his appointment, and on the same day to Miss Caroline Molesworth:

                                              87 Eaton Place, Dec.27th 1852

My dear Aunt,

    I am sure it will give you pleasure to learn that Her Majesty has been pleased to appoint me a member of the Privy Council with a seat in the Cabinet. I am to be the First Commissioner of Works and Public Buildings, and therefore shall have charge of the Royal Palaces and all public buildings and offices except those belonging to the Ordnance and Admiralty. I shall also have charge of the parks of the metropolis, of Greenwich, Richmond, Bushey and Phoenix, and Holyrood Palace; and of the public gardens at Kensington, Kew and Hampton Court.

    I shall have to perform many other duties in connection with the improvement of the metropolis. My office is not a very important or highly paid one, nor one for which I have any particular aptitude, but accompanied by a seat in the Cabinet it is one of much dignity, bringing me into personal contact with the Queen. It will likewise make me acquainted with the details of public business, and in all probability will eventually lead to one of the higher offices in the Government of our country. I believe I am to kiss hands tomorrow.

Your affectionate Nephew, William Molesworth.

Perhaps it was disappointment at not being appointed Secretary of State for the Colonies that caused him to tell his Aunt that the Office of First Commissioner of Works was 'not one for which I have any particular aptitude'. Or was he just trying to sound modest? For surely his life-long interest in gardens, extensive study of trees and all kinds of horticulture, also his Fellowship of the Royal Society made him more suitable for the position than any other conceivable appointee. Indeed, as First Commissioner of Works, he was able to apply himself to undertakings altogether congenial to him. He was responsible for the laying out of Victoria Park, and initiated the ornamental gardening in all the other London parks. His official connection with Kew Gardens was of course a delight to him, a delight which he decreed all citizens of London should enjoy every day of the week – Kew Gardens must no longer be closed on Sundays. He knew that this edict would cause Sabbatarian hackles to rise, and would be regarded as an example of his 'evil agnosticism'. But that did not deter him from immediate action, and Kew Gardens have been open on Sundays ever since for the delight of all London's citizens. Even the Sabbatarians soon ceased to growl.

Everything Molesworth fought for in his Parliamentary life came to pass, although not all in his lifetime: abolition of transportation, self-government of the colonies, the ballot, national education and the end of all religious discrimination. Yet, so fickle is fame, it is for his opening of Kew Gardens on Sundays that he is most immediately remembered. On July 7th 1934, the *Bodmin Guardian* published some memories of Sir William by people who had known him or whose parents had known him. One of their anecdotes, almost certainly apocryphal, is nevertheless so charming that it deserves exact repetition: 'Sir William was not ordinarily accustomed to use his carriage on Sunday afternoons. But one Sunday afternoon, having instructed Matthews, his coachman, to have the carriage at his London residence at a certain hour, he drove off to Kew Gardens. When he pulled up at the entrance the gatekeeper came out of his lodge, waved his arms and shouted that the grounds were closed and on no account could he open them on Sunday. "Open the gates!" ordered Sir William. Reluctantly the gatekeeper obeyed. "Drive on!" Sir William commanded his coachman. And for the first time in history, and, indeed, making London history, Kew Gardens were thus opened on Sundays.'

ALMOST immediately after his taking office, Sir William and Andalusia were invited to stay at Windsor Castle, from February 3rd to 5th. On one of the evenings they were entertained by a performance of *Macbeth* in the private theatre; and the Queen seems, from subsequent correspondence, to have taken a warm liking to Andalusia. William spent much time closeted with Prince Albert – 'I found him to be agreeable with pleasing manner.' The Prince's great interest in science, and of course William having studied in Germany, meant they had much in common. They went through the estimates for repairs at the Castle, and discussed plans for improvements to the National Gallery. The Trafalgar Square building, designed by William Wilkins, had been opened in 1838, the collections having been transferred from a gentleman's town house that had been their previous home at 100 Pall Mall. Sir William, thorough as always, undertook to gather the fullest information possible on all the great European galleries, their merits and demerits, specifications, working plans and estimates of costs.

The equestrian statue of the Duke of Wellington by Matthew C. Wyatt and his son James also came under discussion. This huge sculpture nearly thirty feet high was mounted on Decimus Burton's triumphal arch at Hyde Park Corner, the arch that has variously been known as the Wellington, the Pimlico, the Green Park, or the Constitution Arch. The Duke, heavily cloaked and given an exaggeratedly Roman nose, holds a baton pointing straight between the horse's ears. Prince Albert considered the statue a monstrosity and wanted it removed from the Arch. Sir William agreed that it was 'certainly a hideous object' and referred the Prince to Lord Aberdeen – national hero-worship of the Iron Duke meant that his removal from so prominent, so elevated a position was a very delicate decision to make, indeed one of nationwide importance with political back-lash.

Prince Albert did not get his way. It was not until 1883 that the Duke was hauled down from the arch and finally banished to the coppices of Aldershot. Sir Francis Chantry's more pleasing statue of Wellington outside the Royal Exchange in the City has remained in position to this day. Quite recently there have been suggestions that he should be given a more prestigious position, indeed that the most appropriate position would be near Lord Nelson – mounted on that vacant plinth on the north side of Trafalgar Square.

CHAPTER XVIII — 1853-54

GRAVER concerns than Kew Gardens on Sunday and the Duke of Wellington's statue were involving Molesworth from the beginning of 1853. As a member of Lord Aberdeen's Cabinet, he was present at all discussions about the policy to be adopted towards Russia and Turkey. Foreign politics were an area that he had not studied with the dedicated application that he had given for so many years to colonial matters, so it is not surprising that there seems to have been a degree of vacillation in his opinion regarding the wisdom, or folly, of embarking upon hostilities. In his Cabinet diary he noted on June 11th:

'Affairs of Turkey discussed – we are not bound by any treaty to maintain either the independence or integrity of the Ottoman Empire – question simply of policy – in my opinion not worth while to go to war to preserve for a time the life of an empire doomed to speedy destruction – in all probability such a war would hasten the dissolution of the Turkish Empire – if existence of Turkish Empire would be prolonged, a Grecian Empire might ultimately be established – better than a Russian one at Constantinople. I am convinced that if we get involved in a war with Russia, though it may be popular at the outset, it will speedily become unpopular.'

Molesworth was not present at a crucial Cabinet meeting on October 7th. A note from Lord Clarendon to Delane of *The Times* after that meeting says that if Molesworth had been present he would undoubtedly have sided with Lord Palmerston, who was in favour of declaring war. Does that mean that Molesworth had changed his mind since his diary note in June? – Or was Clarendon mistaken? Lord Aberdeen, while yielding to the majority in his Cabinet who were pressing for an active policy, continued to hope for a peaceful solution right up to the spring of 1854 when war broke out.

A.I. Dasent, in his editing of Delane's letters, comments that

'Sir William Molesworth had become one of the most warlike of Ministers'. On the other hand, Mrs Fawcett, in her life of Sir William, wrote 'Long afterwards, in a public speech in 1887, Bright said: "Lord Aberdeen told me that in the whole Cabinet of which he was the chief there was only one man who backed him up in the slightest degree in favour of peace, and that was Sir William Molesworth." ' Well, both these accounts are hearsay. It is safer to judge his attitude by his own diary note of June 11th – and then accept that, once war was declared, he was enthusiastic for its active prosecution.

Certainly he was seen to have made a *volte-face* by the 'peace-at-any-price' party, whose leaders were some of his old associates in the House of Commons. Bright was particularly scathing, charging Molesworth with inconsistency; and Cobden launched a fierce attack in the House of Commons in which he challenged him to read aloud a speech he had made at Leeds, fifteen years before, in favour of peace. That was at the time when it seemed possible that England and France could go to war over the Eastern question. Molesworth accepted the challenge, and a few days later read extracts from his Leeds speech to the House showing that, on the contrary, he had spoken strongly for an *alliance* with France against Russia for the protection of Turkey: 'We have formed an alliance with Russia, whose interests are hostile to our own in the East. We have lost the alliance of France, the only European power which has an interest equally strong, and a desire equally urgent with ourselves to prevent the occupation of Constantinople by Russia. Who does not perceive that every wound inflicted in France by England, or in England by France, must be a source of rejoicing to the northern barbarian – an obstacle removed from his path to Constantinople?'

Molesworth's concluding extract from his speech of fifteen years earlier was 'Let us say to Russia, we will not permit you to make an attempt to assume to yourself the sovereignty of the Turkish Empire. If you presume to interfere in affairs which are not your own and menace Constantinople, France, united with England, will compel you to desist.'

There is an echo in this of a belligerent letter the young William wrote home from Germany when he was eighteen: 'If there should be a war with Russia I should join the army – a Horse Regiment – slaying Cossacks.'

Home affairs, during these crisis months, were pushed aside in the House of Commons – unnecessarily, Molesworth considered. In January 1854, before war was declared, he had initiated a discussion on the new Reform Bill which was not at all well attended. He proposed representation for the allocation of more urban seats: two to Chelsea and Kensington, one to Salford, one to Edinburgh and one to Glasgow; Middlesex and North Lancashire to have one, not four, additional seats each. He noted in his diary 'Gladstone wished to give another member to each of the Universities. I said that I would rather disenfranchise them.' Molesworth certainly could, at times, set hackles rising. Nothing came of the discussion, the subject being dropped as all attention focussed on the Crimea. Six months later, on June 13th, Molesworth once more tried to get the attention of the House on home affairs. His Cabinet diary comment about it was bitter: 'I made a strong and long speech in the House on the subject of the ballot. My object in so doing was to strengthen my position which had been weakened by silence, and to show that I had not wavered in any of my opinions. A report had been got up probably by Whig intrigue that I was to be shelved with a Peerage. My ballot speech was much liked by most persons except my colleagues.'

One way and another, this summer session was frustrating, dispiriting and more than usually exhausting. There was just one satisfactory achievement: Molesworth sought and obtained from Parliament the necessary funds for rebuilding Westminster Bridge.

IT MUST have been a relief when Parliament was dissolved at the beginning of August. London society also, as was customary, dispersed. Some went to their country estates, some to Continental spas to adjust their health by 'taking the waters' – very necessary for those who had over-indulged in the excesses of the London season. Some made for the moors of Yorkshire or the Highlands of Scotland with invitations from friends to fish and, from August 12th, to shoot – or just to benefit by the bracing air. Doubtless William Molesworth's desire was to benefit by the bracing air of

Cornwall, by the sweet silences of Pencarrow, the balm of his
peaceful gardens, his leather-scented library. Andalusia's desire,
however, was always to do the 'done thing'. It was not in her
nature to refuse invitations from fashionable friends. In August of
the previous year they had been invited to stay with Sir John and
Lady Young in Ireland. They had set out on the 22nd for Holyhead,
staying some days at Bangor on the way; but on reaching Holyhead,
'my wife was deterred from crossing by the storminess of the weather
– we returned to Bangor and finally to London on the 30th August.'
Then there was the long journey to Cornwall. Two wasted summer
weeks.

Now, in this summer of 1854, they made for the Highlands, with
invitations to stay first at Taymouth, Keir and then at Glen Quoich,
Invergowrie, the house of Edward Ellice, known by his friends as
Bear Ellice. At Glen Quoich a fellow guest was Lord Stanley; and
in the malicious style in which the Stanley family enjoyed writing
to each other, he reported to his wife: 'The company here not
amusing. That pedantic and awkward statesman Sir W. Molesworth,
his vulgar spouse, with more imperials and band boxes than would
fit out Lady Aylesbury for a Paris campaign – Nassau Senior and his
daughter, the former instructive but boring, the latter an insipid
statistical young lady. If the Molesworths haunt Scotland I shall for
the future fly the country.'

Happily we have another account of the Glen Quoich house party.
The daughter of Nassau Senior (Lord Stanley's 'insipid statistical
young lady') wrote in her memoirs many years later:

In 1854 we went to Scotland. First to Glen Quoich, the house of the
gentle Bear Ellice. Why he was nicknamed the 'Bear' I never could tell,
except that he had very shaggy eyebrows . . . Among the guests were
Sir William and Lady Molesworth. He was extremely pleasant, simple and
kind, and she was good nature itself and a very accommodating travelling
companion. From Glen Quoich we went to Dunrobin . . . It was in the
days of Harriet, Duchess of Sutherland, the Mistress of the Robes and
friend of the Queen. We used to breakfast in a gallery overlooking the
sea, the pipers playing under the window. We next went to Keir, where we
fell in with the Molesworths again, and we travelled together to Inverary.

In consequence of various misadventures, we approached Inverary at
midnight. We rowed across the loch and walked round and round the
castle, trying to effect an entrance. We had long been given up and we

ought to have been ashamed of ourselves for our untimely arrival, but we were so fascinated by the grandeur of the scene that we were not, I fear, sufficiently penitent.

What happened, one wonders, to all Andalusia's imperials and band boxes throughout their 'various misadventures'?

Whereas the Seniors evidently liked the Molesworths, it seems that Lady Stanley shared her husband's antipathy. She wrote to him from Taymouth on October 6th: 'We have been very well amused with expeditions and pleasant society until yesterday's addition, but Lady Molesworth *me donne sur les nerfs,* she is so ultra-ministerial. However she went to bed last night soon after 9 o'clock.'

An important reason for the Molesworths to be in Scotland this autumn was that Sir William was to be honoured by the Freedom of the City of Edinburgh. It was conferred upon him as a compliment to his position in the Cabinet and in recognition of his distinguished public work. In his speech on receiving the honour, he spoke of his connection with Edinburgh, both by birth and by education:

By birth I am half a Scotchman. I am proud of my Scotch blood, and of belonging to the same family as David Hume, the historian and philosopher. In the University of Edinburgh I was educated under Leslie, Jamieson and other eminent professors. In my youth I was so fortunate as to enjoy the acquaintance and to profit by the conversation of Sir Walter Scott, Jeffrey, Brewster, Sir William Hamilton, Sir John Sinclair, James Mill and other distinguished Scotchmen. I am therefore attached to Edinburgh by feelings of gratitude, affection and admiration; and the strength of those feelings has not diminished by an absence of many years. Since I left Edinburgh I have visited many of the most celebrated cities in Europe, but none of them ever appeared to me to compare in beauty with the metropolis of Scotland.

It must have been a proud day for William's mother, whose decision it had been to take the young baronet to Edinburgh, the city of her birth, for his education.

BY the time Parliament had re-assembled in the late autumn of 1854, the anger of the whole nation had been aroused by reports from Scutari in *The Times,* whose correspondent William Howard Russell was the first reporter ever to have been allowed with the forces. There was no military censorship, and Russell's vivid revelations of the conditions being experienced by the troops came as a terrible shock to the newspaper's readers, who were accustomed to read of nothing but the glory and gallantry of British soldiers, the brilliance of their commanders. Now, in despatches on October 9th, 12th and 13th, Russell revealed the true horrors being endured. Passionately he described the sufferings:

Not only are there not sufficient surgeons . . . not only are there no dressers and nurses . . . there is not even linen to make bandages . . . no preparations for the commonest surgical operations: not only are the men kept, in some cases for a week, without the hand of a medical man coming near their wounds, not only are they left to expire in agony, unheeded and shaken off, though catching desperately at the surgeon as he makes his rounds through the fetid ship, but now . . . it is found that the commonest appliances of a workhouse sick ward are wanting, and the men must die through the medical staff of the British Army having forgotten that old rags are necessary for the dressing of wounds. . . . The worn-out pensioners who were brought as an ambulance corps are totally useless . . . and there are no dressers or nurses to carry out the surgeons' directions and to attend the sick.

In England there were two reactions to Russell's revelations of the plight of the wounded and victims of cholera – also of the mismanagement of the whole campaign, the bungling ineptitude of the commissioners and the disagreements of commanding officers. One reaction was that of those who considered *The Times* was right to publish them; the other was that of those who declared the reports should have been censored. Among the latter was Molesworth. A.I. Dasent writes of him sending a letter to *The Times'* editor, J.T. Delane, 'imploring him to exercise a more rigid censorship over Russell's letters, repeating the parrot cry, which originated in the War Office, that by describing in detail the sufferings of the troops and by denouncing the want of energy in the dispatch of reinforcements, the paper was playing into the hands of the enemy, and providing the Czar with information which it would be desirable to suppress.'

Sir William's close friends the Austins and the Duff Gordons were also in favour of censorship, strongly influenced by Kinglake who championed the fiercely-attacked Lord Raglan: 'Flesh and blood cannot endure the incessant baiting', wrote Sarah Austin. 'The next despotism the world will have to undergo is that of the Press.' But championship of the commanders in the field was certainly not Molesworth's reason for deploring the accounts of mismanagement and unnecessary suffering. It was that he feared the accounts must be of help and comfort to the enemy. And it is relevant to recall here the impassioned speech he made to the House on May 3rd 1836 (quoted in part in Chapter III). In that speech he had moved a motion that a select committee be appointed to enquire into the conduct of the Commander-in-Chief of the Forces in appointing Lieutenant-Colonel Lord Brudenell to the Lieutenant-Colonelcy of the 11th Light Dragoons – Lord Brudenell having been removed from the command of the 15th Hussars by court martial for misconduct. His motion was thrown out, Lord Brudenell's appointment was confirmed. The following year Brudenell succeeded his father and became the 7th Earl of Cardigan – and it was Lord Cardigan who was in command of the Light Brigade at the time of its disastrous charge at Balaclava.

On January 26th 1855, J.A. Roebuck, now Radical Member for Sheffield, brought forward a motion for the appointment of a committee 'to inquire into the condition of the Army before Sebastopol and the conduct of those departments of the Government whose duty it has been to minister to the wants of that Army'. It was a motion of censure on the Government. Lord John Russell, Secretary for War, used this motion as an excuse to resign from the Cabinet. His colleagues considered he had not so much resigned as absconded. Roebuck likened him to a general who, refusing an action in the presence of the enemy, throws down his truncheon and quits the field; then Roebuck advocated, without speaking disrespectfully of Lord Aberdeen, that Lord Palmerston should take his place. The Government was defeated on Roebuck's motion of censure by a majority of 157, more than two to one. Lord Aberdeen at once resigned. The Queen sent for Lord Derby, who did not feel able to form a ministry. Next Lord John Russell was sent for. He attempted to form one, but soon found that his desertion of Lord Aberdeen upon Roebuck's motion had lost him the support of all his Whig friends. Finally the Queen sent for the seventy-year-old Lord Palmerston, who consented to form a ministry.

Lord John Russell was made Secretary of State for the Colonies when he returned from the Vienna Conference. This conference had been arranged with the object of bringing about a cessation of hostilities; but the part Russell had played at it was considered by most people to have been feebly inadequate, and the speeches he made upon his return to be inconsistent with the line he had taken in Vienna. In July, Sir Edward Bulwer Lytton gave notice of a vote of censure on Lord John Russell's conduct of the negotiations. Russell, anticipating that the motion would succeed, resigned his office and left the Government. His place as Secretary of State for the Colonies was offered by Lord Palmerston to Sir William Molesworth.

CHAPTER XIX — 1855

SO – at the age of forty-five Molesworth had attained the office upon which his heart was set, for which his whole parliamentary career had been preparing him, and in which he felt he could best serve Great Britain and her empire. There was universal approval of the appointment; he was seen to be the right man in the right place. As *The Times* wrote on July 22nd 1855, 'It would be difficult to exaggerate the service which during his Parliamentary career the new Colonial Secretary had rendered to the cause of the Colonies, and the degree in which, by so doing, he had consolidated and conciliated the remoter portions of this great Empire . . . If not the founder, he may be fairly termed the regenerator and purifier of that great group of dependencies . . . Much will be expected of such a Minister, and Sir William Molesworth must be indefatigable and successful if he overcomes the formidable rivalry of his own already achieved reputation.'

The transfer of a Minister from one office to another necessitated, at that time, that he seek re-election. Sir William was returned without opposition for Southwark, but a speech which he made to his constituents caused the renewal of a quarrel between himself and the extreme 'peace party' in the House. The subject was a Turkish loan. Three usually antagonistic parties had united in an attempt to defeat the Government: the 'Peace Party', represented by Cobden and Bright; the 'Peelites', who had lately resigned office, represented by Gladstone and Sidney Herbert; and the Conservatives. Molesworth in his Southwark speech had implied that such an unlikely combination smelt of conspiracy. When he returned to the House on August 3rd, Cobden opened the assault by declaring that Molesworth was inconsistent and 'utterly unworthy of the confidence of any political party'. Gladstone followed with a speech in which he said the combination of parties voting against the Government on the Turkish loan had been accidental, not concerted, and therefore had none of the elements of a conspiracy.

Molesworth in his reply accepted Gladstone's word unreservedly; but in reference to Cobden's attack of inconsistency he declared that, while he had been thoroughly at one with the honourable gentleman the Member for the West Riding on the subject of Free Trade, he had *never* shared his views on the possibility of universal peace. Cobden replied with a refusal to withdraw the charges he had made. 'Peace-at-any-Price' men seldom agree to a cease-fire on verbal hostilities.

This somewhat irrelevant hassle was not a happy beginning for Molesworth in his new position; and it must have played a part in undermining his always vulnerable health. The whole of the last year had been a time of accumulating political stress combined with the escalating social obligations that his wife saw no reason to curtail – indeed, saw reason to extend now that he was a Cabinet Minister. His first, and what was to be his only, official act in the House as Colonial Secretary was, on the advice of Sir George Grey, then Governor of Cape Colony, to move a vote of £40,000 to be used for educating and otherwise improving the condition of the Kaffirs. This was moved and carried on the same day, July 18th, at the very end of the summer session.

Nearly always by the time Parliament rose for the summer recess Molesworth was in a state of mental and physical exhaustion. This year, unlike other years, he felt unable to leave London in August. He needed to accustom himself to the responsibilities of his new office, and there was the extra work-load on the whole Cabinet caused by the mounting crisis in the Crimea. He remained in London throughout a hot sultry August and into September. Physically, he was living on his capital, which was fast being reduced. But on September 10th he had the happiness of being able to write to his sister from the Colonial Office:

My dear Mary,
   The south side of Sebastopol has fallen. I send you the telegraph message just received: *Varna, September 9, 9.30.* During the night the Russians have sunk all the remainder of the line of battleships in the harbour. Sebastopol is in the possession of the Allies. The enemy during the night have evacuated the south side after exploding their magazines and setting fire to the whole of the town. All the men-of-war were burnt during the

night, with the exception of three steamers which are flying about the harbour.

The first stages of his illness were assumed to be just a combination of physical and nervous exhaustion, both of which would be cured by a period of rest. Unwisely, Andalusia did not consider it necessary to call a doctor. It was quite clear, however, that he was in no condition to undertake the long journey to Cornwall, and she persuaded him that a visit to Brighton was the best alternative – the sea air would revive him and he would be able to rest quietly. Brighton, however, was neither quiet nor restful if what Joseph Parkes later wrote in a letter to Cobden is to be believed: 'She has been his death. His house, even at Brighton when ill, was a Café – a continual round of company and excitement to a feeble frame, and she kept him in blinkers.'

What Parkes was implying in that last sentence can only be conjectured. Molesworth evidently did attempt to do some work while at Brighton, because the last Cabinet Minute in his handwriting was found on his writing table there and sent up to London on October 18th, four days before his death. Appropriately, the Minute was concerned with the colonies.

Even when they returned to London, it seems that Andalusia was not sufficiently alarmed about William's condition to call his doctor. This was only at last done to placate Mary Ford's distraught pleading, as is shown by an undated letter from Mary to her friend Lady Zetland. This must be quoted in full, since it is the only existing account of William's final days. It was addressed from 41 Lowndes Square, Monday:

The last act of the tragedy is nearly played out and William will soon be no more. He is ill unto death and all hope is gone. For the last six weeks he had been ailing from violent bilious attacks, but as no skilled medical advice was called in I hoped, although uneasy, there was nothing amiss and that these attacks proceeded from an over excited system. Still last week I begged Lady Molesworth would send for Elliotson, or if there was any dislike of him why not try Ferguson. On Monday this advice was acted on. Ferguson came and pronounced William was suffering from gastric fever and most dangerously ill. This was written to me. On Tuesday I came up. I asked that Elliotson might be called in. My prayer was granted. Elliotson has been for twenty years in constant attendance, had pulled him through desperate illness and knew his constitution thoroughly. On Wednesday Elliotson said all hope was gone. He is dying in the most heroic manner with all his faculties about him perfectly resigned and leaves his wealth, his great position, the ambition of his life granted, without a murmur. Yet he has struggled hard for life.

12 o'clock

He still lives but sinking rapidly. Last night when he saw the doctors, he held out his damp cold hand and said, 'Here is a piece of dead flesh' – if he had a particle of constitution left he might have been saved, for the disease has been conquered but the life he has led of constant excitement for the last year and a half without an hour's repose has destroyed him – Oh vanity of vanities.

I have seen him once, he held out his hand to me. I kissed it twice. The face looks so handsome – all fullness gone. The beautiful features so wasted have become quite sculpturesque. The eye is not blue – but the most lovely violet – he suffers no pain. He swallowed during the night a pint of milk – but refuses all stimulants when Johnston the surgeon offered him them this morning. He looked him full in the face and said 'I will take it if you will swear to me I have a chance of life.' He reasons most lucidly. My mother bears up like a Roman Matron and is grand in her sorrow. I have written to you the . . . of my . . . him.

Yrs. affectionately, M. Ford.

Two words in her last sentence are indecipherable. At the same time Richard Ford, Mary's husband, was writing to Henry Unwin from Addington on Oct. 21st 'His system never very strong, has succumbed to a long and late session, to which the overwork of a new office was added just at the moment when repose and the country were most wanting . . . Oh the vanity of vanities! Look at poor Sir William, a young man stretched on his bed and wrestling with death with the heart of a lion, and this just the moment when all his honours were budding thick and the object of a life's honourable ambition gained.'

Another letter from Mary to Lady Zetland, written after her brother's death on October 22nd, tells of his last moments:

October 24th 1855

My dear Lady Zetland,

The great mortal only expired with his last breath. He laid himself out and desired no one should touch him after death. At twelve, as Mrs Cooper, Lady Molesworth's maid who never left him night nor day, went to the door of his room, she was recalled by hearing 'Cooper' said in a quick sharp tone – She rushed to the bed, when my brother convulsively grasped one of her hands, and raising it closed with it one eye while with his remaining hand he performed himself the same last office on the other lid – and then heaved a sigh and the great spirit was . . . [indecipherable].

Our roof is indeed overshadowed. He gave every direction about his funeral – to be plain and unostentatious – to be buried as a gentleman, in some bright sunny spot and that his tomb might be of Cornish granite.

His old servant Maclean was summoned by his dying master with a smile and a parting shake of hands. When all was over the faithful old man shut himself up with the body and stayed the long night with the loved remains, weeping over his bible.

Mary's letter seems to imply that Andalusia was never a watcher in the sick-room, that William did not even ask for her at the end. This may, or may not, have been the case. Allowance must be made for the intense bitterness Mary felt towards Andalusia, whom she believed to be responsible for the early death of her adored brother. William's request to be buried in 'some bright sunny spot' echoes his vow at the time of Elizabeth's death not to be buried in the 'baneful and noxious ancestral tomb' which filled him with loathing; instead to be buried in 'a favourite spot in my grounds under the clear sky'. Now, on his death-bed in London, his thoughts must have travelled to that favourite place in his grounds at Pencarrow.

The 'bright sunny spot' chosen for him by Andalusia was the then fashionable Kensal Green Cemetery at Paddington. With the gas-works in the background and the railway running alongside. As Geoffrey Fletcher wrote of this melancholy, urban cemetery, 'The noise of the railway and the gas-works drowns the song of the birds who hop about the obelisks and mausolea.' Sir William's grave is in one of these mausolea. The door unlocks to a shaft some twenty feet deep, at the foot of which his coffin lies – covered, thirty-four years later, by that of Andalusia. The inscription over the door reads: Sir William Molesworth, Bart.
Born XXIII May MDCCCX
Died XXII October MDCCCLV

A firm adherence to convictions, the result of deep thought, won for him the title of an honest statesman aspiring to regenerate the colonial system. He lived to see his principles established. His early death prevented the completion of his purpose but he left a name his country will remember.

The inscription was composed by his close friend and solicitor, Thomas Woollcombe of Devonport.

FROM all the obituaries in the national press, just a few sentences from that of a correspondent to the *Weekly Dispatch* can be picked out as particularly moving:

We lose in him the entire Radical element of the Cabinet. In that arcanum, he was the anchor and stronghold of democratic principles. Clear and decided in principle, he was practically firm and unyielding. With him in the Cabinet, we felt that the people had indeed a share in the government of the country. . . . By birth he belonged to the aristocracy, but the popular elements in his nature were developed and confirmed by the sunshine and the storms of democracy. In the shiftings and shufflings of political change, we could look to him and say, 'Molesworth is there; 'tis all right, or will soon come right.' The country can ill afford to lose such men at the present crisis, and to lose them too in the very prime and vigour of life. . . . We mourn the reach of thought and the integrity of principle that we have lost. We miss the man.

It was over a week after Sir William's funeral that news reached Australia, not of his death, but of his appointment as Secretary of State for the Colonies. On November 3rd, the *Adelaide Observer* voiced the great satisfaction, indeed the rejoicing, at his appointment to 'a position for which he is eminently adapted above most men of the day . . . all agree that at last the right man is in the right place'. It was not until well into the following year that they learned Sir William was dead. The *Melbourne Newspaper* expressed the loss felt by *all* the colonies: 'Very rarely does any man die whose death is regarded as a public misfortune over so large part of the earth's surface as has been the case with respect to that of Sir William Molesworth. In all climates, and in both hemispheres, the news of his untimely end must have been mourned as that of a man who, after years of probation, has been cut off in the hour of success, and when opportunities of public usefulness – the great purpose of his life – had just opened around him in the direction most congenial to his habits of thought and in the course his political studies had taken.'

PART THREE

1855 – 1888

ANDALUSIA AFTER WILLIAM

That congregated mass of folly, that busy fretful turmoil of conflicting littlenesses which they call 'Society'.

T.H. Lister, *Arlington*

Each autumn Pencarrow was filled with much of what is called the best society in London. Wit, beauty and fashion could not hold us all, and once I was made to sleep in a bothy next door to some snoring gardeners, who kept me awake all night.

Hon. F. Leveson Gower, *Recollections*

Lady Molesworth, although by no means brilliantly intellectual herself, possessed a mysterious power of drawing out clever people and making them talk – a special quality of the highest possible value . . . The way in which she managed to get anyone of exceptional brilliancy or interest, no matter what rank or nationality, to come to her parties was quite wonderful.

Lady Dorothy Neville, *Reminiscences*

CHAPTER XX — 1855-1910

IN HIS Will, Sir William bequeathed to Andalusia everything that did not belong to the Molesworth Trust Estates. She became owner of 'My Leasehold House, number 87 Eaton Place, and all other premises comprised in the Lease made to me by Thomas Cubitt'; also 'All Furniture, Plate, Linen, China, Glass, Prints, Pictures, Bronzes, Statues, Jewels, Articles of Vertu, Carriages, Carriage and Saddle Horses with the Harness and accoutrements belonging thereto, Wines, Liquors, Fuel, consumable Provisions and Brewing Utensils and other Household Effects' . . . in fact everything in the house except certain articles named in the Will as being Molesworth heirlooms. He confirmed the £1,000 a year jointure made to his wife on their marriage, and bequeathed to her a legacy of £10,000. The only other bequests were a £1,000 annuity for his sister Mary Ford, a £50 annuity for his servant Duncan Maclean and the continuance of various small annuities to retired gamekeepers, grooms and gardeners.

This Will could be cited as evidence that William's love for Andalusia was deep and enduring. More cynically, it could be interpreted as a final retort to those who had deplored his choice of a wife. The clause which caused most consternation to the Molesworth family was: 'I declare that my wife during her life and my sister Mrs Ford after shall be at liberty to reside in my Mansion House of Pencarrow' . . . and he directed that 'Whether they reside there or not, my Trustees shall keep up my said Mansion House and the Stables, Office and Garden walls thereto belonging in good repair; but I empower my said wife (and also in such event as aforesaid) my sister Mrs Ford to decide whether the Hothouses, Greenhouses and Ornamental Gardens and Pleasure Grounds shall or shall not be kept up or restored – and I direct my Trustees to be guided by their decision in that respect.' The income from the estates beyond what the Trustees considered necessary for their maintenance 'in manner heretofore' was to be paid to his wife during her lifetime her separate use independently of any husband whom she may marry.'

Thus the heir to the baronetcy, his cousin the Revd. Hugh Henry Molesworth, could not take up residence at Pencarrow until both Andalusia and Mary were dead. In fact, he never got to Pencarrow since he himself died in 1862. Nor did his brother Paul William, 10th Baronet, who died in 1889, less than a year after Andalusia. The 11th Baronet, Lewis Molesworth, Unionist MP for South East Cornwall from 1900-'06, waited twenty-two years before Mary Ford died in her ninety-seventh year in 1910 – only to die himself in 1912 before moving into Pencarrow.

It was indeed a perversion of fate that Andalusia, who had only been a Molesworth for eleven years, should reign alone at Pencarrow for thirty-three years after Sir William's death – that so early death for which the Molesworths, and most of his friends, believed her to be responsible. Was not 87 Eaton Place sufficient for her? – that great London house which William had bought and extravagantly furnished entirely in response to her ambition to be a great London hostess? As they foretold, she spent most of the year in London with frequent visits to Paris; her sojourns at Pencarrow were rare, except in the late summer and early autumn months when her country house-parties took place.

A leather-bound household account book shows that entertaining at Eaton Place was resumed as early as seven months after Sir William's death. It gives dates of dinners, names of guests – also of Andalusia's engagements elsewhere – as well as listing monthly payments for provisions (butcher, baker, grocer, butterman, fishmonger, dairy-man, poulterer) and expenditure by the housekeeper and by Monsieur Blanc the resident chef. On the account-book's fly-leaf there is an inscription in Andalusia's handwriting: A. Molesworth, November 8th 1855, from George Torrington. Since that date is little more than two weeks after Sir William's death, it seems an odd gift for Viscount Torrington to make to the widow, a gift suggestive, perhaps, of friendship sufficiently close for there to be little shared jokes between them – such as Andalusia's extravagance, a subject of gossip in society, a running sore to the Molesworth family. Torrington may have presented the account-book to her with a warning that now *she* must

XV *7th Viscount Torrington — full-page cartoon by 'Spy' in* Vanity
Fair, *April 15th 1876.*
Extract from the magazine's text: *'He is an admitted authority on
nice points, and a judge of hard cases in the social code. The world
has not been unkind to him; and his lot has been cast in pleasant
places; and though poor he has found many kind friends who have
been better than many fortunes to him.'*
*The original of Spy's cartoon, in colour, is at Pencarrow, and has
written at the foot in Mary Ford's handwriting, 'Very like'.*

XVI *Andalusia Lady Molesworth
by E.M. Underdown, 1863.*

*Andalusia in a pony-chaise, with her house-guests. Lord Torrington
is the tall figure pointing.*

XVII   *Picnic party sitting perilously at a cliff edge.*

House-party guests setting out from Pencarrow to visit a local beauty spot, in very Cornish weather.
Sketches by guests in the Visitors' Book.

XVIII *Two postcards sent to Lady Molesworth by the artist E.M. Underdown. Preserved in the Visitors' Book*

watch expenses. Hitherto it had always been William who supervised them. Such a jokey gesture would seem insensitive so soon after his death; but Andalusia cannot have thought so since she wrote the date and donor on the fly-leaf.

George Byng, 7th Viscount Torrington, was Lord of the Bedchamber to King William IV, then Lord in Waiting to the young Queen Victoria. It was he whom she chose to escort Prince Albert to England for the royal marriage. In 1847, Torrington was appointed Governor of Ceylon. Attacked by the Foreign Office for measures he had taken to suppress an insurrection, he returned in 1850 to England and defended himself with complete success. In the House of Lords he was a consistent supporter of all Liberal and free-trade measures, so he and Sir William were political allies and he was a frequent guest at Eaton Place. The personalities of the two men, however, were in total contrast. Torrington became Lord in Waiting to the Prince Consort from 1853. Well-placed in the royal corridors, he was a witty raconteur of near-the-knuckle court gossip,

Lord Torrington. From a daguerreotype by Kilburn. Illustrated London News, *June 7th, 1851.*

and therefore was much sought after by London hostesses. Lady Longford, in her biography of Queen Victoria, describes him as 'a gossiping courtier'; Lady St Helier called him 'a whispering gallery'. He was married, but his wife rarely accompanied him in society. She was, however, included in an October 1866 house-party at Bowood, the Marquis of Lansdowne's seat. Lady Stanley, also there, wrote to her husband: 'Lady Torrington, whom I had always supposed to be in delicate health, is a strong, loud vulgar woman.' This seems to throw light on Torrington being so seldom accompanied by his wife in society. She was not a wife to do him credit. Ill-health would be politely assumed. Another clue is in the diary of Chichester Fortescue, January 6th 1852: 'Talked to the Poodle [nickname for James Byng, Torrington's uncle] about Torrington. He asked me if he had 'made love to the hostess of Nuneham?' [Frances Countess Waldegrave]. Said he had been at that kind of thing all his life, began with the Duchess of Somerset, who was mad about him, married Miss Astley! – "I can't think why he did such a thing" said the Poodle.' Miss Astley, of course, was the 'strong, loud vulgar woman' of Lady Stanley's letter. She was the daughter of Sir John Dugdale Astley, Bart. Torrington was twenty-two when he married her in 1833.

Inevitably the friendship of Andalusia and Torrington came to be regarded, after Sir William's death, as a liaison – as were so many extra-marital friendships in society, some of which may never have trespassed beyond the bounds of *amitiés amoureuses*. It was a generation that had matured as Georgians, not Victorians; affairs, as long as they did not lead to open scandal and divorce, were an accepted part of the aristocratic code. Lord Palmerston, to take just one example, after a long well-known liaison with Emily Lady Cowper, Lord Melbourne's sister, eventually married her in 1839 after Lord Cowper's death – and as Lady Palmerston she was the leading political hostess of her day. Nevertheless, it does seem that Andalusia over-stepped the rules in being seen travelling, less than a year after her husband's death, with Lord Torrington in Paris. Chichester Fortescue noted in his diary, October 6th 1856: 'All of us to the Bois de Boulogne and Pré Catalan, just opened, very gay with flowers; met Lady Molesworth (Andalusia) and Torrington, travelling together!' Etiquette will have required the widow to be still wearing mourning. Black can be very becoming if the complexion is good, and Andalusia was young for a widow – a vivacious forty-six, a widow in full bloom. Perhaps she felt mourning clothes were a defence against gossip . . . Torrington was just acting as her escort. She *must* have an escort – *never* had she travelled abroad without William.

Before that trip to Paris, the dinners at Eaton Place had gathered momentum during the London season of 1856. The account-book recorded ever longer and more impressive guest lists. For instance, on April 9th: 'Ld. Aberdeen, Mr and Mrs Gladstone, Bishop of St Albans, Ld. Panmure and 18 others'; on May 13th, 'the Chancellor of the Exchequer, Ld. and Ly Palmerston, Bishop of Oxford, the Sardinian Minister, the Marchioness of Londonderry'. And of course there were return invitations: February 19th, dined at Lord Lansdowne's: April 6th at Baron Rothschild's. By July the dinners had increased in frequency and in size – fifteen guests on July 10th, four equally large parties following in the same month. In contrast, on July 16th, Lord Torrington dined with Andalusia alone. Also in July, on Sunday 19th, Andalusia went by boat to Greenwich in a party of nine, of which Mr Delane, editor of *The Times* was one. Delane was a friend of Sir William's and had often dined at Eaton Place. Now, according to A.I. Dasent, editor of Delane's diaries, 'he visited Lady Molesworth nearly every week during the season'. Also, this diary records, 'Delane joined Lady Molesworth and Lord Torrington at dinners and other parties and expeditions in Paris in September 1861'.

ABOUT fifteen months after William's death there was an attempt to mend the breach between the Molesworths and Andalusia. A note in the diary on January 22nd 1857 reads simply: 'I dined with the Dowager'. Andalusia herself, of course, was also the Dowager Lady Molesworth, but in the diary 'the Dowager' is William's mother. The original motivation for the *rapprochement* may have been to discuss estate matters, since on the following Sunday Mr Woollcombe from Devonport, one of the Trustees, dined at Eaton Place. Then on Friday 30th a dinner party of seventeen guests included the Dowager and the new baronet, Sir Hugh Molesworth with his wife; also Lady West, wife of Sir John West, Andalusia's first husband's brother. Lord Torrington was there accompanied, unusually, by his wife.

The following week Sir Hugh and Lady Molesworth dined again, with three other guests, including Lord Torrington. Finally in this period of reconciliation the Dowager was present at a Sunday night dinner on February 22nd with eighteen other guests. Notable for their absence from all these dinners were Mr and Mrs Richard Ford. Certainly Andalusia will have invited them; just as certainly Mary will have refused. Her hostility was final. There is just one more entry of the Dowager dining, in July of this year; but there is no way of telling whether there were any further meetings – although, worthy of her Scottish ancestry, she lived on in splendid health until 1877, her ninety-ninth year. One effect of her long life was that at one time there were four Lady Molesworths alive: herself, Andalusia, Sir Hugh's widow and the wife of his brother Paul William who succeeded as 10th baronet.

ANDALUSIA'S chief rival as hostess was Frances, Countess Waldegrave, but she was a friend as well as a rival, since they had known each other from girlhood. Frances was a daughter of John Braham, the celebrated tenor with whom 'Miss Grant' had made her *début* at Drury Lane and with whom she had sung duets at the Bath Assembly Room concerts. Both girls had from socially unpropitious beginnings achieved positions in society beyond the dreams of snobbery. Frances first married the illegitimate brother of the 7th Earl of Waldegrave, then married the Earl when his brother died. When the Earl himself died, he bequeathed to Frances the Waldegrave estate at Dudbrook, also 7 Carlton Gardens in London and Strawberry Hill at Twickenham, the Gothic villa built by Horace Walpole that had become a Waldegrave property. Her third marriage was to elderly, wealthy George Granville Harcourt of Nuneham Park in Essex. Frances continued to be known as Countess Waldegrave. When Harcourt died in 1861 she married Chichester Fortescue, who became Lord Carlington.

Sir Robert Morier described Frances as 'a young wife with immense fortune, beauty and accomplishments, whims without end, gigantic animal spirits, the world-spoiled child with every denomination of admirer flitting about her.' The house-parties at Strawberry Hill and Nuneham were unconventional gatherings, thought by some to be 'too, too beyond – but oh so amusing'. Andalusia had never been to Strawberry Hill with William – he would have been totally out of his element. But nine months after his death she joined a house-party there, after which she was frequently at Strawberry Hill. Lady Morier described her at one of the parties:

There was Lady Molesworth, noisy and good-humoured, who wondered if one *could* know anybody living on the wrong side of Oxford Street; and who, advised of a more moderate dressmaker than her own, asked doubtfully, "Do you think cheap gowns succeed?" . . . She herself lived in Eaton Place where she entertained cheerfully and successfully. Mr A. Hayward, the well-known essayist, diner-out and raconteur, an habitué of both ladies' houses, notes in his *Selected Essays* an amateur performance at Lady Molesworth's of Alfred de Musset's *Il faut qu'une porte soit ouverte ou fermée* before a distinguished audience comprising both French and English royalty . . . A great feature of that world was association with the Orléans princes and their families – the Duc d'Aumale, the Comte de Paris, the Duc de Chartres.

The Prince and Princess of Wales, also the British royal dukes, became friendly with Lady Molesworth from the late 1870s. This probably came about through Lord Torrington, whom they had known since their childhood when he became Lord in Waiting to their father. Even the Queen regarded Lady Molesworth warmly, as a letter to Torrington from the Marchioness of Ely, a lady of the Bedchamber, shows – a very meandering letter:

Balmoral, Dec. 14th 1877

My dear Lord Torrington,

The Queen has desired me to write to you to enquire how Lady Molesworth is as Her Majesty is concerned to hear she has not been strong lately. The Queen has always had a great regard for Lady Molesworth and *knowing* it is not a serious illness wishes me to ask *you* kindly to convey her enquiries to Lady Molesworth and to say, Her Majesty only wishes, *to show how much she remembers* her, but does not wish her to write but to send a message through you, I know you will do this, for the Queen would have asked sooner, only she did not know Lady Molesworth had been unwell, and desires me to say, she thinks it will soon pass over. . . . She has such a regard for Lady Molesworth, you must try to tell her, and, the Queen knows so well how great her affection and loyalty is to her, that you must tell Lady Molesworth, it is not that the Queen thinks she is ill, but knowing

that she has not been strong lately, she would like to feel the Queen thinks about her. Pray send me a line in reply to this, that I can show the Queen. And give Lady Molesworth my most affectionate love, she has ever been a kind and true friend to me. I am writing in great haste to save the post –
Yours sincerely, Jane Ely.

Lady Dorothy Neville was a frequent guest at both Eaton Place and Strawberry Hill, and in her *Reminiscences* she contrasts the rival hostesses:

Lady Waldegrave was by far the cleverer woman of the two: nevertheless her rival scored an easy triumph in her dinner-parties, which somehow or other were always completely successful and a delight to all the guests. Lady Molesworth, indeed, although by no means brilliantly intellectual herself, possessed a mysterious power of drawing out clever people and making them talk – a special quality of the highest possible value. I must add that she took great pains in the selection of her guests, making sure that they should be people certain to get on well together . . . The way in which Lady Molesworth managed to get anyone of exceptional brilliancy or interest, no matter what rank or nationality, to come to her parties was quite wonderful. Samuel Wilberforce, the witty Bishop of Oxford, once said to me: 'I believe if the King of the Cannibal Islands were to come to England, within twenty-four hours he would be dining with Lady Molesworth.' . . . She used to give two different kinds of dinner-parties, some large, of from 15 to 20 people, mostly drawn from the fashionable world, and others small, at which some 6 or 8 of the best brains in London could exchange ideas . . . I remember one dinner at which we were but six – our hostess, Mr Dickens, Lord Torrington, a great musical critic, another literary man and myself. That evening was one of the most agreeable I have ever known; Dickens himself simply bubbled over with fun and conversation, talking in a way which resembled nothing so much as some of the best passages in his books.

The last time before his death that Dickens went to a theatre was with Lady Molesworth and Lord Redesdale, who later wrote of the evening that Dickens' talk 'had all the sparkle of champagne, and kept himself and his companions laughing at the majesty of his own absurdities'.

The anonymous author of *Fifty Years of London Society, 1870-1920*, wrote of Lady Molesworth as 'not only an agreeable, clever, sympathetic and generous-hearted woman of the world, full of tact and *savoir faire*, but cosmopolitan, devoid of all chauvinism and

Lady Molesworth

GEORGE PAINTER,

T⁰ **C. & A. PAINTER,**

(SUCCESSORS.)

Dealers in Turtle, Wholesale & Retail,

SHIP & TURTLE TAVERN,

130, Leadenhall Street, London.

E.C.

TERMS:—CASH.

1886

6 Oct · 1 Quart Thick
Turtle   1 1
Jaw Box   2 6
                1 · 3 · 6

Rec⁴
C. & A. Painter

J W Shipton

8/10/86

Turtle soup was a frequent delicacy at Lady Molesworth's dinner-parties.

197

insular prejudice, and her proficiency in foreign languages and her knowledge of foreign literature were envied by all. She and the widowed Duchesse de Mouchy (devoted friend of the Empress Eugénie) were close friends, and to her house the more distinguished of the people who came over to London in 1870, driven hither by the Huns of of the period, flocked to get the latest war news from France, brought across the Channel by balloon or pigeon-post. The Prince of Wales was often there to greet and solace the refugees. He had no greater admirer than 'Lady Moley', during whose illness the Prince never let a day pass without calling to inquire how she was progressing.'

This raconteur added, 'One cause of her popularity, and that not the least, was that she was credited with possessing that treasure of treasures, a cook second to none.' A fine tribute to Monsieur Blanc.

AT Pencarrow the house-parties included the Prince and Princess of Wales, Lord Kenmore who was Queen Victoria's Chamberlain, the Empress Eugénie and, the year before he died, Napoleon III. The world of music was always well represented: Sir Michael Costa, conductor and composer, Director of Her Majesty's Opera; J.R. Planché, dramatist and English librettist for Offenbach; Henry Fothergill Chorley, music critic of the *Athenaeum*. Sullivan composed most of *Iolanthe* when staying at Pencarrow, shutting himself away from the rest of the house-party. Literary guests included Dickens, Charles Lever, Thackeray, Tennyson, Thomas Hood and Edward John Trelawny, the friend of Byron and Shelley. From the theatre there were Charles and Frank Mathews, Alfred Wigan, Edward Sherard Burnaby and Miss Herbert who was known as the best Lady Teazle of her day – times had moved on since Andalusia's early days when 'the stage' and 'society' were worlds apart. The Hon. F. Leveson Gower wrote of Pencarrow in his *Recollections*: 'Each autumn it was filled with much of what is called the best society in London. Wit, beauty and fashion abounded there . . . Sometimes the house could not hold us all, and once I was made to sleep in a bothy next door to some snoring gardeners, who kept me awake all night.'

On one of the visits of the Duc and Duchesse d'Aumale, the whole house-party went to Bodmin station to greet them. Before the train arrived, so goes the story told by one of the guests, 'Lady Molesworth gave a scream of horror – she had remembered that a fire-screen made of a cavalry standard emblazoned with WATERLOO was in one of the rooms allocated to her French visitors. A groom was sent galloping back to Pencarrow with an urgent message that the defiant banner be removed.' The screen, one of a pair, is now in the drawing-room fireplace at Pencarrow.

The card-game poker was introduced to England by the American

PENCARROW

Friday September 4 1868

PERFECTION

or

The Lady of Munster

a Comedy in one act by
Thomas Haines Bayly,
revised with additions by
J R Planché.

Sir Lawrence Paragon	Sir John Harington Bt
Charles Paragon	M le Bn de Courval
Sam	Mr Planché
Kate O'Brien	Lady Harington
Susan	Mrs Hervey

Prompter and Stage Manager — Capt. Hon. J Vivian.

Vivat Regina.

Amateur theatricals were often one of the amusements at Pencarrow house-parties. J.R. Planché, the distinguished theatrical and musical director, who himself was also a dramatist, was often there to direct the Pencarrow productions.

Minister General Schenck at a Strawberry Hill party. It obsessed the 1870s and '80s, Andalusia becoming among the most obsessed. This may have been a contributing factor to her having at one time to raise a mortgage on the Eaton Place house. There is an anecdote handed down by word of mouth at Pencarrow, originally told by an old man who, when a gardener's boy, started work at sunrise. One morning as he passed by the drawing-room windows, he peeped through a crack in the curtains and saw Lady Molesworth at a card table, a footman standing beside her with a tray of sovereigns.

But it was not all poker at Pencarrow. Picnics, cliff walks, otter-hunting, croquet, billiards, amateur theatricals, concerts – a testament chronicling the charm and the fun of these Pencarrow house-parties is the great visitors' book, begun in 1859. The title page is designed by E.M. Underdown, and carries a long poem by Thomas Hood. There are enchanting sketches by Thackeray, Eastlake and Underdown of picnics and other outings, usually mocking the Cornish weather by umbrellas much in evidence. There are menus and programmes of amateur theatricals; also many poems extolling the hostess and her entrancing gardens. In some of the sketches Andalusia is in an invalid pony-chaise, her guests walking beside it. As early as the 1860s, in letters to Lady Waldegrave from Paris, she had complained of bouts of ill-health . . . 'I can hardly walk up the Rue de la Paix – my knees give less pain, but mounting stairs pains my chest.' There is mention of an ulcer. And there is a rather touching little note from Andalusia to Frances from Eaton Place, undated and marked: 'Dearest Lady Waldegrave – Would you mind asking Lord T. *in the evening* tonight. He undertakes getting me into the carriage, which is my *only* difficulty. I sat him down last night at Mrs Paget's, whither he went, and played Nap etc. with the Prince so there is no difficulty.'

Although Frances was the younger by twelve years, it was she who died first, in 1879. Her adoring fourth husband, Lord Carlington, exchanged many letters with Andalusia at this time, and called frequently at Eaton Place where they sat together talking of Frances. Six years later Andalusia suffered a more devastating loss – the death of Torrington in August 1885. Now there was no Lord T. to help her in and out of her carriage, no one to cosset her in the manner to which she had become accustomed. It was in every sense a bereavement. That the intimate friendship of Lord Torrington and Lady Molesworth was accepted and regarded as permanent as marriage is shown by the Marchioness of Ely's letter to Torrington (quoted earlier) asking him to tell Lady Molesworth how concerned the Queen was that she should be unwell. Further evidence is in a letter of sympathy from the Prince of Wales to Andalusia upon Torrington's death:

April 30th 1884

My dear Lady Molesworth,

I little thought when you so recently wrote to me a kind letter on the sad loss I had experienced that so soon after I should have to write to you and offer you my sincerest condolences – on the loss of one whom I know had been your intimate friend for so many years. I was quite horrified when the news reached me – as I had hoped that Lord Torrington was so much better.

The Queen feels most deeply the loss of one who was for so many years in her service and who had her entire confidence, and so her sons and daughters will always sincerely regard him – having known him ever since we were children and always looked upon him as a true and devoted friend of our family. The Princess expresses with me the firmest hope that your health may not suffer from this sad blow.

I remain, yours very sincerely, Albert Edward.

Torrington's death meant that Andalusia, in addition to her emotional loss, had lost her adviser in money matters – one remembers that early gift of a household account-book. The Molesworth estates were, of course, managed by the Trustees whom William had appointed to 'keep up my place at Pencarrow in the manner heretofore'. But by the mid-1860s the income from the estate became insufficient to keep it up in the manner heretofore, and it seems that Andalusia was meeting the expense of maintaining the house and gardens from her own income. Lord Torrington considered that this she should not have to do. Legal advice was sought, but Counsel's opinion was that 'the Trustees are not entitled to resort to capital for purpose of repairs or improvements, and that the sum in respect of past expenditure should have been provided for out of the income of the Tenant for life and should be made good by her.' Torrington wrote from Windsor Castle on June 30 1873:

I may differ, and as I am not in the Trust and no personal relation or influence in the matter I perfectly admit that you may be quite contented that what I think is of no consequence. My opinion is very simple on the case and it is this: Lady Molesworth has mortgaged her private property for the benefit of the Estate and in my opinion it ought to be charged to the Molesworth Estate – but that you require a bond from Lady Molesworth for access to her for another £3,000 I cannot understand. But as I don't choose as a personal friend of Lady Molesworth to be rudely treated, I must decline any more communication.

One assumes that Andalusia continued to pay for the maintenance of the property from her private income. Of course it could be argued, and doubtless *was* argued by Molesworth relatives, that her private income came from William, and if he were alive he would certainly meet the Pencarrow bills. Also, they may have had a suspicion that Lord Torrington had a personal axe to grind – a suspicion eventually confirmed by Andalusia's Will.

IN 1886, Andalusia became seriously ill and was thought unlikely to recover. Mr Venning of Devonport, who had become the Molesworths' solicitor on the death of his partner Thomas Woollcombe, tentatively suggested to Mary Ford that she might consider making a gesture towards reconciliation with her sister-in-law. Mary agreed; and on October 15th wrote to Mr Venning: 'I have called and inquired for Lady Molesworth this afternoon. If my doing so gives her pleasure it has I assure you given me infinite satisfaction.' Two days later she wrote again: 'The evening of the afternoon of the 15th that I had called to inquire for Lady Molesworth she sent her card along with a note to me requesting me to come and see her the following day – Of course I did so – but I must own I felt very nervous in so doing for it is fifteen years since we have exchanged a word together. The maid and butler warned me I should see a great change in her. When I went into the room she cried a great deal and held my hand the whole time I was with her, which was I think about ten minutes . . . the muscular strength with which she held my hand was *considerable*, and altogether I felt comforted and convinced she is in no immediate peril . . . She requested me to call on her daily. I will do so frequently.'

Sir Victor Houlton, KCMG, who had been Private Secretary to Sir William when he was First Commissioner of Works and then Colonial Secretary, had just the previous month been made a joint executor of Andalusia's Will with Mr Venning and Lord Carlington. He wrote to Mr Venning on October 18th 1886: 'You have no doubt heard from Mrs Ford that she has had two most successful interviews with Lady M. both of them are much the happier with a result due to your diplomacy. You have done a good deed my dear Venning reconciling these two old ladies "avant de partir", for neither can look forward to a very long stay here.' Sir Victor under-estimated Mary Ford's staying power by twenty-two years.

Andalusia rallied and by the following spring resumed her social life; but by the beginning of 1888 she was once more seriously ill – and died, after two days of unconsciousness, on May 16th. She was buried at Kensal Green, lowered onto William's coffin in his mausoleum. An inscription on a brass plate at the side of the mausoleum reads simply:

> Andalusia Grant
> Lady Molesworth, wife of Sir William Molesworth
> Died XVI May MDCCCLXXXVIII

No date of birth. No one knew it. To the last she was coy about her age.

ANDALUSIA's Will, signed on July 13th 1885, the year after Torrington's death, bequeathed 'My estate, property and effects real and personal unto the Rt Hon. George Stanley Byng, Viscount Torrington.' This was the forty-seven-year-old nephew and heir of her *cher ami* – and he, ironically, died the year after this fortune fell into his lap. He was succeeded by his three-year-old son, George Master Byng, 9th Viscount Torrington.

There was a three-day sale at Christie's in King Street on July 7th to 9th 1888 of the most valuable contents of 87 Eaton Place – silver, porcelain, pictures, decorative furniture, etc. and of the late Lady Molesworth's dazzling collection of jewellery. The articles were on view for two days previously, and according to the Press 'the position which the deceased owner of them held in the fashionable world, no less than the rare beauty of most of the goods exhibited, attracted to Christie's showroom a large number of private persons and dealers.' The item which realised the highest price was 'a brilliant necklace, with numerous graduated pendants which promptly went to a private purchaser for £745. The total sum raised was £11,062.10.10. – in present-day currency, over a quarter of a million pounds. A sale by the auctioneering firm of George Gouldsmith of the less valuable furniture and effects raised another £929. The auction of the ground lease of 87 Eaton Place and 1 Lyall Mews took place on June 27th. The sum raised for this 'Fashionable Town Residence of a Family of Distinction' cannot be traced; but since the lease had sixty-eight years more to run, it would have been considerable. Added to all this, there was the £10,000 legacy left by Sir William to Andalusia. Gall and wormwood surely to the Molesworths that all this should be inherited by an unrelated three-year-old boy that Andalusia had probably not even seen.

There were a few items that Andalusia bequeathed in her Will to Mary Ford – in particular 'a small enamel Miniature of my late Husband set with diamonds and containing some of his hair'. Also to Mary Ford for life, and afterwards to the Trust, 'my furniture and effects at Pencarrow; the Portrait of myself by Ross, and the portraits by Chalon of my late Husband and myself which are at my residence 87 Eaton Place, and my books at Pencarrow shall devolve as heirlooms.' The portrait of Sir William by Sir Watson Gordon she bequeathed to the Trustees of the National Portrait Gallery; and 'to Sir Paul William Molesworth, 10th Bart. the group in silver presented by the Wharfingers of Southwark to my late husband'.

EPILOGUE — 1888-1910

EXACTLY three months after Andalusia's death, Mary Ford took up residence at Pencarrow. She was now seventy-two years old and had been a widow for thirty years – after seven years of marriage Richard Ford had died of Bright's disease in 1858, leaving 17 Park Street, the Ford family's London house, to Mary for life. From Pencarrow she wrote on August 15th to her step-son Sir Clare Ford:

> My journey to the Far West was long and to me full of sad memories. At Bodmin Road I had to change trains for Bodmin and at quarter to 9 p.m. I got into my carriage for my Father's home. It was a moderately clear evening. My carriage was open and as I drove through Bodmin it seemed to me as if the whole town had turned out of doors so full were the streets of people all staring at the solitary old lady dressed in deep mourning. On, on I sped and when I neared the Lodges the road was lined with vehicles of all sizes and shapes and forms filled with people who saluted me. There was literally an army of men on foot and on horseback. They did not stop the carriage, but all took off their hats . . . On reaching Pencarrow I was given a tremendous cheer and I went out and curtseyed and thanked them warmly for the kindness of their reception . . .
>
> Pencarrow is a Princely possession and requiring a princely income to keep it up. I have been over the gardens this morning and walked about the grounds. The trees are in splendid leaf, and those that I left small have grown into almost fine forest trees – what a paradise William has created and how little he ever dreamt that the last survivor of his family would now be in possession.

And the 'last survivor' resolved forthwith, not only to maintain William's paradise but to enhance it – replanting wherever the thirty-three years since William's death had made it necessary, importing rare specimens from other countries as he had done. Her work was recognized internationally in 1891 when she was awarded the Knightsian Medal by the Royal Horticultural Society for the best collection of coniferous trees in England.

In the newly built Truro Cathedral, consecrated in 1887, a

Pencil drawing of Pencarrow by Lady Molesworth-St Aubyn.

memorial was erected on the north wall of the Jesus Chapel 'To three famous Cornishmen, patriots and statesmen: Sir John Eliot, 1592 – 1632; Sidney, Earl of Godolphin, 1645 – 1712; Sir William Molesworth, Bart., 1810 – 1855'. In Bodmin, the foundation stone of a library was laid on April 27th 1896, a gift to the people of the borough from Mr John Passmore Edwards 'as a memorial to the late Rt. Hon. Sir William Molesworth, Bart., Secretary of State for the Colonies.' It was a gift splendidly appropriate to Sir William's love of learning and his belief in, and work for, national education. The building was opened on May 24th in Queen Victoria's Jubilee year, and is still Bodmin's Public Library today. In Egloshayle Church, Mary Ford commissioned a marble wall memorial to be erected 'In memory of Mary Lady Molesworth, mother of the Rt Hon. Sir William Molesworth, Bart., MP – Statesman and philosopher, famed for his vigorous support

of the principles of colonisation continuously rendered; and of
whom on his decease it was aptly said that for singleness of
mind, honesty of purpose, clearness of judgement, faithfulness
of conduct, courage in difficulties, and equanamity in success he
never was surpassed* – Also of Francis Alexander Molesworth, one
of the founders of Wellington, New Zealand, whose perseverance,
courage, endurance of hardship and devotion to his adopted country
has rendered his name 'ceraperannius' in that country.' But Mary
Ford's most personal labour of love was to catalogue in nineteen
great red-leather albums all William's letters, and all family letters
pertaining to William, from his childhood until his death – also
relevant press-cuttings and letters from friends and politicians.
There are no letters to or from Andalusia in 'these albums, no
press-cuttings referring to her. Only in an album embossed ROYAL
LETTERS did Mary acknowledge the existence of her sister-in-law
by writing on the first page: 'These letters addressed to Andalusia
Lady Molesworth came into my possession on her death in 1888
who for many years enjoyed the society and acquaintance of these
distinguished people. Mary Ford, August 7th 1881.'

The first letter, dated Sandringham 1877, is from Albert Prince
Consort; the last item is a telegram from 'The Empress Queen',
Berlin, January 3rd 1885. There are numerous notes from Edward
Albert Prince of Wales, mainly responding to invitations to dinner.
Letters from the other royal dukes are there, the royal grandchildren
and European royalty – Leopold King of the Belgians, Marie
Henrietta of the Belgians, Sophia Queen of Holland. But it has to be
said that the majority of these letters are thank-you notes for flowers
or other presents received at Christmas, Easter, on birthdays and
wedding anniversaries. Andalusia knew the importance of keeping
in touch. The only interesting letters in the album are those of the
Marchioness of Ely to Lord Torrington on behalf of the Queen, and
of the Prince of Wales to Lady Molesworth on the death of Torrington
– both quoted in the last chapter.

MARY Ford, despite her age, spent some time every year in the

---

*A passage quoted from Lord Palmerston's letter of sympathy to Lady
Molesworth on the death of her husband, dated October 27th 1855.

London house her husband had bequeathed to her for life. There she entertained a wide circle of friends from literary and artistic circles. Her health remained excellent until a short time before she died in 1910, her ninety-fifth year. In her Will she expressed the desire to be buried under the trees in the churchyard of St Conan's (the little church built for Washaway village on Pencarrow land in 1883) – 'in a plain wooden coffin in the unbricked ground and to have placed over my grave a granite block and on it a granite cross similar to the one in the Rockery at Pencarrow'. She desired 'mine to be a walking funeral and that I may be carried to my grave by my retainers who are Gardeners, Gamekeepers, Carpenters and Weedmen on the Pencarrow Estates not exceeding thirty in number.' She asked that there should be no flowers at her funeral, just a cross laid on her coffin of evergreen sprigs from different species of pines. Everything was planned as a final tribute to her beloved brother – a simple Cornish funeral as she knew he had wished his own to be, a peaceful tree-shaded resting place in Pencarrow land.

BIBLIOGRAPHY

Alice Acland. *Caroline Norton*. Constable, 1948.

Anon. *Fifty Years of London Society, 1870-1920*. Eveleigh Nash Company, 1920.

George Douglas 8th Duke of Argyll. *Autobiography & Memoirs, 1823-1900*. Ed by the Dowager Duchess of Argyll. 2 vols. John Murray, 1906.

Philip Henry Bagenal. *Life of Ralph Bernal Osborne, MP*. For private Circulation. Richard Bentley, 1884.

Jessie Buckle. *Joseph Parkes of Birmingham, & the Part he played in Radical Reform Movements from 1825-45*. Methuen, 1926.

Thomas & Jane Welsh Carlyle. *Collected Letters*, Ed by Charles Richard Sanders. Duke University Press, Durham, North Carolina, 1981.

David Cecil. *Lord M., or the Later Life of Lord Melbourne*. Constable, 1954.

Henry Fothergill Chorley. *Autobiography, Memoir, & Letters*. Compiled by Henry G. Hewlett. 2 vols. Richard Bentley, 1873.

Arthur Irvin Dasent. *John Thadeus Delane, Editor of 'The Times'. His Life & Correspondence'*. 2 vols. John Murray, 1908.

Thomas H. Duncombe. *The Life & Correspondence of Thomas Slingsby Duncombe*. 2 vols. Hurst & Blackett, 1868.

Lady Eastlake. *Mrs Grote — A Sketch*. John Murray, 1880.

John Ebers. *Seven Years of the King's Theatre*. William Harrison Ainsworth, 1828.

Hugh Edward Egerton. *Selected Speeches of Sir William Molesworth, Bart., PC, MP. on Questions Relating to Colonial Policy*. Ed with an Introduction. John Murray, 1903.

T.H.S. Escott. *Social Transformations of the Victorian Age*. Seeley & Co., 1897.

T.H.S. Escott. *Society in the Country House*. T. Fisher Unwin, 1907.

Fawcett, Mrs Millicent Garrett. *Life of the Right Hon. Sir William Molesworth, Bart. MP, FRS.* Macmillan, 1901.

Geoffrey S. Fletcher. *The London Nobody Knows.* Hutchinson, 1963.

Richard Ford. *Letters.* Ed by R.E. Prothero, MVO. John Murray, 1905.

Charles C.F. Greville. *Memoirs.* 2nd & 3rd vols. Ed by Henry Reeve, 1874 & 1885.

Harriet Grote. *Collected Papers, Prose & Verse, 1842-62.* John Murray, 1862.

Harriet Grote. *The Personal Life of George Grote. Compiled from Family Documents, Private Memoirs, & Original Letters.* 2nd ed. Murray, 1873.

Harriette Grote. *The Philosophical Radicals of 1832. Comprising the Life of Sir William Molesworth & some Incidents connected with the Reform Movement from 1832 to 1842.* For Private Circulation. Pub. Anon by Savill & Edwards, 1866.

Joseph Hamburger. *Intellectuals in Politics — John Stuart Mill & the Philosophic Radicals.* Yale University Press, 1965.

Augustus J.C. Hare. *The Years with Mother.* 3 vols. George Allen, 1896. Ed with Notes & Introduction by Malcolm Barnes, Century Publishing, 1984.

Diana Hartley. *The St Aubyns of Cornwall 1200-1977.* Barracada Books, 1977.

Abraham Hayward. *A Selection from his Correspondence from 1834 to 1884.* Ed by Henry E. Carlisle. 2 vols. John Murray, 1886.

Edgar Johnson. *Charles Dickens — His Tragedy & Triumph.* Allen Lane, 1977.

Doris Langley Moore. *Ada, Countess of Lovelace.* John Murray, 1977.

R.E. Leader. *Life & Letters of John Arthur Roebuck, PC, QC, MP with chapters of Autobiography.* John Murray, 1897.

Hon. F. Leveson Gore. *Bygone Years — Recollections.* John Murray, 1905.

E.H. Lewin, editor. *The Lewin Letters. A Selection from the Correspondence & Diaries of an English Family 1756-1884.* 2 vols. Archibald Constable, 1909.

Elizabeth Longford. *Victoria R.I. Weidenfeld & Nicholson, 1965.*

Sir John Maclean. *The Parochial & Family History of the Deanery of Trigg Minor in the County of Cornwall.* Vol. I. Nichols & Son, Parliament St, 1873.

John Stuart Mill. *Autobiography,* Preface by John Jacob Cross. Columbia University Press, New York, 1924.

Nancy Mitford, editor. *The Stanleys of Alderley. Their letters between 1851-1865.* Hamish Hamilton, 1939.

William Nassau Molesworth. *The History of England from the Year 1830 to 1874.* Chapman & Hall, 1874.

Lady Morgan. *Memoirs: Autobiography, Diaries & Correspondence.* Ed by W. Hepworth Dixon. 2 vols. Chapman & Hall, 1881.

John Morley. *The Life of Richard Cobden.* 2 vols. Chapman & Hall, 1881.

Lady Dorothy Nevill. *Reminiscences.* Ed by Ralph Nevill. Edward Arnold, 1906.

Cyril Noall. *A History of Cornish Mail & Stage Coaches.* D. Bradford Barton, 1963.

T.P. O'Connor. *Lord Beaconsfield — A Biography.* Chatto & Windus, 1884.

Hesketh Pearson. *The Smith of Smiths, being the Life, Wit & Humour of Sidney Smith.* Hogarth Press, 1984.

J.R. Planché. *His Recollections & Reflections — A Professional Autobiography,* 2 vols. Tinsley Brothers, Catherine St, Strand, 1872.

J. Polsue. *Lake's Parochial History of the County of Cornwall.* Vol I. W. Lake, Truro, 1867-73. Repub. 1974 by E.P. Publishing Ltd in collaboration with Cornwall County Library.

Una Pope Hennessy. *Charles Dickens,* 1812-1870. Chatto & Windus, 1945.

Lord Redesdale. *Memories.* Hutchinson, 1915.

T. Wemyss Reid. *Richard Monckton Milnes, 1st Lord Houghton — Life, Letters, & Friendships.* 2 vols. Cassell, 1890.

John Arthur Roebuck. *Life & Letters, with Chapters of Auto-biography.* Ed by Robert E. Leader. Edward Arnold, 1897.

Janet Ross. *Three Generations of Englishwomen. Memoirs & Correspondence of Susannah Taylor, Sarah Austin, & Lady Duff Gordon.* T. Fisher Unwin, 1893.

Lady St Helier (Mary Jeune). *Memories of Fifty Years*. Edward Arnold, 1909.

M.C.M. Simpson. *Many Memories of Many People*. Edward Arnold, 1898.

Sydney Smith. *Letters*. Ed by Mrs Austin. 2 vols. Longman, Brown, Green & Longman, 1855.

Ray Strachey. *Millicent Garrett Fawcett*. John Murray, 1931.

Margot Strickland. *The Byron Women (for Lady Lovelace)*. Peter Owen, 1974.

W.M. Thackeray. *Letters & Private Papers*. 4 vols. Ed by Gordon H. Ray. Oxford University Press, 1945.

W.M. Thackeray. *Pendennis — His Fortunes & Misfortunes, His Friends & His Greatest Enemies*. 1850.

William Thomas. *The Philosophic Radicals. Nine Studies in Theory & Practice, 1817-1841*. Clarendon Press, Oxford, 1979.

Sir George Otto Trevelyan, Bart. *The Life & Letters of Lord Macaulay*. 2 vols. 1st pub. 1876. O.U.P. 1961.

Edward Twycross, editor. *The Mansions of England & Wales. County of Cornwall*. C.J. Greenwood, Dalston, 1846.

Gordon Waterfield. *Lucie Duff Gordon*. John Murray, 1937.

R. Roslyn Wemyss, Mrs. *Memoirs of Sir Robert Morier*. 2 vols. Arnold, 1911.

Sir Algernon West, KCB. *Recollections, 1832-1886*. 2 vols. Smith Elder, 1891.

George Woodbridge. *The Reform Club 1836-1978. A History from the Club's Records*. Privately printed for Members of the Reform Club in association with Clearwater Publishing Inc., New York & Toronto, 1978.

Cecil Woodham-Smith. *Florence Nightingale, 1820-1910*. Constable, 1950.

Cecil Woodham-Smith. *The Reasons Why*. Constable, 1953.

Cecil Woodham-Smith. *The Great Hunger. Ireland 1845-49*. Hamish Hamilton, 1962.

Thomas Woollcombe, editor. Notices of the later Sir William Molesworth, Bart., MP, Secretary of State for the Colonies. Printed for private circulation. London 1857.

Osbert Wyndham-Hewett. *Strawberry Fair. A Biography of Frances, Countess Waldegrave, 1821-1879*. John Murray, 1958.

Osbert Wyndham Hewett. . . . *And Mr Fortescue. A Selection from the Diaries of Chichester Fortescue, Lord Carlington.* John Murray, 1958.

Edmund Yates. *His Recollections & Experiences.* 2 vols. Richard Bentley, 1884.

INDEX

Numbers in italics refer to illustrations
W.M. refers to Sir William Molesworth